Media and the British Empire

Media and the British Empire

Edited by

Chandrika Kaul

First published 2006 by
PALGRAVE MACMILLAN
Houndmills, Basingstoke, Hampshire RG21 6XS and
175 Fifth Avenue, New York, N.Y. 10010
Companies and representatives throughout the world

PALGRAVE MACMILLAN is the global academic imprint of the Palgrave
Macmillan division of St. Martin's Press, LLC and of Palgrave Macmillan Ltd.
Macmillan® is a registered trademark in the United States, United Kingdom
and other countries. Palgrave is a registered trademark in the European
Union and other countries.

ISBN-13: 978–1–4039–4882–3 hardback
ISBN-10: 1–4039–4882–8 hardback

This book is printed on paper suitable for recycling and made from fully
managed and sustained forest sources.

A catalogue record for this book is available from the British Library.

Library of Congress Cataloging-in-Publication Data
Media and the British Empire / edited by Chandrika Kaul.
    p. cm.
  Includes bibliographical references and index.
  ISBN 1–4039–4882–8 (cloth)
  1. Great Britain—Colonies—In mass media. 2. British—Foreign
countries—Historiography. 3. British—Foreign countries—Press
coverage. 4. Great Britain—Colonies—Press coverage. 5. Great
Britain—Colonies—Historiography. 6. Imperialism—Press
coverage. 7. Imperialism—Historiography. I. Kaul, Chandrika.
DA16.M395 2006
  909'.0971241—dc22
                                                                 2005044512

10   9   8   7   6   5   4   3   2   1
15 14 13 12 11 10 09 08 07 06

Printed and bound in Great Britain by
Antony Rowe Ltd, Chippenham and Eastbourne

To
Lawrence Ishan Anand

Contents

List of Illustrations

Foreword

My 25-year career reporting for the BBC in South Asia was a history of the damage governments can do to their own cause by pursuing what they believe are methods which will guarantee them the media coverage they want. I came to believe that the power of the media does not equal the power or effectiveness of its message, and that no matter what efforts are made to drown out alternative messages they will somehow be heard.

For almost the whole of my career the electronic media in all the countries of South Asia were controlled by Ministries of Information. This was the era of the transistor revolution when cheap sets spread shortwave radio listening to the remotest corners of South Asia. Because the Government-controlled media were broadcasting propaganda, and poor and rich alike were quite able to discern this, millions and millions of listeners used to tune in to the BBC regularly for what they felt was impartial news. Whenever I asked villagers why they listened to the BBC they used to say, 'Because it gives true news, and gives it first.' Yet the BBC's voice was difficult to hear because it came crackling across the shortwave, it was difficult to find amidst all the other crackles, and it was broadcast for only comparatively short periods. Governments commanded the long and medium waves with their far superior signals, and stayed on air 24 hours a day. Their power was far greater than the BBC's.

Needless to say, the credibility of the BBC, and its consequent popularity, frustrated governments and was sometimes even seen by them as a threat to their security. On two occasions the BBC was seen as such a threat that the British Government allowed itself to be dragged into the battle of the airwaves. The BBC was in the eye of the storm during the movement against the Pakistani Prime Minister Zulfiqar Ali Bhutto, after his controversial electoral victory in 1977. I had to sit in the press gallery of the National Gallery and listen to Bhutto launching an impassioned attack on me. Shortly after that I was summoned by the British High Commissioner to be told that the BBC's reporting was damaging British relations with Pakistan and so he thought I should leave. I replied that the BBC had been intending to give me a break, but his intervention meant that I would have to stay on for at least two more weeks. During the dreadful riots in which thousands of Sikhs were massacred after the assassination of the Indian Prime Minister Indira Gandhi in 1984, the British High Commissioner in Delhi called in all the British correspondents and warned them that if they didn't tone down their coverage, they would be thrown out. The riots didn't last long enough for us to put that threat to the test.

History shows us that the alternative sources of information which spring up when governments try to control its flow change as the means for disseminating information change. In my case, as I have said, it was the transistor radio which gave the BBC its extraordinary influence in South Asia. History also shows us that new media do not necessarily replace older forms of transmitting information. Britain might well have lost the First World War if it hadn't been for the army they recruited in India. The British Government realised that if damaging reports about the progress of the war were not countered, the stability of the country from which that crucial manpower was being drawn, and the loyalty of the soldiers once they were recruited, would be threatened. The Governments in Britain and in India therefore used all the most modern technologies and techniques to get their message across and to combat hostile sources of information. There was one pre-modern medium which they had particular difficulty in controlling: the rumour mill. One of the official bulletins, personally scrutinised by the Viceroy before it was carried by the news agencies, stated that 'wild rumours were still circulating in bazaars'. The bulletin admitted that in spite of the rumours' wildness every effort needed to be made to prevent 'the credulous' believing them.

When Indira Gandhi imposed a State of Emergency, censored the press and told the Director General of All India Radio that credibility didn't matter and he should just broadcast what he was told to broadcast, she forgot India's penchant for rumours. She didn't think of the little teashops all over the country where people were gathering to pour scorn on the censored newspapers and eagerly discuss the rumours in the bazaar. But when the Emergency was over and an election was declared, she discovered the power of the rumours about her slum destruction and mass sterilisation campaigns which had filled the information vacuum, the credibility gap, left by the censored press and the tightly controlled official media. After she had been trounced in the election she said to me, 'I have been defeated by rumours.' That was not the whole truth, but nor was it entirely untrue. There is another lesson for governments in Indira Gandhi's defeat. Sensitive governments realise the value of receiving as well as sending out information. Because independent sources were blocked by her own emergency regulations, Indira Gandhi was not aware of the damage the sterilisation campaign was doing to her reputation.

Many people have been convinced by Marshall McLuhan that 'the medium is the message'. But my experience as a journalist has taught me that the message does not necessarily reach its destination. The impact of rumour has shown me that when rival media put out different messages it isn't always the most powerful one that goes home. I've learnt from the failure of government-controlled media that overstated messages lead people to look for other sources of information. These and other important lessons are reinforced by history, particularly by the history of imperial Britain.

Britain's media relations with its Indian Empire and its colonies were peculiarly delicate, because in most cases imperial rule was a partnership. Britain could never have ruled India without securing Indian partners. India may have come under British rule by conquest, but there was no question of holding it by force. Keeping partners on side required a very subtle message; it had to persuade those it was addressed to that it was in their interest to be ruled by foreigners. It had to counter hostile messages without resorting to crude propaganda or coercion. That is why a study of those relations is so fascinating.

I draw encouragement from the history of media relations between Britain and the Empire. In the latter days of the Indian Empire Britain was opposed by perhaps the most effective journalist of the twentieth century: Mohandas Karamchand Gandhi. Winston Churchill and many others in Britain scorned the power of his message, thinking that the pen and the voice of one eccentric man who rejoiced in his own poverty, whose own paper the *Harijan* was not officially addressed to the opinion-makers but to the poorest of the poor, who had no voice on the radio, could not possibly compete with the media power in the Government's hands. But they learnt the hard way that the power of the media does not correspond directly to the power of the message. So for those fearful of the power of the media today which is spreading a global culture, Gandhi and the difficulties the mighty British Empire had in getting its message across give hope that the present cultural imperialism will not have it all its own way. These essays show that there will always be resistance to a message, no matter how powerful the media. My experience, and my reading of these essays, also lead me to believe that the more powerful the media the more likely it is to provoke others to send out their messages, and the most powerful media does not always win.

Mark Tully

Notes on the Contributors

Alain Canuel received his PhD from the Université de Montréal for his research in international radio broadcasting. Since 1998, he has been working with the Networks of Centres of Excellence of Canada program. Until recently, he was Secretary-Treasurer for the Canadian Science and Technology Historical Association.

Philip Cass was born in Papua New Guinea and has worked as a journalist and academic in Australia, PNG, Fiji, the UK and the United Arab Emirates. He has a special interest in Pacific media history and is currently Acting Assistant Dean of the College of Communication and Media Sciences at Zayed University, Abu Dhabi.

Denis Cryle lectures in media and communication studies at the Central Queensland University in Australia. He has published extensively on print media at both regional and national levels, and is compiling a 25-year history of Rupert Murdoch's *Australian* newspaper.

Ross Harvey is Professor of Library and Information Management at Charles Sturt University, Australia. His publications explore aspects of New Zealand and Australian newspaper history, especially of the nineteenth century, and also the preservation of cultural heritage material in both print and digital forms.

Deana Heath is lecturer in South Asian and World History at Trinity College, Dublin. She has published a number of articles on colonialism and censorship, and is currently working on a book on the governmentalisation of the obscene in India, Australia and Britain in the late nineteenth and early twentieth centuries.

Chandrika Kaul is lecturer in Modern British and Imperial History at the University of St Andrews, Scotland. Her research interests include the British press and Empire 1850–1950, the Indian press, and communications in world history. She is author of *Reporting the Raj, the British Press and India 1880–1922* (Manchester, 2003), the first detailed monograph examining the British press coverage of India. She is currently working on a history of the Empire/Commonwealth Press Union.

John Lambert is an Associate Professor in the Department of History at the University of South Africa, Pretoria. His research interests include a study of white, English-speaking identity in South Africa and of the interrelationship between that identity and Britishness.

Joanna Lewis is a lecturer in Imperial and African History at the Department of International History, London School of Economics. She is author of *Empire State Building: War and Welfare in Colonial Kenya* (Oxford, 2000).

Su Lin Lewis completed her MA dissertation on colonial Penang's cosmopolitan English press at the School of Oriental and African Studies, University of London in 2004. She has worked as a journalist and aid worker in Thailand and Indonesia, and writes occasionally for the *Times Literary Supplement*.

John M. MacKenzie is Professor Emeritus of Imperial History at Lancaster University, and holds honorary professorships at the Universities of Aberdeen, St Andrews and Stirling. He has been general editor of the Manchester University Press 'Studies in Imperialism' series for more than twenty years and is currently completing a book on the Scots in South Africa.

Philip Murphy is Reader in Imperial and Commonwealth History at the University of Reading. He is author of *Party Politics and Decolonization: The Conservative Party and British Colonial Policy in Tropical Africa 1951–1964* (Oxford, 1995), and *Alan Lennox-Boyd: A Biography* (London, 1999). He has recently finished editing the Central Africa volume in the series *British Documents on the End of Empire* (London, 2005).

Tim Pratt was educated at the University of Manchester. He has published on the British media and Indian affairs in the *Journal of British Studies*, and has reviewed for *Contemporary South Asia*.

Ian St John studied for a doctorate at Nuffield College, Oxford. He is the author of *Disraeli and the Art of Victorian Politics* (London, 2005) and has published several articles on nineteenth-century politics. He has worked with David Butler on the Nuffield Election Studies, and was assistant author to Martin Westlake on *Kinnock: The Biography* (Little, Brown, 2001). He currently teaches history at Haberdashers' Aske's School, Hertfordshire.

Sir Mark Tully was BBC Delhi correspondent for more than twenty years and has continued to live in India since his retirement. He has written several books on India and continues to write and broadcast about that country.

Susan Williams is a Senior Research Fellow at the Institute of Commonwealth Studies, University of London. Her publications include *Ladies of Influence: Women of the Elite in Interwar Britain* (Penguin, 2000) and *The People's King: The True Story of the Abdication* (Penguin, 2003). She is currently writing a book about the marriage of Seretse and Ruth Khama, and the birth of Botswana: *Colour Bar: The Triumph of Seretse Khama over British Imperialism and Apartheid South Africa for the Love of His Wife and His Nation*.

Philip Woods has taught history at Thames Valley University, London, since 1974. He also teaches for New York University in London and St Lawrence University. His research is on the British use of film for propaganda in India.

1
Introductory Survey

Chandrika Kaul

'The only true history of a country', wrote Thomas Macaulay, 'is to be found in its newspapers.' Yet, in the past, scholars of imperial history and of the media worked in essentially compartmentalised spheres. With a few notable exceptions, such as the propaganda studies associ-ated with the First World War,[1] the overwhelming tendency of histo-rians has been to utilise the media – the press in particular – in an illustrative fashion, neglecting to give due deference to understanding the media forms themselves or acknowledging their function and impact within the imperial context. It was seen as easy copy and used – and often abused – as such. However, the connections between media and the British Empire have attracted rapidly growing scholarly interest in recent years, engaging the attention not merely of historians, but of students of media, literary culture and politics. It is an interest to which the quality and variety of contributions in this collection bear testimony.

Media and the British Empire seeks to provide a platform for some of this innovative research, with the emphasis on adopting an integrative approach to the study of the imperial experience, incorporating the role of the media in shaping the political, economic, social and cultural dynamics of the British colonies and Dominions, viewed from both the peripheral perspective of the colonised, as well as the metropolitan gaze of the colonisers. Thus, while the use made of the press by government departments like the Colonial Office and such major metropolitan figures as Winston Churchill is analysed, so too are the activities of critics of empire like the Chartists, the colonial challenges to the impe-rial news systems within Australia and New Zealand, and the impetus to cosmopolitanism provided by the English-language press in late colo-nial Penang. In their distinctive fashion, each of the contributors,

1

themselves drawn from the various parts of the former Empire, seeks to place the role of media in the context of the Empire and in the process also throw light on the history of the media itself – in each case exhibiting sensitivity to the problematic relationship between media and the practice of imperial domination, of the economics of news collection and distribution, as well as the differing viewpoints of producers and consumers.

A brief note about the terminology employed is perhaps apposite. There has been continuing debate about theories of communication as opposed to theories of media. Before the 1960s, H.-F. Dahl observes, the term media itself was not in general academic use. However, it was with the advent of electrical means of communication that 'the collective phenomenon of the media came into existence as a nascent system and hence deserves the attention of historians under that name'.[2] The study of communication can be seen to refer to 'the communicative process and its effects', whereas the study of media essentially deals with 'institutional levels'. The first offers 'the broader approach', while the media are 'well defined and delimited, although pouring out an overwhelming, almost ubiquitous, output'.[3]

Yet to adopt a rigid distinction between these two perspectives would be artificial and counter-productive in our context. Historical work on the Empire should encompass both emphases. This is no more than to say that the study of Empire today is essentially interdisciplinary. Hence the interchangeable use of the terms communication, communication media and media in this collection, which are taken to mean 'both a structure and a system' compounded of the distinct entities like the press, wireless, etc., and at the same time mutually interdependent and tied together within a cultural, economic and political system.

Within the constraints of a single volume, this collection has been designed to be as comprehensive as possible. The communication media examined include electric telegraphs and news agencies, newspapers (national, provincial and local), books and printed ephemera, newsreels and wireless. In geographic terms the essays cover South Africa, Kenya, Central Africa and Bechuanaland (chapters 2–5), Britain and the Indian subcontinent (chapters 6–9), Australia, New Zealand and Papua New Guinea (chapters 10–13), Canada (chapter 14) and Malaya (chapter 15). Inevitably, though, there are omissions. Thus, it has not been possible to accommodate the distinctive case of Ireland. Photographic and cinema studies have similarly been excluded. However, in each of these instances, the reader has been well served by recent books – for Ireland these include de Nie's *The Eternal Paddy* and Potter's edited collection. Similarly, Ryan's *Picturing Empire* offers a stimulating insight into 'the visualisation' of the empire through photography, and Choudhry has tackled 'empire cinema', focusing on how it 'constructed the colonial world' and the ways in which such constructions were received by Indians.[4]

Each essay in *Media and the British Empire* focuses on one or more of the key communication media forms to illustrate a particular set of issues in a specific imperial setting. Yet, it is useful to appreciate the cross-media culture of past societies and the extent to which media forms are complementary and cumulative. Thus Canuel argues that as the industrialised countries spread wireless telegraphy around the world, they superimposed a new international communications network on the existing telegraphic system; while Cryle observes that the telegraph news agencies before the Great War had to compete with the colonial press for a share of the market in the Antipodes. This contention holds even truer, of course, for the writing of media history itself. As James Curran has argued in *Media and Power*, the challenge is both to produce integrated media history as well as to integrate media history itself into more mainstream history.[5] (Interestingly, this has connotations similar to the challenge faced by imperial historians in Britain till a couple of decades ago.) It is as well to remember, for instance, that it was Lord Northcliffe, press magnate and proprietor of the *Daily Mail* and *The Times*, who sponsored the first wireless broadcast in Britain featuring the renowned Australian singer Dame Nellie Melba, or that the British press supported the BBC's monopoly of broadcasting and vetoed advertising on it, or, as Paddy Scannell has contended, cinema influenced BBC radio broadcasting in significant ways from the late 1920s.[6] To advance a theoretical framework that encompasses the field of media and empire in its entirety is premature at this stage and probably impossible, just as it is impossible to talk about the British Empire as a single entity, even less to posit a single theory to explain its rise and fall. It is, nevertheless, hoped that these empirically-based studies with respect to content, methodological approaches and regional perspectives will serve to open still wider the potential for future research in the area.

* * *

The nineteenth century marked the culmination of a series of remarkable advances in communications technology and the media. A world which entered the century travelling in horse-drawn carriages and transmitting information by the recently developed device of semaphore, departed it sending word of events by electric telegraph and travelling in a steam train. To understand the critical developments in imperial history during this period it is imperative that attention be given to shifts in the underlying communication media environment.

The systems of communication and the media both within Britain and in her world-wide Empire underwent a revolutionary change by the end of the century. The telegraph network – accessibly described by Standage in *The Victorian Internet*[7] – attained maturity and became, for the first time, a viable medium for mass commercial use and an invaluable asset in imperial defence; the railway system expanded rapidly – India, for instance, acquired the fifth largest rail network in the world; steamships using the Suez Canal reduced journey times between Britain and her eastern interests to between three and eight weeks; the printing process was transformed with inventions like rotary machines creating the conditions for the press to become a mass-production capitalist industry; news agencies based on the concept of instantaneous electronic communication rose to prominence, and Reuters successfully carved up the international news market and established its dominance on the basis of Britain's worldwide formal and informal Empire; the typewriter began to be widely used; the camera became portable and ubiquitous; the first motion films were made; the successful wireless experiments were undertaken; and the telephone made its appearance. The consequences of these changes were many and profound, for in one sense the whole point about the British Empire, and that which most struck contemporaries, was its dissolution of space. The miracle of new technology, it was believed, had broken the tyranny of distance and allowed Britain to administer and control the affairs of an empire of unparalleled geographic reach. Empire was about communications, and communications were about breaking down the conceptions of near and far. The impact of new communication and media technology have been well surveyed in the researches of Innis, *Empire and Communications*; Grant, *Technology and Empire*; McLuhan, *Understanding Media*; Williams, *Communications*; Headrick, *The Tools of Empire*; Adas, *Machines as the Measure of Men*; Deibert, *Parchment, Printing and Hypermedia*; Crowley and Heyer, *Communication in History*; and Marvin *When Old Technologies were New*.[8]

From the early nineteenth to the mid-twentieth centuries, Great Britain was a supreme *communication media power*; that is to say, it possessed unparalleled capacity to report and transmit news, information and ideas, as well as transport people, soldiers and produce, around the world. Britain was also the predominant *imperial power*, that is, it controlled and directed the affairs of large parts of the world. These were two distinct states of affairs. Yet there were close and reciprocal links between the two. It was communication media power that helped create and sustain imperial power, and this power in turn reinforced and shaped the development of communication media power. The essays in this book trace and analyse the intimate relationship between the British Empire and the media systems that it nurtured between the end of the Napoleonic Wars, when the basis of the Empire was laid, to the 'wind of change' in Africa which marked the end of her pretensions to be the imperial superpower. Rather than being primarily metropolitan or peripheral, the emphasis of the essays is on the relations between the two. Communication media did not merely underpin the metropolitan–peripheral relationship, they dynamically shaped its evolution.

Although the complementarity between media and empire was seminal, the nature of the relationship between the two was paradoxical. Britain's imperial commitments distorted the development of communication and media systems within her various colonies and Dominions and compromised their effectiveness. At the same time, the imperial relationship helped to create and sustain new forms of media and cultural expressions within the constituent parts of her Empire, which were frequently successful in withstanding metropolitan pressures and in which peculiarly local concerns developed and flourished.

Media and the British Empire: themes

While the case studies in this collection reveal the complex interplay of different media landscapes and the diverse and divergent contexts of Britain's far-flung Dominions and colonies, several key themes are discernible.

Communications and empire

The infrastructure of the communication system and the impact of new technology lie at the core of any appreciation of an empire–information– media network and the creation of an imperial media culture. Harold Adam Innis, who is generally considered the founding father of this genre of research, proposed in the early 1950s a theoretical framework for analysing the bias of media towards space- or time-saving characteristics and its consequences for imperial expansion. Traditionally, media systems had permitted the transfer of information through time. It was the shift towards the more ready transmission of information across space, particularly from the eighteenth century onwards, that permitted the articulation of global empires. However, communication systems have always to be embodied in institutions which operate and deploy them, and these institutions, while helping to form the politics of imperial government and ruling elites, are themselves subject to their influence and agendas.

Thus, Donald Read in his study of Reuters, *The Power of News*, argues that, despite its adherence to independence and impartiality, the company remained an imperial institution with close links to metropolitan and colonial governments. The relationship with India is a case in point.[9] However, there were areas of the international news market that remained 'surprisingly tenuous', including the Antipodes, and this provides the subject of Cryle's study (chapter 11), which examines colonial challenges to the imperial news and cable system, as it impacted on Australia and New Zealand in the period 1870–1912. He analyses the alliance formed between the Australian and New Zealand Press Associations (NZPA) in order to counter the market presence of Reuters, and outlines the politics of the Pacific cable as an alternative to the Eastern Telegraph Company at the turn of the century. Cryle contends that the colonial press played a significant role, as a competitor in the first instance and as an ambivalent mouthpiece for competing cable and public interests in the second.

The criticisms emanating from these press associations were based on both commercial factors – the high cost of cabled news – and the fact that 'its news was not sufficiently local'. Cryle notes the 'rapidity with which cabled information had become integral to colonial administration and business' before the Great War and the fact that colonial governments played a significant role in mediating and subsidising news and convening inter-colonial communication policy which involved participation in international conferences. Such developments were also of immense concern to the press of the Empire and one of its most visible institutional responses took the shape of the Imperial Press conferences and Empire Press Union, which forms the subject of Kaul's study (chapter 8). British, colonial and Dominion press representatives meeting for the First Conference in London during 1909, and in subsequent conferences in different parts of the Empire, reiterated their conviction of the importance of maintaining cheap and efficient communication links between the various parts of the Empire by way of telegraph cables (and later wireless and airplanes) for press use so as to create and enhance imperial cohesion, increase inter-imperial knowledge, and serve the needs of imperial security and defence: 'You cannot build a durable empire on ignorance,' claimed Stanley Reed, editor of the *Times of India*.

The importance of press associations and news agencies in the development of an imperial press network has been contended by Potter, Boyd-Barrett, Rantanen, Kaul and others. However, Harvey (chapter 12) puts this argument to the test by analysing the microsphere of the local press – in his case the *Inangahua Times*, published in the remote mining town of Reefton, New Zealand. The development of the NZPA in 1878 shaped the way in which news was sourced and its distribution, with its monopoly imposing a cohesiveness to the information relayed and opening the possibility of manipulation by government. Focusing on the 1890s, Harvey demonstrates how, despite acute financial constraints, the *Inangahua Times*' proprietor, Mrs Potts, went to extreme lengths to continue her subscription for overseas and imperial cable news from the NZPA. Despite this, Harvey contends that the *Inangahua Times* 'remained determinedly a local newspaper' and is sceptical about the notion of 'mutual interdependence' between Britain and the Dominions as a consequence of the imperial press system developing from the late nineteenth century.

The hardware of imperial communications is the subject of Canuel's study (chapter 14). He notes how the completion in 1902 of the submarine cable linking Vancouver to Australia made Canada an essential link in the British imperial communications network, which had begun in 1866. There is 'no doubt', in Canuel's mind, 'that this technology brought a certain unity to the British Empire and that the cable monopolies often anticipated or favoured Imperial needs'. However, the Great War proved critical in turning the 'world of wireless into the world of radio by passing from the electric to the electronic era', at the same time that the political status of Canada was being transformed. The consequences of these developments were manifest during the Second World War, when the Canadian Government, despite its sympathy for British war aims, affirmed the right to have an independent policy *vis-à-vis* wireless beam stations and the radio, regarding this sophisticated technology for influencing opinion as a powerful new weapon with which to assert their national identity on an international stage. Hence, while radio, argues Canuel, 'did not rid itself fully of the stigmata of imperialism', it would be incorrect to conclude that peripheries could not control this technology and claim a measure of autonomy. 'From this point of view, the dichotomy of centre versus periphery constitutes the substrata of communications.' Even so, as the influence of the British experts and the BBC on the content and form of the wireless programming demonstrates, old ties of loyalty and deference were hard to break.

In their respective ways, each essay in this section affirms in the imperial context the importance of electric communications, from the spread of the telegraph in the 1870s–1890s to the use of the wireless and electronic radio in the 1940s. However, while communication technology served to bind metropole and periphery ever closer together and link the various parts of the Empire, it was simultaneously the focus for a power struggle between colonial interests and those of the centre. The greater political freedoms enjoyed by the Dominions of Australia, New Zealand and Canada were translated into a greater independence to decide communication policy and address local and regional commercial imperatives, while at the same time adhering to the imperial demands. As such these case studies serve as a useful reminder against taking a position that is too technologically determinist.

The metropolitan impact of empire: the presence of India in British politics and media

While the importance of the centre–periphery dynamic is generally acknowledged, there are still relatively few in-depth appreciations of the use of the metropolitan media to pursue imperial themes. Until recently, India, despite being the largest of Britain's imperial possessions, was largely absent from studies on the impact of empire on the metropolis and the media. Recent publications have begun to fill this lacuna. Kaul's *Reporting the Raj*, for instance, examines the treatment of Indian issues in the national newspaper press in the critical 1880–1920s period. She considers the nature of Fleet Street coverage, the role of Reuters and telegraph communications in shaping the news agenda, and the attempts made by the India Office – especially under the impetus of the Great War and a publicity-conscious Secretary of State, Edwin Montagu – to incorporate the press management function into government strategy.[10] Two collected volumes of essays also deserve attention. Peers and Finklestein's volume *Negotiating India in the Nineteenth-Century Media* concentrates on Indian coverage in the periodical press of nineteenth-century Britain, tackling issues of race, gender, national identity, technology, education, the army, etc., while some contributors to Codell's *Imperial Histories, National Co-Histories and the British and Colonial Press*, which examines 'the intersecting national and imperial discourses' in the Victorian press, study Indian representations in specialist publications like *The Imperial Gazetteer* and *The Journal of Indian Art and Industry*.[11]

Academic attention has, of course, been devoted to analysing press responses to individual events and issues, and none more so than those surrounding the Great Rebellion, or 'Mutiny', of 1857–8.[12] Pratt (chapter 6) discusses how a specific interpretation of these events was used in an attempt to bolster the cause of radical politics in Britain, in particular the depressed fortunes of the Chartist Movement and the leadership claims of Ernest Jones. Through commentary, analysis and future predictions in *The People's Paper*, Jones argued that the dissatisfaction of both the Indian insurgents and the Chartists sprang from a similar source – the underlying corruption of the English political system. Thus members of both groups were not reactionaries but political reformers. Pratt claims that the deficiencies in the communication and information networks between India and Britain at this time created a news vacuum which Jones successfully exploited for his propaganda. It was only subsequently when 'eye witness' accounts began to appear in Fleet Street and the rumour-mongering began in earnest that the power of his narrative began to be undermined.

St John's study of Winston Churchill (chapter 7) provides another example of a British politician seeking to use India for domestic advantage and the central role occupied by the press in this process. When the Conservative leadership backed Irwin's plans for reform in India, Churchill joined Lord Rothermere, owner of the mass circulation *Daily Mail*, to mobilise middle-class opinion, not only against the reforms, but also against Stanley Baldwin's leadership of the Conservative Party. This study demonstrates the need for care in the handling of the domestic impact of empire news. Though Churchill was supported by the *Mail*, politicians generally assumed that the newspaper's readers were not that interested in India: media power in this instance did not translate into political power. Second, as St John argues, press opinion was a multilayered phenomenon: it was the heavyweight political press, especially *The Times*, that was influential in policy debates concerning India and this press favoured reform. St John reminds us, finally, that imperial–press politics, like any other, operated through individuals. The fact that neither Churchill nor Rothermere in the 1930s inspired trust was a key factor in the failure of their campaign. Even so, the conclusion of his study underpins a central contention of this volume: that British press coverage of Churchill's campaign helped to discredit the reform process *within India*. It was these imperial cross-currents, as Indian nationalists read Churchill's attacks on Gandhi and the princes saw that British opinion was divided, that ultimately sabotaged the 1935 India Act, with profound consequences for the nature of Britain's ultimate departure from India.

In contrast to the campaigns of individual politicians, Kaul's study of India in the context of the Imperial Press Conferences and the Empire Press Union (EPU) from 1909 to 1946 (chapter 8) offers an institutional perspective, examining the contradictions inherent in the case of a subject colony operating in an association extolling the virtues of a 'free' press and communication. Indian participation in the early years was largely through the British editors and journalists who represented the powerful Anglo-Indian press which formed an integral part of the British scheme of things in India. It was only from the 1930s, and especially with the impact of the Second World War, that a radical shift occurred towards greater Indian presence in the composition of the delegation. To some extent these developments reflected the influence of the EPU ethos, which was based on equality for members of the British imperial 'family' and the intention of creating a forum for discussion which was consciously pan-Empire. To a further degree this was also due to the conviction of generations of liberals from Thomas Macaulay onwards that free speech and association was necessary for the emergence of a successful polity within the subcontinent. The dilemma for this liberal theory of the press was that Indian newspapers had always to operate in the context of autocratic imperial control. While the press had been predominantly a British-owned and operated concern, this dichotomy had generally been obscured. But as the twentieth century progressed, with the nationalist movement acquiring more sophisticated means of propaganda, the press itself striving to become less partisan and more critical, and individual editors like Arthur Moore of the *Statesman* working harder to place the Indian and Anglo-Indian press on an equal footing, the cracks in the edifice were prised apart ever wider. Indian participation in such an international forum like the Imperial Press conferences and the EPU thus supplied a further impetus to such developments. The growing international exposure enjoyed by Indian journalists brought with it an increasing self-confidence and an enhanced ability to articulate the inequalities under which they had to operate – drawing, in the process, attention to the nature of the government's media manipulation and censorship.

Society and culture

The study of imperial culture and its associated theme of 'cultural imperialism' has attracted a range of inspiring research in recent decades. Notable contributions have included the Manchester Imperialism series, beginning in the mid-1980s with MacKenzie's treatises on propaganda and popular imperialism in Britain in the 1880–1940s, the

Subaltern studies of South Asian history, the seminal impact of Said's *Culture and Imperialism* and *Orientalism*, as well as the works by Hall, Hyam, Bratlinger, Bhabha, Burton, Nandy, Spivak and McClintock – all of which have served to galvanise this genre of historical research and emphasise the importance of writing co-histories.[13] The media in its widest sense, including all forms of institutions and products that embed and serve to transmit notions of identity, race and culture, form an important avenue for such exploration.

Operating in this tradition, Heath argues (chapter 10) that with the growing cultural interconnectedness of the Empire, there had emerged by the late nineteenth century something like a giant literary web, with Britain at its centre. Given its imperial claim to a 'civilising mission' – to inculcate British notions of morality and civility – metropolitan concern arose over the diffusion of 'unwholesome' literature – books, magazines and photographs – from Britain to its subject populations. Consequently, moral regulation and censorship came to be seen as necessary, to maintain not only the 'purity' of the English 'race' and culture, but also the unity and purpose of the Empire. Therefore, governments began to institute the framework for an imperial system of moral censorship to regulate such trade. Australia and India were the largest imperial markets for British books and publications and there-fore became particular targets of this moral crusade. Yet in both cases the implementation of this policy proved problematic. In Australia the system of censorship, though modelled on Britain's, aimed also to protect Australia from British culture and ultimately make her the new moral centre of the Empire. In the case of India, for instance, despite some initial enthusiasm, the practical difficulties proved insurmount-able, and by the early twentieth century Indians turned against British cultural importation, with the nationalists using it as yet another lever to reject its moral authority to govern. Thus, Heath contends that by the 1920s there was, paradoxically, a general conviction that British culture itself was degenerate and a danger to the empire's moral welfare.

Lewis's study of the colonial culture of 1930s Penang (chapter 15) takes issue with the genres of intellectual discourse surrounding the emergence of nationalism influenced by Anderson's seminal study of the impetus to nationalism provided by the growth of 'imagined communities' through the impact of print and the vernacular press.[14] She argues that such a perspective does not take due account of the cultural heterogeneity of port cities – an aspect she focuses on when examining the context of one of Penang's most popular newspapers, the English-language *Straits Echo*. Under Chinese ownership and edited by a

Ceylonese, the paper championed English as a vehicle for cross-cultural agency, and Lewis analyses how debate in the paper's columns over a range of issues, such as the position of women and diasporic loyalties, created a discourse of cosmopolitanism that advocated intercultural co-operation as an alternative to the ethno-nationalisms of Malaya's major ethnic communities: Malay, Chinese and Indian, which sought to preserve and promote separate identities.

Important insights into the origins of the press culture of South Africa are provided by John MacKenzie's study (chapter 2), which analyses the evolution of a free press and the general efflorescence of an intellectual and literary culture in the Cape in the early nineteenth century by means of an examination of the prominent role of the 'Scotch Independents' including John Philip, Thomas Pringle and John Fairbairn. He discusses their struggle with the colonial authorities over freedom of expression and traces the influence of the attitudes and ideas imbibed in Scotland in the formation within the Cape of a 'bourgeois public sphere' which was 'intellectual, religious, political *and* mercantile all at once'. This was reflected in the insistence among members of the Scottish diaspora on the importance of a free press as well as in the establishment of institutions like the South African College, literary and scientific societies, schools, a South African Museum and a Botanic garden.

This cultural revolution in the Cape was stymied throughout the early nineteenth century by the political machinations of governors, despite moves at reform in the civil service and the introduction of liberal measures which had an impact on issues of race and slavery, legal equality, corruption and the relationship between the English and Dutch communities. In these controversies too, the Scots, claims MacKenzie, played a prominent role. Yet, ironically, despite their opposition to the 'autocratic imperialism' of these years, the Scots were themselves 'heavily implicated' in types of cultural imperialism. 'The press they created was free ... to propagate their own distinctive social, educational, economic and political views, often closely bound up with their Scottish intellectual and educational backgrounds.'

In contrast to the *Straits Echo*, which was the antithesis of a colonial mouthpiece, Lambert's study of the English language press in South Africa from the 1890s through to the 1960s (chapter 3) reveals a press culture catering for a minority community and whose 'leitmotif' was 'loyalty to the imperial ideal'. At the risk of alienating educated Afrikaner opinion, such press coverage 'reflected their sense of British identity and their belief in the superiority of the British way of life. They also reinforced them.' This imperial ethos included, for instance, a reverence for monarchy such that even mild irreverence, as displayed by the Johannesburg *Star* on the death of Queen Victoria's grandson, the Duke of Clarence, in 1892, resulted in attempts 'to lynch the editor and physical attacks on the newspaper's offices'. News was dominated by the London connection, with Reuters playing a leading role and Fleet Street papers like the *Daily Mail* serving as a medium for influencing peripheral opinion with metropolitan imperial perspectives. However, although the press was British-'oriented' it was not 'controlled' from London, and local interests – in particular the Randlords, who dominated the gold industry – realised the value of using the press to further their interests initiating 'a process that was to see intimate links created between the English-language press, mining capital and imperialism'. Lambert paints a disquieting picture of the ebb and flow of South African politics in the twentieth century, linking the role of the partisan press and journalists to the ensuing culture of distrust between its communities.

The challenges confronting a press operating within a western paradigm and under non-indigenous ownership in a postcolonial context forms the subject of Cass's study of newspaper coverage of the 1969 Bougainville crisis in Papua New Guinea, focusing on the only English daily newspaper the *Post Courier* (chapter 13). The proposal to mine copper ore in Bougainville brought to the fore unresolved issues of race, ethnicity and tradition bequeathed by the decision, in 1898, to include Bougainville in German New Guinea, despite the fact that it was ethnically and geographically part of the British-controlled Solomons. In the controversy as to whether the copper should be mined at all and in whose interests, the *Post Courier*, which showed some sympathy with the plight of the Bougainvilleans, provided an important forum for debate. Interestingly, the idea of 'creating a united and unified nation was central in all the media' and in a 'complete reversal' of the usual case of newly developed countries, the Australian-owned newspapers and the government radio service displayed several characteristics of developmental journalism, including such functions as the promotion of a sense of national identity as a means of uniting disparate tribal and language groups. Symbolically, the Bougainville mine fulfilled such a role in the *Post Courier*. Yet, overall, the chief lesson to be drawn from the paper's coverage, according to Cass, is 'that when the media in a colony is owned by expatriates, however well intentioned it may be and however sympathetic towards the aspirations of the indigenous peoples, it will still see things through the eye of the colonial power'.

What the case studies in this section reveal is the complexity of the social and cultural context within which print media functioned and were utilised by a range of consumers. Issues of 'moral censorship', political ideology, racial purity and ethnic difference, cultural imperialism and cosmopolitan projects all shaped press responses to issues generated either at the centre or within the localities. Press involvement in the imperial projects differed widely, from the partisan press in South Africa to the modernising one in Malaya. They show how despite metropolitan pressure – in the case of Papua New Guinea from Australia, in the case of India from Britain – peripheral societies were able to oppose political and cultural directives and utilise tradition and customary law to advance their perceived interests. They also reveal how the institution of the press itself was imagined as the cultural harbinger of different visions of progress whether it be the free thinking enlightenment of the Scots at the Cape or the self-conscious cosmopolitanism of the English-speaking communities in Penang.

Government media management and political propaganda: the context of the retreat from empire

Though the government–media nexus has existed in varied forms throughout history, the twentieth century witnessed a particularly intense and concerted attempt to 'manage' the media and disseminate official propaganda particularly in western societies, linked in no small measure to the fact that politicians were operating in an age of mass media and democracy with rapid advances in technological sophistication of the communication network, and a high incidence of war and conflict. J. A. Spender, the influential editor of the *Westminster Gazette* whose career spanned the late nineteenth and early twentieth centuries, reflected on the shift in attitudes that had occurred by 1939:

> When I first came on the scene, these relations were irregular and capricious and both sides pretended that they did not exist. How much of a pretence that was may be seen from the numerous memoirs and other records in which Victorian statesmen are revealed in intimate touch with editors and journalists and endeavouring to use newspapers, sometimes for their private and sometimes for public purposes. The rigid virtue which is sometimes attributed to the statesmen of former times is mostly a myth. It has always been highly improbable that members of a Government would keep their hands off their principal means of communicating with the public

and influencing opinion. They never have, but there has generally been a flavour of the illicit in their relations with newspapers.[15]

The explicit use by the British Government of the press, newsreels and cinema to disseminate propaganda received critical impetus from the Great War, which also gave birth to the institution of the Information Office within Whitehall, with, as Taylor observes, the Foreign Office – traditionally the most conservative of government departments – leading the way.[16] By the time of Spender's speech, as Cockett demonstrates, Chamberlain, the Foreign Office and the Downing Street press office were all heavily implicated in the manipulation of the press over appeasement, the success of the endeavour owing not a little to, in the words of Koss, 'the epidemic of self-restraint' exercised by the press.[17]

Developments similar to those witnessed in 1919 in Whitehall took place *vis-à-vis* imperial interests too. The India Office saw an information officer installed in 1921, with the subsequent formation of the Information and Publicity Department.[18] Within India the Government was keen, as Israel contends, to counter the increasingly sophisticated nationalist propaganda and information networks during the interwar years.[19] One area in which the Government retained technological advantage over nationalists was in the sphere of propaganda with newsreels. This has traditionally been a neglected source, but Woods (chapter 9) helps to correct this deficiency by painting a vivid picture of the deployment of propaganda around the events of August 1947 under the watchful eye of the publicity-conscious Viceroy, Lord Mountbatten. Newsreels, which were regularly shown in British cinemas under wartime arrangements, received high exposure and 'more than any other form of mass medium, have defined the way in which we see the first major decolonisation of the twentieth century'. As conceived by the Government, the 'transfer of power' to Indians (and Pakistanis) was not a humiliating surrender, but part of Britain's imperial mission; thus the official image of the independence celebrations was to be a positive affirmation of Britain's role overseen by a photogenic couple who had persuaded both the new nations to remain within the British Commonwealth. Unfortunately, there was no Indian newsreel to challenge such an official perspective. Thus Woods cites the example of the British Paramount newsreel editor cutting out scenes of Indian ceremonial rituals which accompanied the assumption of power in the Constituent Assembly in New Delhi around midnight on 14 August. Instead, he started coverage the next morning with the swearing-in of Lord Mountbatten as the first Governor-General of independent India.

Overall, the image of decolonisation portrayed (in contrast to Pakistani coverage) was 'positively euphoric'. Despite a more nuanced approach to events following independence, such as the partition riots, in general, Woods argues, the newsreels represent one of the ways in which 'decolonisation was made understandable and perhaps palatable to British audiences'.

Following Indian independence the postwar years witnessed the rapid disintegration of Britain's imperial edifice. Official manipulation of the British media during these years of imperial uncertainty can provide fruitful insights to complement the Indian case study. Two books published in the mid-1990s have explored this theme with some success. Shaw focuses on the Eden Government's handling of the media during the Suez Crisis and its repercussions, while Carruthers has examined how the British Government controlled the flow of information and influenced its interpretation when dealing with counter-insurgency in Cyprus, Malaya and Kenya during 1945–60.[20] Kenya, along with Central Africa, forms the subject of Murphy and Lewis's essay (chapter 4) in which they analyse the Colonial Office's press management in 1959, arguing that the relationship with the press was 'highly complex', 'fraught with contradictions' and aspects of it 'remain obscure'. Through encouraging positive spin on stories, leaking supportive reports that had not been intended for publication, utilising sympathetic MPs to raise issues in Parliament and combat pressure group criticism, and maintaining close links with its 'inner circle' of journalists, the Colonial Office 'proved remarkably successful' in managing newspaper comment regarding the treatment of Mau Mau suspects in Kenya's detention camps and its aftermath. However, with regard to Central Africa, where it was the Nyasaland Emergency that grabbed media attention, the authors claim that henceforth the Colonial Office was less effective and came under 'intense scrutiny', despite their attempts to pursue a policy of 'constructive engagement' with the media.

Remaining with the African continent, Williams (chapter 5) personalises the impact of official policy by focusing on the decision of Clement Attlee's Labour government in 1950 to exile Seretse Khama, Chief of the largest tribe, the Bangwato, from the British protectorate of Bechuanaland. Done ostensibly to avoid internecine conflict and help usher in the democratic process by diminishing the rule of chiefs, the real reason – which the media were quick to point out – was a response to pressure exerted by South Africa and Southern Rhodesia whose white minorities were opposed to Seretse's marriage to Ruth Williams, a white

Englishwoman. Seretse's case was taken up by sympathisers in Britain like the MP Fenner Brockway, who campaigned along with supporters in Bechuanaland. And with many of the latter being wealthy and well educated, their 'most effective weapon was their use of the media to influence international public opinion – the government's only real area of weakness'. Williams describes the virtual failure of the damage-limitation exercise of the Government, not only in Britain but within Bechuanaland – for instance, in the attempts of their information officer Nicholas Monsarrat to appease the international media gathered in the capital Serowe. Thus, despite the exile being permanent, in 1956 the Khamas were allowed to return to Bechuanaland and Williams claims one of the reasons for this was the adverse publicity which the Government had been unable to manage or limit. In 1966 Seretse became President of the newly independent Botswana.

These case studies reveal the importance of both official and, perhaps much more so, the unofficial and 'behind the scenes' contact between members of the fourth estate and government, and the limits to the success of such ventures. They suggest that it is in moments of crisis or potential weakness that governments are most assiduous about media manipulation and the media is most influential. However, Mark Tully reminds us in the Foreword of the danger to governments themselves of excessive attempts to manipulate the media, as well as serving as a warning to both members of the media and officials that it is not always the loudest voice which is heard – and with often unexpected consequences.

Notes

1. For instance, R. S. Lambert, *Propaganda* (London: Thomas Nelson & Son, 1938); H. D. Lasswell, *Propaganda Technique in World War One* (London, 1927); W. Lippman, *Public Opinion* (New York: Free Press, 1929).
2. Hans-Frederik Dahl, 'The Pursuit of Media History', *Media, Culture and Society*, vol. 16 (London and New Delhi: Sage, 1994), p. 556.
3. Ibid., p. 557.
4. M. de Nie, *The Eternal Paddy* (Madison: University of Wisconsin Press, 2004), S. J. Potter (ed.), *Newspapers and Empire in Ireland and Britain* (Dublin: Four Courts Press, 2004); P. Chowdhry, *Colonial India and the Making of Empire Cinema* (Manchester: Manchester University Press, 2000); James R. Ryan, *Picturing Empire* (London: Reaktion Books, 1997).
5. J. Curran, *Media and Power* (London: Routledge, 2002).
6. P. Scannell and D. Cardiff, *A Social History of British Broadcasting* (Oxford: Blackwell, 1991).
7. T. Standage, *The Victorian Internet* (London: Phoenix, 1999).

8. H. A. Innis, *The Bias of Communication* (1951, Toronto: University of Toronto Press, 1995 edition) and *Empire and Communications* (1950, Toronto: University of Toronto Press, 1986 edition); M. McLuhan, *The Gutenberg Galaxy* (Toronto: University of Toronto Press, 1962), *Understanding Media: The Extensions of Man* (London: Ark, 1964 edn.), *The Medium is the Message* (New York: Bantam 1967); M. Adas, *Machines as the Measure of Men* (Ithaca, NY: Cornell University Press, 1989); E. Havelock, *Preface to Plato* (Cambridge, MA: Harvard University Press, 1963); J. Goody (ed.), *Literacy and Traditional Societies* (Cambridge: Cambridge University Press, 1968); C. Marvin, *When Old Technologies were New* (New York: Oxford University Press, 1988); D. Crowley and P. Heyer (eds.), *Communication in History* (New York and London: Longman, 1991); D. R. Headrick, *The Tools of Empire* (New York: Oxford University Press, 1981) and *The Tentacles of Progress* (New York: Oxford University Press, 1988); R. J. Deibert, *Parchment, Printing and Hypermedia* (New York: Columbia University Press, 1997), R.Williams, *Communications* (Harmondsworth: Penguin, 1962).
9. D. Read, *The Power of News* (Oxford: Oxford University Press, 1992, 1999); Chandrika Kaul, *Reporting the Raj, The British Press and India 1880–1922* (Manchester: Manchester University Press, 2003), chapters 2, 5 and 7–9.
10. Ibid.
11. D. Finkelstein and D. M. Peers (eds.), *Negotiating India in the Nineteenth-Century Media* (London, Macmillan, 2000), Julie. F. Codell (ed.), *Imperial Co-Histories National Identities and the British and Colonial Press* (London: Fairleigh Dickinson University Press, 2003).
12. E. Palmegiano, 'The Indian Mutiny in the mid-Victorian Press', *Journal of Newspaper and Periodical History*, 7 (1991): 3–11; Finkelstein and Peers, *Negotiating India*, pp. 84–134; .J. Bender, 'Mutiny or Freedom Fight' in Potter, *Newspapers and Empire*, pp. 92–108.
13. J. M. MacKenzie, *Propaganda and Empire* (Manchester: Manchester University Press, 1984), (ed.), *Imperialism and Popular Culture* (Manchester: Manchester University Press, 1986), (ed.), *Popular Imperialism and the Military, 1850–1950* (Manchester: Manchester University Press, 1992); E. Said, *Culture and Imperialism* (London: Chatto and Windus, 1993) and *Orientalism* (New York: Routledge, 1978); C. Hall (ed.), *Cultures of Empire* (Manchester: Manchester University Press, 2000) and *Civilising Subjects* (Cambridge: Polity 2002); R. Hyam, *Empire and Sexuality* (Manchester: Manchester University Press, 1990); A. Burton, *Burdens of History* (Chapel Hill, NC: University of North Carolina Press, 1993); A. Nandy, *The Intimate Enemy* (Delhi: Oxford University Press, 1983); A. McClintock, *Imperial Leather* (New York: Routledge, 1995); G. Spivak, *In Other Worlds* (New York: Routledge, 1985); H. Bhaba, *The Location of Culture* (London: Routledge, 1994).
14. B. Anderson, *Imagined Communities* (London: Verso, 1983).
15. The Fourth Annual Imperial press conference of the Empire Press Union (London: EPU, 1939), p. 22.
16. P. Taylor, 'Publicity and Diplomacy', in D. Dilks (ed.), *Retreat from Power* (London: Macmillan, 1981), vol. I, pp. 48–9; see also Taylor, *Projection of Britain* (Cambridge: Cambridge University Press, 1981).
17. R. Cockett, *Twilight of Truth, Chamberlain, Appeasement and the Manipulation of the Press* (London: Weidenfeld and Nicolson, 1989); S. Koss, *The Rise and Fall of the Political Press in Britain* (London, Fontana 1990 combined volume), p. 984.

18. For a discussion of the early development of the Information department at the India Office, see Kaul, *Reporting the Raj*, pp. 151–4.
19. M. Israel, *Communications and Power* (Cambridge: Cambridge University Press, 1994).
20. S. L. Carruthers, *Winning Hearts and Minds* (London: Leicester University Press, 1995), T. Shaw, *Eden, Suez and the Mass Media* (London, I. B. Tauris, 1996).

2

'To Enlighten South Africa': The Creation of a Free Press at the Cape in the Early Nineteenth Century

John M. MacKenzie

The early nineteenth century has usually been interpreted as a period of autocratic rule in the colonies of the British Empire. The Napoleonic Wars produced systems designed for the exigencies of global conflict. A rapidly expanding empire had to be assimilated at a period before modern colonial bureaucracies – and their London headquarters – had been fully established. Moreover, governorships tended to be in the hands of military figures. After 1815, a continuing network of military governors, often connected with the Duke of Wellington and other key figures in the Peninsula campaigns, were sent to the colonies, not least to save them from the half-pay status of the unemployed officer.[1] They were invariably conservative, generally Tory in sympathies, and all their experience and predilections led them to be anxious about the possibility of the spread of a seditious Jacobinism in the Empire. They were therefore disposed to maintain the tight clamps on associations and on publishing of all sorts, which had been imposed during the era of the wars with revolutionary and Napoleonic France.

In India, for example, regulations were issued in 1799 to maintain tight controls on the press. The East India Company administration had been worried about the scurrilous nature of some of the early English journalism in Bengal, notably that of James Augustus Hicky. By the end of the century three anxieties had combined in stimulating these efforts at repression: the damaging effects of social scandal on the reputation of the Government; the growing dissent of an emergent Indian elite; and the possibility of revolutionary contamination from France. More-over, the number of printing presses in India had been growing to what the Company found an alarming degree. The regulations decreed that all newspapers had to be inspected by a high-ranking official, and editors had to comply with censorship on pain of deportation from the subcontinent.[2] These gags were maintained for twenty years after the end of the Napoleonic Wars, a period marked by many struggles to establish civil freedoms, including that of the press. Two Scots, Dr Charles Maclean, surgeon and Aberdeen graduate, and a minister, Rev. James Bryce, set about trying to establish press freedom during the imperious rule of the Marquess Wellesley.[3] Press freedoms were not fully restored until the governor-generalship of Charles Metcalfe, acting on the advice of T. B. Macaulay. They were often revoked by subsequent 'gagging acts', as the political temperature rose to fever pitch in the later nineteenth and early twentieth centuries.

From the British conquest of the Cape from the Dutch in 1795 (interrupted only by the Batavian Government interlude between 1803 and 1806),[4] the new colony became a vital staging post on the route to India. All East India Company and royal naval vessels heading to the East called there on outward and homeward voyages. They were joined increasingly by those of private companies. Regiments often served in both India and the Cape. As the nineteenth century wore on, many Anglo-Indian military officers and civilians began to use the Cape as a place to take their leaves. It was also closely connected to St Helena, particularly during the period of Napoleon Bonaparte's exile there, as well as to Indian Ocean islands such as Mauritius and Ceylon (Sri Lanka). The trades of South-East Asia and of China were also routed, on the outward voyages, via the Cape. The colony was thus of great strategic significance in the British global system, and its own economy developed considerably (with the usual cyclical checks) during the first half of the nineteenth century.

The combination of such strategic importance with a strong military presence and a potentially rebellious population of Dutch colonists, not to mention a considerable number of slaves and recurrent frontier wars, ensured that the early British governors were not likely to be enamoured of freedom of association or expression. In May and July 1800 the Governor Sir George Yonge issued regulations for the establishment of a printing press and the publication of newspapers by the firm of Walker and Robertson, better known at the Cape as ship hirers and merchants in the import/export business.[5] These regulations were closely connected with others banning any association which was perceived to be Jacobin in its tendencies (which effectively covered all societies that might at any time criticise the colonial authorities). Thus the Government was to exercise complete control, and indeed eventually took the first private press into official ownership. The *Cape Town Gazette*, an official sheet containing announcements of regulations, ordinances and appointments, remained the only publication.

Once again, it was Scots who were at the centre of the struggle to create freedom of expression. Scotland was itself a cockpit of publishing and of the press, and Scots were at this time spreading Enlightenment ideas imbibed at the Scottish universities to various imperial possessions. At the Cape, the long-standing Tory Governor Lord Charles Somerset, who ruled by autocratic proclamation between 1814 and 1826, was determined to frustrate such developments, viewing them as potentially productive of seditious and even republican ideas.[6] But by the 1820s, a group of Scots had arrived at the Cape determined to establish the institutions they had known in Scotland.[7] They included George Greig, an experienced printer who imported a printing press, Archibald Robertson who became an influential Cape Town bookseller and publisher, and, above all, John Fairbairn who was to edit, and later own, *The South African Commercial Advertiser*, which became involved in all the contentious issues of the day. Fairbairn had been a friend of the writer, poet and settler Thomas Pringle while still in Edinburgh, and they now teamed up on a number of projects, including publishing.

The point about all of this activity, however, is that the press was part of a wider intellectual ferment, connected in a variety of ways to the establishment of literary and scientific societies, to frontier and 'native' policy, to the abolition of slavery, and to missionary endeavour, particularly as personified by yet another Scot, the London Missionary Society superintendent, Dr John Philip. The press, which Somerset made strenuous but failing attempts to suppress, was part of a wider creation of a bourgeois, intellectual and also commercial public sphere. The Scots were motivated not just by the ambition to influence matters of governance, religion and frontier settlement, but also to create banking, insurance and commercial institutions. The press was a vehicle for all these concerns, much influenced by Adam Smith and other figures of the Scottish Enlightenment. By 1853, the efforts of this group (in league with influential Dutch and English allies) culminated in the establishment of representative government at the Cape.

Somerset and the 'Scotch Independents'

Three Scottish figures dominated this tempestuous period at the Cape, and the developments of the 1820s can only be understood in terms of their background. The first of these to arrive was Dr John Philip (1775–1851), the highly influential superintendent of the London Missionary Society.[8] Philip was the son of a handloom weaver from Fife, and born therefore into a social group that was to be most disadvantaged by the developing industrialism of the period. Well schooled, he worked at a mill in Dundee in the 1790s, an experience which contributed to his sense of social injustice. By 1799 he believed he had a vocation and went to the Congregationalist college at Hoxton to train as a minister. He was duly ordained in the Congregationalist Church, then increasingly powerful in Scotland, and in 1804 became minister of a church in Aberdeen. There he began to display his radical tendencies, his belief in the relationship between religion and politics, and his search for a particular kind of practical and involved evangelicalism. He was also a powerful and popular preacher, frequently filling a large church to capacity.

In 1817, Philip decided to accept an invitation by the London Missionary Society to take over the position of superintendent at the Cape and landed there in February 1819. He quickly became a highly controversial figure. His house in Cape Town was visited by all the most notable divines and missionaries of the period, as well as by influential secular figures. He soon had many critics within the ecclesiastical as well as the lay worlds of the Cape. He was seen as assuming episcopal powers, as entering too enthusiastically into the secular realm, in both Cape Town itself and the frontier. He was critical of fellow missionaries and earned the enmity of other celebrated Scots, such as Robert Moffat, the LMS missionary at Kuruman. But in his distinctive courting of both secular and religious controversy, he clearly saw the press as a significant ally. He was an assiduous propagandist for his ideas, whether from the pulpit, through pamphlet and book publishing, or newspaper articles.

Thomas Pringle (1789–1834) arrived the year after Philip and in very different circumstances.[9] He went to the Cape as leader of a party in the 1820 settlement, a government-supported migration scheme designed to settle the eastern Cape frontier and supposedly help protect it from the incursions of southern Nguni people. Pringle, whose group was patronised by Sir Walter Scott, was an unlikely figure to be involved in such a venture. He was a disabled writer and journalist, poet and campaigner, a sensitive figure in appearance and character, who was to become the leading publicist for the settlers' plight on the frontier. Two years after their arrival, after a series of disasters on the frontier, Pringle left for Cape Town with the intention of agitating for greater support for the settlers.

When Pringle arrived in Cape Town from the frontier, he was appointed sub-librarian of the city's public library. This helped to position him within the small Cape elite group interested in establishing literary, scientific, educational, religious and publishing institutions and ventures in the colony. He was soon joined by John Fairbairn (1794–1864), a friend from Edinburgh student days, who was to be perhaps the central figure in the press agitation and was also highly influential in many issues and developments at the Cape over the next three decades. Fairbairn shared Borders origins with Pringle.[10] He went to Edinburgh University in 1810, and by 1812 had formed a firm friendship with Pringle. Fairbairn started in the Humanities, but in 1812 moved to medicine, attending classes in chemistry, pharmacy, anatomy, surgery and physics. Although he subsequently abandoned his medical studies, he must have developed broad interests which were to stand him in good stead in his subsequent activities at the Cape. He and Pringle were active in the Edinburgh Literary Society. In 1817 he went to teach in Newcastle upon Tyne, where there was a Scottish colony. He soon joined the celebrated Literary and Philosophical Society in the city, founded in 1794. He was a member from 1818 to 1823 and read many papers before its members. This society, and others like it, would have represented many liberal, humanitarian and Romantic views.

But Fairbairn's links with Edinburgh were far from broken. Pringle had become the joint editor of *Blackwood's Edinburgh Monthly Magazine* (more commonly known as *Blackwood's*), which was intended to be a Tory response to the Whig *Edinburgh Review*. After a few issues (it is possible that he was out of sympathy with its politics) Pringle moved on to edit Constable's *Edinburgh Magazine*, and Fairbairn contributed to the latter from 1817. He continued to do so from Newcastle, often providing translations of German (and occasionally French) poetry, notably by Goethe and Herder, as well as original work of his own. Thus, Pringle and Fairbairn helped to maintain Edinburgh's links with the European Romantic movement. In 1819, Pringle announced to his friend that he had decided to join the 1820 settlement scheme and tried to persuade Fairbairn to join him. The latter declined. But Pringle kept up the pressure from the Cape, and in 1823 Fairbairn relented and set out for the colony. In a letter to Pringle, he wrote: 'Your hint about Magazines and Newspapers pleases me exceedingly. What would hinder us from becoming "Franklins of the Kaap"?'[11] The reference is to Benjamin Franklin (1706–90), who set up a printing press in Philadelphia, bought the *Pennsylvania Gazette* in 1729 and established a reputation as a journalist. Fairbairn, exhibiting a strong sense of history, clearly felt that he and Pringle could chart a similar course at the Cape almost a century on. They must also have realised that they could make a bigger mark in the smaller and pioneering world of the Cape than they could in Edinburgh or Newcastle. In Cape Town, Fairbairn and Pringle founded a Classical and Commercial Academy, which opened in December 1823. Soon, many of the Cape notables were sending their sons to this school, its name presumably indicative of the notion that this was to be something more than a grammar school, combining classical and practical studies.

Philip, Pringle and Fairbairn joined a small, but highly influential group of Scots at the Cape, a number of them members of the mercantile and shipping elite. They dominated some of the professions. Their centrality in the founding of the major cultural, scientific and intellectual institutions of the time brought them into shifting alliances with other ethnic components of the white population, notably the Dutch and the English. In all these activities they brought distinctive Scottish training and attitudes to bear on the administrative and developmental problems of the Cape. In many ways they were attempting to replicate the intellectual and cultural life of contemporary British cities, notably Edinburgh. Schools, the South African College, literary and scientific societies, a South African Museum, later a botanic garden and above all a free press were not ends in themselves. They were designed to introduce some of the intellectual, humanitarian and evangelical ferment of the day, a transplantation of the contemporary norms of their class from Europe to the southern tip of Africa. In all of this, there was no sense that cultural and capitalist enterprises were in conflict. The essence of their philosophy was that the two were mutually and appropriately supporting. The bourgeois public sphere that they set about creating and dominating was intellectual, religious, political *and* mercantile all at once. They were wholly eclectic in their interests. Frontier, missions, slavery, the status of the Khoi (then known as the Hottentots), commercial developments and the political influence of the settlers were all grist to their mill. And to them a central characteristic of such an outpost of enlightened activity was the existence of a free press as a printed forum for their ideas and an exchange of views.

This is well illustrated by the activities of these leading Scots at the Cape between the 1820s and the 1850s. The educational activities of Pringle and Fairbairn, of which Philip would have approved, seemed to represent a relatively uncontroversial start to their 'improving' aspirations. Soon, however, their ambitions were to lead into a period of considerable turmoil in Cape Town. The Edinburgh student friends were quickly mixed up with other Scots individuals, not just John Philip, but also George Greig, Alfred Robertson, the merchant

H. E. Rutherfoord and Archibald Robertson. Merchants, printers, divines and intellectuals were all united in wishing to see an end to autocracy and all forms of coercion and monopolistic restriction. The new press would thus become a hotbed of controversy, a turbulent centre for resistance to established power, a factional flag that would stimulate efforts at suppression by the Governor and inspire the hatred of settlers, as well as fierce tussles between the Cape metropole and frontier interests.

Thomas Pringle first applied to establish a literary periodical in January 1823. He was working in league with a Dutch cleric, the Rev. Abraham Faure, and their idea was to publish a monthly magazine, alternately in English and Dutch, mainly devoted to literary and intellectual topics, and designed, as Pringle put it, 'to enlighten South Africa'.[12] They pledged themselves to avoid the discussion of all 'agitating or controversial topics'. The idea was approved by the Cape colonial secretary Colonel Bird, but Somerset soon overruled his subordinate's decision.[13] Somerset may have been aware that, as in Edinburgh, supposed literary periodicals were Trojan horses for much wider concerns. Greig tried in July 1823 and was again refused, despite promising to exclude 'personal controversy' and any discussion of 'the policy or administration of the Colonial Government'. Indeed, it may be that Greig had the limited intention of supplying commercial information and offering space for advertisements. By December 1823, the Secretary of State in London had intervened and Pringle was permitted to publish. Fairbairn and Pringle co-operated in the issue of the *South African Journal*, a quarterly intended to be mainly literary in its content. Meanwhile Rev. Faure proceeded to issue what became, in effect, a Dutch rival, *Nederduitsch Zuid-Afrikaansche Tijdshrift*, which drew much less notice from the authorities and survived from 1824 to 1843. Greig discovered that there appeared to be no ban on the publication of newspapers (only periodicals) and set about publishing the *South African Commercial Advertiser*, which he then offered to Pringle and Fairbairn for their editorship. The paper was to contain a mix of poetry with law reports (including a case involving a critic of the Governor),[14] and politically sensitive material, such as the fortunes of the eastern Cape settlers, as well as thinly veiled attacks on despotic government (portrayed as a characteristic of continental Europe, though few readers would have failed to draw the inference that the Cape was another example).[15] The *Advertiser* was, of course, being closely watched in Government House and soon incurred the ire of the Governor. He set about attempting to censor it by insisting that the Fiscal, the senior law officer, should see all copy and have the right to ban publication (by this time the *Advertiser* had reached issue 18). To this, Fairbairn and Pringle asserted their intention 'never to compromise our birthright as British subjects by editing any publication under censorship'.[16] The *Advertiser* had been provocative in a number of ways. One editorial intoned, 'No Government has yet been found capable of resisting, for any protracted period, the united voice of Public Opinion'.[17] The paper had, perhaps cheekily, applied for the same postage facilities enjoyed by the *Gazette*.[18] The epigraph of the paper also asserted, 'The mass of every People must be barbarous where there is no Printing'.[19]

Somerset's general state of paranoia was not helped when a poster libel circulated in Cape Town, accusing him of a sexual relationship with Dr James Barry, a military doctor who also treated the Governor and was known to enjoy a close friendship with him. Barry was the son of an Irish artist, but his formative years had been spent in Edinburgh, where he had studied medicine. Clearly, the accusation of what was believed to be a homosexual relationship was a very serious one for the time, although the story is greatly complicated by the fact that after his death, Barry was discovered to be a woman.[20] The libel contributed to the highly fevered atmosphere at the Cape and contributed greatly to Somerset's sense of being under serious personal attack.

Somerset broadened his assault on those he perceived to be his enemies by undermining the Fairbairn–Pringle school. He considered this to be a 'seminary of sedition', a hotbed of Jacobinism, and that the teachers were instilling 'the disgusting principles of Republicanism' in their pupils.[21] The numbers of pupils duly declined. Meanwhile, the *Commercial Advertiser* was closed.[22] Somerset ordered that Greig's press should be sealed, but the Fiscal and his officers failed to seal the type. Greig proceeded to bring out a remarkable pamphlet, produced on wetted paper with mallet and planer, without the help of the press. Greig and his employees worked all night on this, and distributed hundreds of copies from the windows of Greig's premises, creating the sensation Somerset no doubt wished to avoid.[23]

Somerset next ordered the confiscation of Greig's press and his type, enraging Philip who considered it to be the property of the LMS. Greig himself was banished from the colony. This must have been galling for him since he had originally been disposed to be much more cautious about opposing the Government. Somerset's heavy-handed policies had thoroughly radicalised him. (He later returned to the Cape and published, among other things, the valuable *South African Almanac* of 1832.) Greig's press was sold to William Bridekirk, the owner of yet another newspaper, the *South African Chronicle and Mercantile Advertiser*, which had been published for a year. Bridekirk was pro-Government, but his *SA Chronicle*, roundly condemned by Fairbairn, lost money and closed in 1826. Toadyism did not pay.

Somerset also refused to contemplate Pringle and Fairbairn's efforts to found a South African Literary Society, no doubt designed to shadow the equivalents in Edinburgh and Newcastle. Indeed, Fairbairn often referred to Edinburgh as the ideal model for the intellectual and press community.[24] The Governor asserted that he would 'oppose and thwart everything without exception which emanated from them [Pringle and Fairbairn], or in which they were concerned'.[25] The meetings of the society were declared to be illegal under the 1800 anti-Jacobin regulations, and it was not re-founded successfully until 1829. Indeed, Pringle was so loathed by Somerset that when a committee was formed in 1824 to found a Presbyterian church in Cape Town, assurances had to be given that Pringle was not involved in the project.[26] Pringle, prudently perhaps, chose to resign his post as sub-librarian of the public library and returned, for a period, to Glen Lynden on the eastern Cape. Thoroughly frustrated by the atmosphere at the Cape, he was preparing to return to Britain (which he did in 1826), where he would become the secretary of the Anti-Slavery Society. From this influential position he maintained his interest in conditions at the Cape. Pringle was described by Somerset as an 'arrant Dissenter'[27] (which was inaccurate, since he was a member of the Established Church of Scotland), and the Governor characterised the whole group as 'Scotch Independents', dabbling in politics and dangerous to the running of the colony.[28]

However, Somerset was grappling with complex forces. A scion of the highest ranks of the British nobility, he found himself facing individuals of much lower social standing who were exerting an influence beyond anything his upbringing could have envisaged. These people seemed, therefore, to be undermining a natural social order. He would have noted their adherence to ideas of legal equality, their religious dissent (in its broadest sense) and their notions of influence, if not power, open to talent – which he would have found disturbing – much more than their beliefs in a stable social hierarchy or their fundamental concern for the primacy of property – with which he could have found common cause. Moreover, not only was he facing an apparently radical, enlightened group of Scots, he was also far from getting his own way in London. There he faced the Colonial Secretary, Bathurst, and a permanent under-secretary, James Stephen, who were at least partly drawn into the evangelical network and felt increasingly uncomfortable with Somerset's autocratic style. The Colonial Office considered, for example, that his treatment of Greig had been illegal. Bathurst contemplated dismissing Somerset, but drew back from doing so, no doubt fearing the alienation of important patronage networks. It is indicative of colonial governance in the period that he had been Governor since 1814, yet getting rid of him was not easy. He returned to Britain for another of his extended leaves in 1826 and was replaced in 1827 after a change of government in London. To a considerable extent it was the Scots, in alliance with many in the merchant class, who engineered his downfall.

Reform after Somerset

The press, educational and intellectual conflict of the years 1823–25 were part of a wider struggle which ran through the 1820s and early 1830s, including the governorships of Somerset's two successors, Sir Richard Bourke (a Whig who acted during Somerset's final leave) and Sir Lowry Cole. The establishment of a more organised administrative civil service and the removal of patronage and corruption had been recommended by a Commission of Enquiry appointed in 1822, which reported in 1826. This was paralleled by the introduction of a whole range of liberalising and humanitarian measures which appeared to transform the character of colonial governance, legal arrangements in respect of race and slavery, and the relationship between English and Dutch-speakers at the Cape. Scots were at the centre of all these controversies. First of all, press freedom had in fact been further delayed. Although the *Commercial Advertiser* had resumed publication in 1825, it was again closed between 1827 and 1829.[29] Fairbairn, who had published a condensed version of the first eighteen issues in 1826 to offer evidence for the history of the conflict and the value of the paper, continued to campaign with great vehemence. His preface to the condensed digest expressed his loathing for despotic power and pronounced it the duty of every subject to resist. He pledged himself to denounce maladministration and injustice and proposed that the *Commercial Advertiser* would be the 'advocate of our real and essential rights and privileges'.[30] In 1827 he departed for London, funded by a public subscription, to lobby the Colonial Office, where he encountered a sympathetic William Huskisson, briefly Secretary of State. The result was ordinance 60 of 1829 which, though stopping short of full freedom for the press, none the less offered guarantees unknown before.

The *South African Commercial Advertiser* had been out of commission during the heady days of 1828, when John Philip had agitated for ordinances (50 and 51) giving some semblance of equality before the law to Khoi and also the right of Africans to cross the frontier for labour, strictly controlled by passes. But it was fully involved in the debates leading up to the abolition of slavery. With the departure of Pringle, Fairbairn remained the most notable journalist and editor, fiercely throwing himself into every issue of the day. He was a passionate abolitionist, as were some of the other Scots. If the ordinance respecting the Khoi affected the Afrikaans stockholders and frontiersmen, the abolition of slavery was to damage the economic position of the substantial Dutch wine growers and arable farmers of the Cape, some of whom also operated as elite figures in Cape Town itself. In the later 1820s their fortunes were in any case at a low ebb, partly because their wine no longer received any protection in British markets and partly because its export had been damaged by its allegedly poor quality. The conditions of slavery had been ameliorated to a certain extent by new regulations in 1826 (and all slave laws were consolidated in 1830), but by the end of the decade the humanitarian/evangelical faction, headed by Thomas Fowell Buxton, Bishop Wilberforce and Zachary Macaulay, was gaining the ascendancy in London. In the Anti-Slavery Society, Thomas Pringle (who often gave sanctuary to blacks in his London home) was able to bring knowledge of the situation at the Cape. Pringle died in 1834, shortly after Emancipation came into force. Since it was followed by several years' forced 'apprenticeship', he never saw the slaves securing their full freedom.

During this period Philip acted as a key go-between for metropolitan interests and local concerns. He used his connections with the powerful evangelical network in London to maintain pressure on the moves to emancipation. He was also a frequent contributor to the *Commercial Advertiser* under the pseudonym 'Colonist'. Some of the earliest issues had included material and editorials on the question of slavery, but anonymity cloaks whether these were written by Fairbairn or Philip. They had also been involved in the Philanthropic Society, founded in 1828 to help deserving slaves and slave children to purchase their freedom. Once again it represented an alliance of evangelical and mercantile interests. Pringle and Philip both made donations, and Fairbairn became a prominent committee member. After the abolition of slavery in 1833–4, Philip and Fairbairn had one more triumph. In 1834 a Vagrancy Act was proposed which they believed would have overturned the provisions of ordinance 50. They set up a fierce opposition to the measure, including in the pages of the *Commercial Advertiser*, which led to its disallowance by the Government in London. It earned them the undying enmity of both Dutch and English colonists at the Cape and on the frontier.

Greig and the dissemination of the press

From 1830, newspapers began to flourish in centres outside Cape Town – Grahamstown, Port Elizabeth and Graaff Reinet. The struggle of Greig, Fairbairn and Pringle resonated through the nineteenth century and became a frequent touchstone for press and political freedoms, though increasingly framed in terms of white rights. In Grahamstown, the publication of a newspaper was undertaken by a printer, L. H. Meurant (1812–93), who had been apprenticed to Greig and who had helped to produce the 'Facts'. There too the Governor, Donkin, had attempted to confiscate a press, but Meurant brought out the *Grahamstown Journal* in December 1831.[31] Though it saw its own freedoms as being closely connected to the struggle in Cape Town, it became so identified with settler interests that it was soon totally out of favour with Fairbairn, who was identified with an opposing humanitarian faction.

Yet another of Greig's protégés was a Scot from New Lanark, David Dale Buchanan (1819–74). He reached the Cape in 1829 and studied under John Philip. He became an infant teacher and later worked for Greig for a number of years. In 1840, he founded his own newspaper, *The Cape Town Mail*, aided by a gift from Greig of an old press and type. In 1846, he moved to the new colony of Natal and founded the first newspaper there, the *Natal Witness*, which survives to this day. Buchanan had thoroughly imbibed the radicalism of his mentors and used the *Witness* to pursue anti-authoritarian and humanitarian issues.[32]

The press and cultural institutions

Just as Greig's influence spread through the activities of Meurant and Buchanan, so the cultural and polemical interests of Fairbairn and others infused all types of printing and publishing. These often took the form of contentious pamphleteering and much recourse to the law. A number of additional newspapers appeared at the Cape, including the Dutch *De Zuid Afrikaan* in 1830, founded by an influential Dutch advocate, Christoffel Brand.[33] Such a plurality of journals helped to widen the fissures between different groups of colonists and between the English speakers and the Dutch. This was exacerbated by the sequence of reforms enacted in the later 1820s. But in some realms Scots, English and Dutch were able to co-operate. These included the founding of the

South African College (and Governor Cole regarded its founding group as anti-British, by which he presumably meant anti-English or anti-Establishment),[34] the recreation of a Literary and Philosophical Society, and the emergence of the Scientific Institution, all in 1829.[35] (The latter two amalgamated in 1832.) Literary and scientific publishing were now well established. Pringle's successor as librarian, Alexander Johnstone Jardine, also a Scot from the Borders and active from 1824 until 1845, edited the journals the *South African Chronicle* and the *Cape of Good Hope Literary Gazette*.

The Scientific Institution published the *South African Quarterly Journal* between 1829 and 1831 and again from 1833 to 1836, edited by a Scottish military doctor, explorer and ethnographer Andrew Smith and the austere Presbyterian divine James Adamson.[36] Fairbairn's *Commercial Advertiser* supported all these developments, as well as the founding of a significant botanical garden in 1848. Fairbairn was also heavily involved with a number of social and commercial developments, ranging from temperance to shipping, banking[37] and insurance. In 1848–9, he greatly increased his popularity at the Cape by leading a powerful, and successful, opposition to the landing of convicts at the Cape. This helped to give him credibility in his campaign, initially in alliance with Philip, for arrangements for representative government which included a 'colour-blind' franchise with a low property qualification, permitting some non-white voters (the number was never to be considerable) to qualify for the voters' rolls. In turn, the pressure exerted on this issue by Fairbairn and Philip was to arouse renewed hostility.

Nevertheless, Fairbairn was elected to the first assembly, although he failed to secure the speakership, which he had coveted. He continued to edit the *Advertiser* until 1859 and also published an annual *Trade and Economic Review* in which he accurately predicted the various turns in the fortunes of the colony. Throughout, he regarded himself as a crusading, social-reforming editor. His paper was also self-reflective, constantly weighing up its role and significance in society. If he had become somewhat less liberal in his later years (notably in his support for the Masters and Servants Ordinance of 1856), his intellectual and commercial approach confirms that his 'notion of "the people" was set up against both an idea of aristocratic patronage and, at the other extreme, a disorderly underclass'.[38]

After Fairbairn's death, the *Commercial Advertiser* continued to be published until 1869. But his example continued to be influential. F. S. Watermeyer, who married Fairbairn's daughter, founded the *Cape of Good Hope Observer* in 1849, at least partly influenced by the Fairbairn model. By the second half of the nineteenth century, many papers and journals were being published at the Cape, catering for a wide range of constituencies, including women, missionaries, the Dutch community, Jews and even Spiritualists, as well as the newly emergent black readers. The Scottish mission at Lovedale at the eastern Cape used its increasingly active press – which trained Africans and printed bibles, books and periodicals – to publish for an African audience from at least as early as 1862.[39] By this time, the Tenth Muse governing the periodical press, as Anthony Trollope put it, had firmly taken up residence in southern Africa.[40]

It is noticeable however that, as the numbers of newspapers and journals increased, the liberal and radical tendencies of the earliest examples waned. The original publications like the *South African Journal* and the *Commercial Advertiser* appeared in an atmosphere of danger. They courted closure in order to make their point and for the sake of developing resistance and controversy. But perhaps more significantly, they illustrate the fact that early colonial publishing efforts were not in any sense single-mindedly and overtly political in nature and newsgathering in content. The early captains of the press at the Cape were interested in much wider interests and endeavours. It was entirely in keeping with the Romantic and Evangelical movements, which so many of the early protagonists of a free press represented, that their literary, scientific and religious concerns were deeply interpenetrated with their liberal humanitarianism (though it always had its limits), their search for some forms of social and political freedoms, as well as their commercial ambitions. But in all of this they were primarily interested in the transfer of sets of European norms to be transplanted into a southern African environment. And the manner of that transplantation was as much Scottish as English. The activities of Fairbairn, Pringle, Philip, Greig and others casts a strange light on the over-frequent use of the world 'Anglicisation' with reference to this period in Cape history. If these Scots strenuously opposed the autocratic imperialism of the early nineteenth century, they were themselves heavily implicated in forms of cultural imperialism. The press they created was free, at least for a season, to propagate their own distinctive social, educational, economic and political views, often closely bound up with their Scottish intellectual and educational backgrounds. If the white-owned press had become somewhat more 'acclimatised' by the second half of the nineteenth century, it was to the realisation that the maintenance of colonial freedoms had become ever more bound up with the interests of the white colonists.

Notes

1. Chris Bayly, *The British Empire and the World, 1780–1830* (London: Blackwell, 1989); and, in more detail, Zöe Laidlaw, *Colonial Connections* (Manchester: Manchester University Press, 2005).
2. J. Don Vann and Rosemary T. Van Arsdel, *Periodicals of Queen Victoria's Empire: An Exploration* (London: Mansell, 1996), pp. 175–84.
3. John M. MacKenzie, 'On Scotland and the Empire', *International History Review*, XV, 4 (1993): 734.
4. During this period the colony was returned to the Dutch under the terms of the Treaty of Amiens.
5. H. C. Botha, *John Fairbairn in South Africa* (Cape Town: Historical Publication Society 1984), p. 16. For Walker and Robertson, see J. L. Meltzer, 'The Growth of Cape Town Commerce and the Role of John Fairbairn's *Advertiser*, 1835–1859', *Archives Year Book of South African History* (1994), pp. 110ff.
6. For a sympathetic account of Somerset's governorship, see A. K. Millar, *Plantagenet in South Africa: Lord Charles Somerset* (Cape Town: Oxford University Press, 1965). Some modern historians have also attempted to reinstate his reputation.
7. It should be remembered that the struggles of William Cobbett and William Hone to establish a free press in London were very recent, with climactic events taking place in 1816–17. See Ben Wilson, *The Laughter of Triumph: William Hone and the Fight for a Free Press* (London: Faber and Faber, 2005).
8. For Philip, see Andrew Ross, *John Philip: Missions, Race and Politics in South Africa* (Aberdeen: Aberdeen University Press, 1986). For a good account of the period – though the understanding of the Scottish background of some of the protagonists is often flawed – see Timothy Keegan, *Colonial South Africa and the Origins of the Racial Order* (London: Leicester University Press, 1996), chapters 3 and 4.
9. Thomas Pringle, *Narrative of a Residence in South Africa* (London: Moxon, 1935); Angus Calder, 'Thomas Pringle (1789–1834); A Scottish Poet in South Africa', in *English in Africa*, 9:1 (1982): 1–28; Pringle, *Some Account of the Present State of the English Settlers* (London and Edinburgh: n.p., 1824).
10. There is a substantial literature on Fairbairn. In addition to Botha and Keegan, see Meltzer, 'The Growth of Cape Town Commerce'; Kirsten McKenzie, 'The *South African Commercial Advertiser* and the Making of Middle-class Identity in Early Nineteenth-century Cape Town', MA diss., University of Cape Town, 1993; ' "Franklins at the Cape": the *South African Commercial Adviser* and the Creation of a Colonial Public Sphere, 1824–1854', *Kronos*, 25 (1998–9): 88–102.
11. John Fairbairn to Thomas Pringle, 2 March 1823, quoted in J. Meiring, *Thomas Pringle: His Life and Times* (Cape Town: Balkema, 1968), p. 80.
12. Eric A. Walker, *A History of Southern Africa* (London: Longmans, 1962, first published 1928), p. 160. See also McKenzie, 'The *South African Commercial Advertiser*', p. 5.
13. A fuller account of these events can be found in John M. MacKenzie, *The Scots in South Africa* (Manchester: Manchester University Press, forthcoming), chapter 3.

14. A brief account of this case can be found in Monica Wilson and Leonard Thompson (eds.), *The Oxford History of South Africa*, South Africa to 1870 (Oxford: Clarendon Press 1969), pp. 315–16.
15. See the copies of the *Commercial Advertiser* held at the Archives of the Western Cape, Cape Town.
16. Pringle, *Narrative of a Residence*, p. 186.
17. *Commercial Advertiser*, 7 April 1824.
18. Archives of the Western Cape (ACW), GH 1/38, no. 570.
19. This may be a quotation from Samuel Johnson, though I have been unable to trace the precise source.
20. Rachel Holmes, *Scanty Particulars: The Strange Life and Astonishing Secret of Victorian Adventurer and Pioneering Surgeon, James Barry* (London: Viking, 2002). James Barry was certainly a close friend of Lord Charles Somerset and acted as medical adviser to him and his family. Holmes speculates that Barry may have been a hermaphrodite.
21. Botha, *Fairbairn*, p. 25; Keegan, *Colonial South Africa*, p. 97.
22. Reasons for closure can be found in AWC, GH 1/39. no. 592.
23. George Greig, 'Facts connected with the stopping of *the South African Commercial Advertiser*', A facsimile reproduction produced by the Africana Connoisseurs Press, Cape Town, 1963.
24. McKenzie, 'South African Commercial Advertiser', p. 43.
25. Botha, *Fairbairn*, p. 28.
26. Frank Quinn and Greg Cuthbertson, 'Presbyterianism in Cape Town: the History of St. Andrew's Church 1829–1979' (Cape Town, 1979), p. 7.
27. Wilson and Thompson (eds.), *Oxford History*, p. 315. Somerset used this term to explain to Bathurst why he had refused to contemplate the publication of Pringle's original *South African Journal*. Somerset was not always down on Scots. On the contrary, he was instrumental in the recruitment of a number of Scottish ministers for the Dutch Reformed Church and several Scots teachers to develop the Cape educational service.
28. Keegan, *Colonial South Africa*, p. 98.
29. Complaints against false statements can be found in AWC GH1/58, no. 840, 1826 and papers on the second suppression in GH 23/8, no. 19.
30. Botha, *Fairbairn*, pp. 38, 47.
31. Meurant was half-Swiss, half-English and was born at the Cape. His father apprenticed him to Greig. In old age he wrote a celebrated book which set out to describe the heroic efforts to achieve a free press at the Cape and the manner in which he took this tradition to the frontier at Grahamstown. L. H. Meurant, *Sixty Years Ago or Reminiscences of the Struggle for the Freedom of the Press in South Africa and the Establishment of the First Newspaper in the Eastern Province* (Cape Town: S. Solomon 1885), reprinted in a facsimile edition by Africana Connoisseurs Press, 1963.
32. Balasundram Naidoo, 'David Dale Buchanan as Editor of the *Natal Witness*, 1846–1856', *Archives Year Book for South African History*, Vol. 40 (1977), Pretoria 1982, pp. 121–248.
33. H. C. Botha, 'Die rol van Christoffel J. Brand in Suid-Afrika, 1820–1854', in *Archives Year Book of South African History*, Vol. 40 (1977), Pretoria 1982, pp. 1–116. *Die Zuid-Afrikaan* is treated on pp. 23–53 and *passim*.

34. Botha, *Fairbairn*, p. 137. See also W. Ritchie, *The History of the South African College, 1829–1918*, 2 vols. (Cape Town, T. M. Miller 1918).
35. Saul Dubow, 'Literary and Scientific Institutions in the 19th-Century Cape Colony', in Dubow, *A Commonwealth of Knowledge* (forthcoming). I am grateful to Professor Dubow for sending me a copy of this and for his permission to make use of it.
36. Vann and Van Arsdel (eds.), *Periodicals*, p. 262.
37. Fairbairn's first plea for a bank to be founded on the Scottish principles appeared in the *Advertiser* on 15 February 1826.
38. McKenzie, "Franklins of the Cape" ', p. 98.
39. Vann and Van Arsdel (eds.), *Periodicals*, pp. 254–86. See also R. H. W. Shepherd. *Lovedale South Africa 1824–1955* (Lovedale: Lovedale Press, 1971).
40. The quotation is from *The Warden*, chapter 14.

3
'The thinking is done in London': South Africa's English Language Press and Imperialism

John Lambert

In recent years the resurgence of interest in questions of identity in Britain and the former Dominions of the British Empire has had a marked effect on historiographical studies of what has come to be called the 'British world'. In South Africa this has led to the appearance of a number of studies of British, or as they were known by the early twentieth century, English-speaking, South Africans.[1] Although part of the same imperial diaspora that saw British settlers populate Canada, Australia and New Zealand, the experience of English-speaking South Africans differed markedly. Unlike their cousins in the Dominions, they were a minority within white society, which in turn was a minority within the wider society. This was to affect the way in which they viewed themselves, as both South Africans and as British. It was also to have a direct bearing on the way in which the English-language press developed in South Africa.

Of all of the Dominion newspapers, the English press in South Africa has possibly had the most negative publicity. From the 1890s until the eve of the Republic in 1961, it was accused by its critics of promoting British above South African interests and of being subservient to British capitalism.[2] No single work has yet appeared on the English press during South Africa's 'imperial' period, 1806–1961. Most studies concentrate on the apartheid years,[3] while other works are either studies of individual newspapers or newspaper groups,[4] or the reminiscences of editors.[5]

The purpose of this chapter is to do what these studies do not attempt, to examine the complex relationship between the English press, British South Africans and the British Empire during South Africa's imperial years, a relationship that changed as conditions within both the Empire and southern Africa altered. It was made more complicated by the dominant role played by the mining interest in the subcontinent after the discovery of gold on the Witwatersrand in 1886. The accusation that the press was subservient to British capitalism is on one level true, for many English newspapers were inextricably bound up with the development of mining capital.

The history of the press in South Africa began with the annexation of the Cape to the British Crown and the arrival of the first British settlers in 1820. In 1824, Thomas Pringle and John Fairbairn started the Cape's first newspaper, the bilingual *South African Commercial Advertiser*.[6] Pringle and Fairbairn brought to the Cape a firm belief in the British right to free expression. Despite attempts by the administration to censor the paper, a Press Ordinance in 1828, together with further legislation in 1859, established the freedom of the press in British South Africa.[7]

The expansion of British settlements in the interior from the 1830s saw a vibrant newspaper culture develop. By the 1870s, newspapers that were to become household names in South Africa and many that still appear today were to be found throughout the subcontinent. In Cape Town, the *Cape Times* and the *Cape Argus*, on the Cape eastern frontier, the *Graham's Town Journal* and Port Elizabeth's *Eastern Province Herald*. In the neighbouring colony, Pietermaritzburg's *Natal Witness* and the *Natal Mercury* in Durban while in the Orange Free State, the *Friend* was published in Bloemfontein. Like the *South African Commercial Advertiser*, many early newspapers were bilingual, catering for Dutch and British colonists.

Had the tradition of a bilingual press continued, South Africa might have been spared the cultural and political estrangement between British and Dutch/Afrikaners which was to bedevil South Africa's history. But it was not to be. While most of the smaller country papers remained bilingual and catered for the requirements of both sections of the white community,[8] the large urban papers were soon appearing only in English. This reflected the political and cultural dominance of the British in the Cape and Natal, and steadily marginalised Afrikaners in these colonies. In reaction, the Afrikaners sought to protect their language and culture. As early as 1830, in Cape Town, they founded *De Zuid Afrikaan*, while in the 1870s the first Afrikaans-language newspaper, *Die Afrikaanse Patriot*, appeared.[9]

Despite their desire to protect their language and culture, the Cape Afrikaners and their press remained loyal to the Empire and the monarchy.[10] To the north, in the Transvaal, the South African Republic was established in 1852. After various vicissitudes, it was annexed by Britain in 1877, a short and inglorious annexation that ended when an

Afrikaner force defeated the British at Majuba in 1881. While Majuba humiliated the British, it increased Afrikaner self-confidence, beginning a process that was to lead to the Anglo-Boer War of 1899–1902.

The defeat of the Transvaal and Orange Free State during that war and their annexation as British colonies, followed by the establishment of the Union of South Africa in 1910, was meant to usher in a new era in which British and Afrikaner would work together as South Africans in a Dominion firmly committed to the British Empire. Under the leadership of the two defeated Afrikaner generals, Louis Botha and Jan Smuts, who now preached conciliation and acceptance of imperial ties, a broad South Africanist identity was given a political home in the South African Party (SAP), which governed the Union between 1910 and 1924. But, bitter at their defeat, many Afrikaners rejected both South Africanism and imperialism. In 1914, the Afrikaner National Party (NP) was founded by Anglo-Boer War general, Barry Hertzog, and gained rapid support amongst Afrikaners. The establishment of *Die Burger* in 1915 provided it with a newspaper committed to disseminating nationalist, anti-imperial ideology.[11]

The history of the English press in South Africa is very different. Their position as a minority influenced British South African attitudes to Britain and to imperialism. Unlike Afrikaners and Blacks, who experienced imperialism as a conquering, destructive force, British South Africans saw it as a positive expansion of imperial rule throughout southern Africa. This view was reflected in most English newspapers.

The English press provided a significant barometer of British South African society. Although English newspapers were read by Afrikaners, who until the twentieth century did not have a daily newspaper, and by the small but growing group of literate Blacks,[12] it catered essentially for English-speakers. Its traditions were shaped by men like Fairbairn and Pringle who had successfully fought for the freedom of the press and by a series of great nineteenth-century owner-editors. Men like Frederick St Leger of the *Cape Times*, Francis Dormer of the *Cape Argus* and founder in 1886 of the Argus Printing and Publishing Company, and Sir John Robinson of the *Natal Mercury*, set standards of journalism which their successors were to strive, not always successfully, to maintain. They began a tradition that was to last into the 1930s of editors and senior journalists being recruited from British newspapers like *The Times*, the *Yorkshire Post* and *Liverpool Post*. They modelled their papers on their British counterparts and sought to maintain British press traditions. In small communities in which the personality of an editor was more important than it is today, they played a prominent role, often becoming members of parliament and, in the case of Sir John Robinson, prime minister of Natal.[13]

The arrival of the telegraph in the second half of the century heralded a communications revolution that brought South Africans into close contact with Britain. As cable communication was costly, a virtual monopoly of news between Britain and South Africa was cornered by the Reuters Telegram Company. Founded in London in 1851, Reuters built up a network of agencies throughout the Empire and by the 1880s controlled news entering and transmitted from South Africa, and the distribution of domestic news within the subcontinent. The major English newspapers also had their own offices in London by the 1900s, but their attempts to break Reuters' monopoly failed, although they resulted in the formation in 1909 of the Reuters South African Press Agency with Reuters remaining the basic distributor of news to and within South Africa. It was to lose its monopoly of domestic news only in the 1930s when the South African Press Association was formed. Throughout the imperial period, South African newspapers remained dependent on British news, for example, in the 1950s, 80 per cent of the editorial content of the Argus group's newspapers was cabled from London.[14] This dependence on British news saw the English press accused of being incapable of formulating its own policies. As 'Dawie' of *Die Burger* put it in 1946, the 'thinking is done in London and cabled to South Africa'.[15]

The news selected by Reuters had a strong imperial bias which appealed to South Africa's English press. The acceptance by that press of Reuters' British worldview reflected the ties of kinship and loyalty which bound English-speaking South Africans to Britain. Newspapers reflected their sense of British identity and their belief in the superiority of the British way of life. They also reinforced them. Imperialism was all pervasive in newspaper pages, from the royal coat of arms many carried on their mastheads to news columns with headlines like 'Home News', 'The Old Country', 'The Motherland' and 'Our Navy'. While this alienated Afrikaner readers, few English-speakers questioned it.

The leitmotif of the press was loyalty to the imperial ideal. Newspapers carried detailed reports glorying in imperial achievements and military victories. Generals like Gordon or Wolseley were cult figures in South Africa as much as in the rest of the Empire. The icon on which imperial pride focused was Queen Victoria. From the 1880s, as the British Crown was transformed into an imperial monarchy, South Africans shared the perception of Victoria, the imperial matriarch, caring for the greater British family. This view of the monarch as the centre around which the Empire revolved continued after Victoria's death, the Crown represented as the 'one material link which embodies and represents the spiritual unity of the Empire'.[16] Editors preached the gospel of loyalty to the monarch[17] and newspapers carried regular features on the Royal Family, devoting whole issues to royal weddings, coronations and deaths, and particularly to royal visits. News that might reflect negatively on the Royal Family was censored. Public reaction to supposed slights to individual members was sufficient to make editors hesitate before publishing. In January 1892, the Johannesburg *Star* published a mildly irreverent piece on the death of Queen Victoria's grandson, the Duke of Clarence. It resulted in attempts to lynch the editor and physical attacks on the newspaper's offices.[18]

Devotion to the monarchy and the imperial ideal did not extend to British governments, nor did it imply an automatic acceptance of imperial policies, particularly those affecting southern Africa. The English press was British-oriented, but it was not controlled by the British Government. During the mid-Victorian years of unchallenged British political predominance in the subcontinent, editors frequently criticised British policies and officials, particularly when imperial policy conflicted with colonial interests or when British Governments pursued policies they believed were detrimental to English-speaking interests in the subcontinent.[19]

The Conventions that granted independence to the Transvaal and the Orange Free State in the early 1850s were castigated as a deliberate betrayal by the British Government of imperial interests in the interior.[20] During the following years editors regularly condemned any indication of maladministration in the fledgling republics and called for British intervention. The discovery of diamonds at Kimberley in the late 1860s opened new trading possibilities to the Cape and Natal and saw many editors first urge, then welcome, a British resumption of a forward policy in southern Africa, culminating in the annexation of the Transvaal in 1877.[21]

Britain's forward policy was a disaster, leading to humiliating military reverses, first at the hands of the Zulu at Isandlhwana in 1879, then by the Boers at Majuba in 1881. This latter battle led to the retrogression of the Transvaal. British South Africans, unaccustomed to imperial defeats, expressed their anger in anti-government demonstrations including burning the Prime Minister, William Gladstone, in effigy. The press shared this anger, the *Natal Mercury* proclaiming that it would be 'mere folly to talk hereafter of British sovereignty or of British prestige in South Africa'.[22]

The discovery of gold on the Witwatersrand in 1886 changed the position of the press in South Africa as radically as it changed the subcontinent. The white population of the Transvaal increased rapidly as a large *Uitlander* (foreign) community, mainly British, settled on the Witwatersrand. Viewed with suspicion by the republic's President, Paul Kruger, this community was to become a vocal opponent of the Boer Government. From the start the mining magnates, the Randlords, who came to dominate the gold industry realised how useful the press could be to further their own interests, beginning a process that was to see intimate links created between the English-language press, mining capital and imperialism. Cecil John Rhodes was one of the first magnates to try to manipulate the press. By the early 1890s, he had interests in the *Cape Times* and the Argus Company, encouraging the latter to expand into the Transvaal where it bought the Johannesburg *Star*. Both as a mining capitalist and as Prime Minister of the Cape from 1890, he saw the conservative republican oligarchy in the Transvaal as a threat to his ambitions and began planning its overthrow.[23]

By the mid-1890s, the Corner House Group of Wernher-Beit & Eckstein had become the dominant mining group in the Transvaal and the most important shareholder in the Argus Company, effectively controlling its editorial policies. The Corner House's main concern was obviously to secure the financial and economic success of its mining interests. While its owners were prepared to support a reformed republican government if it could provide stable and efficient working conditions, they were equally ready, if necessary, to play the imperial card to gain their own ends. By 1895, Lionel Phillips and Percy Fitzpatrick believed that British intervention was essential and began using the Group's control of the Argus Company to agitate for it.[24]

In many of the major English newspapers they found willing collaborators. By the 1890s, the tone of the press was becoming more stridently imperial, reflecting the growth of a new aggressive and jingoistic imperialism in Britain and the eagerness of English-speaking South Africans to embrace its values. The new imperialism was fed by British papers like the *Daily Mail* which promoted an exaggerated imperial patriotism and a Social Darwinist conviction of British superiority. Although these sentiments pervaded the whole Empire, in South Africa they cannot be seen in isolation from the humiliation of Majuba. The British defeat continued to rankle, while the growing wealth of the Transvaal threatened the dominance that English-speakers assumed as their right. The English press was accordingly a willing convert. The Argus newspapers actively preached the imperial gospel while the *Cape Times* under St Leger's successor, Edmund Garrett, previously a colleague of the future High Commissioner, Sir Alfred Milner, on the *Pall Mall Gazette*, firmly advocated imperial expansion in the subcontinent.[25]

Not all newspapers accepted the new imperialism. The small village newspapers were generally lukewarm, while papers that opposed it included the Pretoria *Press* and the Johannesburg *Times* in the Transvaal and, in the Cape, the *South African Telegraph*. Here too, however, mining interests dictated policy for these papers were owned by J. B. Robinson, a rival of Rhodes and the Corner House who hoped to strengthen his position by supporting the Transvaal Government.[26] In Natal, where economic dependence on the railway link with the Witwatersrand dictated policy, Sir John Robinson, now the colony's Prime Minister, played down imperial interests in the *Natal Mercury* so as not to alienate Kruger.[27]

By the end of 1895, Rhodes was ready to strike against the Transvaal Government. With the connivance of men like Phillips and Fitzpatrick, a raiding party under Leander Starr Jameson invaded the republic from Bechuanaland with the intention of linking up with an *Uitlander* uprising in Johannesburg. The raid was premature. The *Uitlander* leaders were in disarray, and the raid ended in an ignominious surrender of the leaders near Krugersdorp.

Despite the leverage Rhodes and the Corner House had over much of the Transvaal and Cape press, the raid caught editors as much off guard as it did the general public. Only the editor of the Johannesburg *Star*, Frederick Hamilton, was implicated in the conspiracy and he was arrested and tried for treason.[28] Editors were equally caught by surprise at the upsurge of English-speaking support for Jameson. Throughout British South Africa the raid was seen as an attempt to revenge Majuba and received loud and vigorous support. Faced with this emotional response, editors like Garrett who, despite his support for Rhodes, felt that the raid was a blunder, played for time. Although he successfully resisted Rhodes's attempts to influence his policies,[29] his editorials following the raid provide an excellent example of an editor reacting to public opinion rather than leading it. The day after the raid, Garrett was uncertain what line to follow, but as the public clamour grew so the *Cape Times* came out firmly in support of Jameson.[30] Other newspapers also bowed to public opinion. The *Cape Argus* referred to 'gallant Jameson and his lion-hearted lads',[31] while the editor of the Johannesburg *Times* was dismissed by J. B. Robinson for referring to the raid as a 'glorious procession of the Anglo-Saxon race'.[32]

Newspapers that attacked Jameson fared badly. The *South African Telegraph*'s coverage outraged Capetonians, leading to the paper's closure in September 1896.[33] In Durban where the *Natal Mercury* was the only Natal newspaper to condemn the raid,[34] the surge in pro-*Uitlander* sentiment among English-speaking Natalians forced the editor to modify his attacks.

The failure of the Jameson raid did not put an end to the Randlords' scheming and in the following years even opponents like J. B. Robinson became convinced that only Britain could provide the effective government the industry required.[35] In this, they were encouraged by the appointment in 1897 of Sir Alfred Milner as High Commissioner. Any hesitation on the part of the Randlords to call for radical changes in the Transvaal was removed once Milner made it obvious in 1899 that he was determined to assert British supremacy in South Africa.

The Randlords rallied press support for Milner. A new imperialist newspaper, the *Transvaal Leader*, was established while, on the advice of the editor of the London *Times*, the Corner House appointed a fervent imperialist, William Monypenny, editor of the *Star*, with instructions to publicise *Uitlander* grievances and argue for British suzerainty.[36]

These years saw no diminution in the mass hysteria that had gripped English South Africans during the raid. Their jingoist sentiments became ever more vocal and were given expression in the pro-imperial South African League and in the *Uitlander* Council, founded in 1899 to protect *Uitlander* interests. Many miners rejected the *Uitlander* Council as the mouthpiece of mining capital rather than of working-class interests. To encourage their resistance to the Randlords, the Transvaal Government subsidised a new anti-imperial and anti-capitalist *Standard & Diggers' News* of Johannesburg.[37] In the republic the *Pretoria News* also opposed the demands for British intervention, as did the Bloemfontein *Friend* and Cape Town's *South African News*. But these were exceptions. The English press generally threw itself wholeheartedly into the anti-Kruger campaign, publicising 'abuses' of British rights in the Transvaal and calling for British intervention. By the second half of 1899 even newspapers with no connection with the Randlords, such as in the smaller mining communities on the Witwatersrand, were calling for intervention, while in Durban the *Natal Mercury* had converted to the imperial cause.[38]

English newspapers have to share much of the blame for inflaming passions and hardening attitudes between British and Afrikaner during these years, in the process also strengthening anti-imperial attitudes in the Afrikaner press. Francis Dormer blamed the 'seditious excesses of the *Uitlander* papers' for the outbreak of the war.[39] The correspondent for the *Manchester Guardian*, J. A. Hobson, agreed, accusing the capitalist press in the Transvaal and the Cape of slavishly publishing sensationalist reports the Randlords fed them in order to mislead English-speaking South Africans and which 'stirred up rebellion in the Transvaal' and provoked 'the armed intervention of an outside nation'. Hobson further argued that as the editors of newspapers like the *Star* and the *Cape Times* were agents for British newspapers, they deliberately published news intended to incite opinion in Britain.[40]

Although Hobson's accusations must be treated with caution, it cannot be denied that the Corner House appointed editors like Monypenny, who it knew would support imperialist policies, and that they financed the many thousands of pounds needed by editors to cable propaganda to the British press. What Hobson failed to appreciate, however, is that at this critical moment in South African history, the interests of the Randlords, of the press in both South Africa and in Britain, and of British South Africans coincided. The Randlords tried to manipulate the situation to gain their own ends, but editors and the British in South Africa were willing accomplices.

The Anglo-Boer War consolidated the alliance between British imperialism and South Africa's English press. The newspapers lamented British losses, rejoiced in British victories and shared the hysteria of the imperial press when first Ladysmith and then Mafeking were relieved. The fall of the republics to imperial forces in 1900 saw pro-republican newspapers like the *Standard & Diggers' News* closed, while in the Cape the editors of the *South African News* and *Ons Land*, were imprisoned for libel.[41] A strict censorship was imposed in the new colonies. In Bloemfontein, the *Friend*, whose editor, Arthur Barlow, had reluctantly supported the Orange Free State's participation in the war, was taken over by the military administration. Rudyard Kipling was appointed editor, initiating an extremely jingoist policy, which Barlow believed did incalculable harm both to English South Africans and to the Empire.[42]

Pre-war newspapers like the *Star* were not allowed to resume publication until 1902. After the Treaty of Vereeniging ended the war, Milner tried to secure a press supportive of his policy of Anglicising the Transvaal and of making South Africa the lynchpin of the Empire. On Kipling's recommendation, a staunch imperialist, Sir Maitland Park of the *Allahabad Pioneer*, was appointed editor of the *Cape Times* in 1902, a post he held until 1921. Milner also appointed the equally staunch imperialist Vere Stent as editor of a revived *Pretoria News* and in 1905 secured the editorship of the *Star* for a member of the Kindergarten, his private secretary, Geoffrey Robinson (later Dawson, editor of the London *Times*).[43]

The transfer of control from Kruger's republic to Milner directly benefited the Randlords, who returned to Johannesburg by 1902. The death of Rhodes that year saw the Corner House become the most powerful financial group in South Africa, controlling the Central Mining and Investment Corporation, De Beers, the National Bank and the Argus Company. With the Group's main office now in London, first Sir Lionel Phillips then, after 1915, John Martin were in charge of its South African operations. Under their control the Argus Company expanded to include *The Friend, Natal Advertiser* (later *Daily News*), *Diamond Fields Advertiser* and the *Pretoria News*.[44] The links between the Argus Company, the mining interest and British capital were strengthened when Martin became president of the Chamber of Mines and a director of the Bank of England. Like his predecessors, he spent a large part of each year in London.[45]

The Argus Company was not unchallenged. In 1902 the *Rand Daily Mail* was founded in Johannesburg. Until 1904, Edgar Wallace, war correspondent for the London *Daily Mail* and a convinced Milner imperialist, was editor, and in that year the newspaper was bought by the mining magnate, Sir Abe Bailey. Until his death in 1940, Bailey controlled the paper's policy and that of the *Sunday Times*, which was founded in 1906. After 1940 the Bailey Trust controlled the newspapers until they were formally linked in the South African Associated Newspapers (SAAN) Company in 1955.[46]

With control of most urban newspapers in the hands of the Argus Company and Bailey, real power in the English-language press ultimately resided in their hands. As shrewd businessmen, however, Bailey, Phillips and Martin were aware that their newspapers could not survive without the support of advertisers and that advertisements were aimed at what the reading public wanted. They accordingly had to cater for English-speaking needs and to do so they had to give their editors considerable leeway. Nevertheless, they appointed editors who would promote their interests and were constantly in touch with them, explaining the policies that they wanted them to follow.[47] On major issues, they were not prepared to allow these policies to be flouted. In 1938, Martin ruthlessly made this clear when he demanded the resignation of the editor of the *Cape Argus*, D. E. McCausland, for ignoring his instructions that no *Argus* editor should criticise the British Government's handling of the Sudetenland crisis. Although his demand was regarded as unprecedented, it emphasised the extent to which the Corner House would go to protect British interests.[48]

The need for owners to intervene to protect imperial interests was rare, however, largely because there was seldom a conflict of interest between them and their editors and, more importantly, because the emphasis the mining interest placed on the importance of the imperial connection harmonised with English-speaking sentiments. For example, until 1961 there continued to be little to distinguish the imperial policies of the independent newspapers from those controlled by mining capital. If anything, independent newspapers like the *Natal Witness* and the *Natal Mercury* were more stridently imperial. As the fate of anti-imperialist newspapers like the *South African Telegraph* suggests, they could not survive unless they printed what their readers wanted to read.

As has been seen, both the Randlords and English-speaking South Africans had welcomed the transfer of power in the Transvaal to Britain and had supported Milner and looked forward to a future in which British and imperial interests would control the subcontinent. Yet, within less than a decade, they found themselves confronted with a situation in which political power, not only in the former republics but throughout South Africa, passed into Afrikaner hands. The return to power in 1905 in Britain of a Liberal Government opposed to the Unionists' policies towards southern Africa saw responsible government granted to the former republics, followed in 1910 by the establishment of the Union of South Africa. Numerically superior in three of the Union's four provinces, Afrikaners dominated its political life and, for the next half-century, South African politics revolved around a struggle for power between moderate Afrikaners like the ex-Boer generals, Louis Botha and Jan Smuts, committed to a South Africanism based on loyalty to the Empire and English–Afrikaner cooperation; and a growing Afrikaner republican nationalism led by Barry Hertzog and D. F. Malan.[49]

In this situation there was a danger that English-speaking South Africans and their press would become politically marginalised. The press was uncertain which political party could best protect English interests and during the first decade of Union varied its support between two parties. The Unionist Party was essentially an urban, English-speaking party committed to placing the interests of the Empire first. It reflected mining interests but, as it had no Afrikaner support, could not achieve power on its own. By contrast, the willingness of Botha's SAP government to work with the mining interest encouraged support for that party. The choice between the two was resolved in

1920 when the Unionists were absorbed by the SAP under Smuts, who had become Prime Minister in 1919. This move, which would have appeared radical in 1910, resulted from the rapid growth of Afrikaner support for Hertzog's NP, which was formed in 1914 and by 1919 advocated separation from the Empire. During the First World War the SAP had committed itself to full participation in the struggle. While this drove many of its Afrikaner supporters into Hertzog's camp, it reduced the differences between the SAP and the Unionists. From 1921, Smuts and the SAP, broadly representing English, moderate Afrikaner, and mining interests and committed to maintaining the British connection, received the support of the English-language press. Unlike the Afrikaans press, however, which was dominated by the NP, the SAP could never take the support of English newspapers for granted. The Argus Group's editors, for example, were not allowed to belong to political parties.[50]

Throughout the Union period, English newspapers continued to reflect British cultural values and to stress the importance of South Africa's economic and political ties with the Empire. During the First World War editors gave almost unquestioning support to the imperial war effort. The press's strident jingoism and its intolerance of Nationalist opposition to the war antagonised its Afrikaner readers, strengthening support for the NP.[51] By 1924, the NP had become the largest political party and, with the support of the small, mainly English-speaking Labour Party, formed a government with Hertzog as Prime Minister. In the following years, when government policy appeared to threaten South Africa's British heritage, the English press defended it stridently. Newspaper opposition to an attempt to drop the Union Flag was instrumental in its retention as a national flag in 1927.[52]

The English press's support for the Empire and imperial symbols confirmed the Afrikaner belief that it was anti-South African and controlled by imperial capitalists. In 1918, in one of his many attacks on English newspapers, Hertzog labelled them the greatest supporters of the Empire in South Africa, claiming that 'but for the Jingo newspapers, they would hear less of striving after Empire and more of South Africa and Africa's interests'.[53] Hertzog's attack carried weight in 1918, but became less valid as South Africa and the Empire changed. Picking up any English newspaper of the 1920s and 1930s reveals a people, and a press, that remained intensely British, committed to the Empire and to British cultural values, resolutely monarchist and obsessed with news of the Royal Family, yet, at the same time, coming to terms with their South African identity. This was particularly so after the acceptance of the Statute of Westminster in 1931 and, in 1934, of South Africa's

Status Acts, which legally enacted the Union's position as a sovereign independent state within the Empire.

By 1934, the Depression had forced Hertzog to accept fusion with the SAP to form a new United Party Government in which he was Prime Minister with Smuts his deputy. Under these circumstances the English press, with the exception of the *Natal Mercury* which threw its support behind the small, breakaway ultra-British Dominion Party, rallied to the new Government. Like English-speaking South Africans generally, however, the press found it difficult adapting to a Government that had to accommodate both SAP and NP views. Many editors did so only because the more extreme Nationalists under Malan broke away to form a Purified Nationalist Party and they were afraid that it would attract Afrikaner support.[54]

The outbreak of the Second World War, Hertzog's resignation after being defeated in a neutrality vote and the appointment by the Governor-General of Smuts as Prime Minister laid the tensions within English society to rest. The Government's commitment to fighting on the side of its Commonwealth partners saw the English give full expression to their dual loyalty to Britain and to South Africa. After two decades of uncertainty, the English press came into its own again. As in 1914 it played a notable part in the war, spread pro-British propaganda, raised funds for the British and South African armed forces and encouraged imperialist sentiments. By 1945 it had reason to be proud of its part in South Africa's war contribution.[55]

After 1945, the English press's commitment to the British ideal continued and was never more evident than in 1947 when, in a great outpouring of devotion and loyalty, newspapers welcomed George VI and his family to South Africa. *Die Burger*'s Dawie believed that the editors' 'slavish' attitude to the Royal Family encouraged republicanism in South Africa[56] and the Royal Visit starkly revealed the dichotomy between the English and Nationalist press. The latter was regarded as out of tune with the times and it was only in 1948 that the full realisation of how powerful Afrikaner nationalism and its press had become was revealed when the NP won the general election.

The NP's victory ushered in a period which was to end the political influence of the English press for the rest of the century. After 1948, it became an 'opposition' press, supporting a declining United Party and unique among the media in opposing government policies. Despite their political impotence, English newspapers remained the most important vehicle of communication, providing all South Africans with most of their news. With only four Afrikaans-language daily newspapers in the Union in 1950 compared to 13 English-language papers,[57] many Afrikaners continued reading English newspapers, causing Joel Mervis to comment, apropos of the *Sunday Times*, '[p]eople vote for the party which the paper dislikes, and they read the paper which the party dislikes'.[58]

It is an observation that holds good for the whole English press.

Like the United Party, the English press remained committed to the Crown and Commonwealth. But it was impossible to ignore the fact that the days of Empire were over. Reluctantly but inevitably English South Africans accepted Britain's post-war decline and that they had been cast adrift in a country and a world increasingly alien to them. Although their cultural and economic ties with Britain showed few signs of diminishing, apathy crept into the Group and its press. As the symbols of British imperialism disappeared, the response of the press was very different from what it had been in the past, accepting what it knew it could not prevent. As South Africa became more isolated from the outside world, so the newspapers turned inward, seeking to protect the cultural and economic position of the English in South Africa, rather than in a British and imperial context.

The English press had one last fight to wage as an 'imperial' press. In 1960 the Government announced a referendum on forming a republic for October. In the following months the press fought a grim, rearguard action, aware of its powerlessness to prevent the change, but refusing to acknowledge the possibility of defeat. It hammered home the message not to 'break the links that bind your future to a great past',[59] concentrating on the importance of the Commonwealth connection and the contribution played by the Crown to South Africa.[60] In the referendum, English-speaking South Africans overwhelmingly rejected the republic.[61] The press's reaction to the news in March 1961 that South Africa could not remain in the Commonwealth was one of dismay and shock, the *Cape Times* lamenting that South Africa had been 'thrown out of the group of the most tolerant, the most civilized, the most fair-minded peoples in the world'.[62]

On 31 May 1961, the Republic was proclaimed in Pretoria. During the previous days English newspapers carried sombre editorials stressing South Africa's debt to Britain and the Crown, and deploring the breaking of links with the Commonwealth. On 30 May they bade farewell to the Queen and to over a century and a half of the British presence. Symbolically, on 1 June 1961, the *Cape Times* dropped the Royal Coat of Arms from its masthead. For South Africa, and for the English press, it was the end of an era.[63]

Despite its campaign against the Republic, the English press accepted the constitutional change and, in the following years, concentrated far more on opposing the Government's apartheid policies and increasing autocratic tendencies. Although the dominant capitalist interest controlling the English press by the 1960s was the Anglo-American Company which retained its predecessors' strong economic ties with British capital, there was little hankering after an Empire that no longer existed. After 1961, English-speaking South Africans found it difficult identifying with a post-imperial, multi-ethnic Britain. They also, and particularly after UDI in Rhodesia in 1965, resented what they saw as the British betrayal of their colonial kith and kin, leaving them to the mercy of African nationalism. By the 1970s, as part of a beleaguered and ostracised white community, the English were turning their backs on their British past. Instead, they sought to preserve their position as part of a privileged white minority by accepting an implicitly racist consensus with Afrikaner nationalism. It is to their credit that in the face of an increasingly oppressive press censorship, most English newspapers remained true to their traditions of maintaining the right to report fully on all news. But while the press fought to retain its freedom from government control, it remained subservient to the forces of mining and financial capital that had done so much to shape it during the imperial period. In this way it continued to serve the interest of white, English-speaking South Africans in maintaining the status quo instead of trying to reach a *modus vivendi* with the new forces of African nationalism. The consequences of this failure remain to be told.

Acknowledgement

I acknowledge the financial support of the University of South Africa.

Notes

1. For a discussion of some of these works, see J. Lambert, 'South African British? Or Dominion South Africans? The Evolution of an Identity in the 1910s and 1920s', *South African Historical Journal*, 43 (November 2000): 197–222; and 'An Identity Threatened: White English-Speaking South Africans, Britishness and Dominion South Africanism, 1934–1939', *Kleio*, XXXVII (2005).
2. See J. A. Hobson, *The War in South Africa: Its Causes and Effects* (London: James Nisbet, 1900), p. 215; *Dawie, 1946–1964: 'n bloemlesing uit die geskrifte van Die Burger se politieke kommentator*, saamgestel deur Louis Louw (Kaapstad, Tafelberg, 1965), p. 4, translation; *The Star*, 3 October 1960.

3. These do, however, include useful introductions on the imperial period. See M. Broughton, *Press and Politics of South Africa* (Cape Town and Johannesburg: Purnell & Sons, 1961); W. A. Hachten and C. A. Giffard, *The Press and Apartheid: Repression and Propaganda in South Africa* (London and Basingstoke: Macmillan, 1984); E. Potter, *The Press as Opposition: The Political Role of South African Newspapers* (Totowa, NJ: Rowman and Littlefield, 1975).

4. See particularly S. Haw, *Bearing Witness: The Natal Witness, 1846–1996* (Pietermaritzburg: The Natal Witness, 1996); J. Mervis, *The Fourth Estate: A Newspaper Story* (Johannesburg: Jonathan Ball, 1989); G. Shaw, *Some Beginnings: The Cape Times, 1876–1910* (Cape Town: Oxford University Press, 1975) and *The Cape Times: An Informal History* (Cape Town: David Philip, 1999); *Today's News Today: The Story of the Argus Company* (Johannesburg: The Argus Printing & Publishing Co., 1956); T. Wilks, *For the Love of Natal: The Life and Times of the Natal Mercury, 1852–1977* (Durban: Robinson, 1977).

5. See H. Flather, *The Way of an Editor* (Cape Town: Purnell, 1977); G. A. L. Green, *An Editor Looks Back: South African and Other Memories, 1883–1946* (Cape Town and Johannesburg: Juta & Co., 1947); M. Green, *Around and About: Memoirs of a South African Newspaperman* (Cape Town: David Philip, 2004).

6. The *Cape Town Gazette and African Advertiser*, published 1802–4 during the first British occupation of the Cape contained mainly government notices.

7. For the origins of the press in South Africa, see Potter, *Press as Opposition*, pp. 30–3.

8. As late as 1950, 65 of South Africa's 95 country newspapers were bilingual, see *A Short History of the Newspaper Press in South Africa, 1652–1952* (Cape Town: Nasionale Pers, 1952), pp. 33–6.

9. H. Giliomee, *The Afrikaners: Biography of a People* (Cape Town: Tafelberg, 2003), p. 196.

10. Ibid.

11. For a discussion on South Africanism and the Nationalist rejection of it, see Lambert, 'South African British?' *passim*.

12. An independent black press emerged in the 1880s reflecting the views of the new black petty bourgeoisie. This press tended to be politically moderate and pro-imperial, seeing the British Government as a protector of black interests. It was only from the 1930s that it became a militantly left-wing resistance press. See L. Switzer (ed.), *South Africa's Alternative Press: Voices of Protest and Resistance, 1880s–1960s* (Cambridge: Cambridge University Press, 1997).

13. Shaw, *The Cape Times; Today's News Today;* Wilks, *For the Love of Natal,* all *passim*.

14. G. Storey, *Reuter's Century, 1851–1951* (London: Max Parrish, 1951), *passim*.

15. *Dawie*, p. 4, translation.

16. *Cape Times*, 12 May 1937.

17. See *The Pretoria News*, 9 November 1903; *Cape Times*, 6 May 1935; *Natal Mercury*, 2 June 1953.

18. *Star*, 23 January 1892.

19. See Shaw, *The Cape Times*, p. 3; *The Natal Witness*, 25 February 1879; Haw, *Bearing Witness*, p. 114.

20. See *Natal Mercury*, 4 October 1854.
21. C. F. Goodfellow, *Great Britain and South African Confederation, 1870–1881* (Cape Town: Oxford University Press, 1966), *passim*.
22. See Wilks, *For the Love of Natal*, p. 93.
23. For a discussion of Rhodes's policies, see M. Tamarkin, *Cecil Rhodes and the Cape Afrikaners: The Imperial Colossus and the Colonial Parish Pump* (London: Frank Cass, 1996), *passim*.
24. R. Hyam and P. Henshaw, *The Lion and the Springbok: Britain and South Africa since the Boer War* (Cambridge: Cambridge University Press, 2003), p. 40; R. Davenport and C. Saunders, *South Africa: A Modern History*, fifth edition (Basingstoke: Macmillan, 2000), p. 220.
25. *Today's News Today*, p. 120; Barlow, 'The Clouded Face of Truth', p. 9; G. A. L. Green, *An Editor Looks Back*, pp. 149–50.
26. G. Shaw, *South African Telegraph versus Cape Times*...(Cape Town, Centre for African Studies, University of Cape Town, Communications no. 3, 1980), *passim*.
27. J. Lambert, 'Sir John Robinson and Responsible Government, 1863–1897: The Making of the First Prime Minister of Natal', MA diss., University of Natal, 1975, pp. 232–3.
28. *Today's News Today*, p. 96.
29. Shaw, *The Cape Times*, p. 5.
30. Shaw, *Some Beginnings*, pp. 75–80.
31. *Cape Argus*, 4 January 1896.
32. Shaw, *South African Telegraph versus Cape Times*, pp. 8–9.
33. Ibid.
34. *Natal Mercury*, 7 January 1896, 'Ubique'.
35. Davenport and Saunders, *South Africa*, p. 99.
36. A. N. Porter, *The Origins of the South African War: Joseph Chamberlain and the Diplomacy of Imperialism, 1895–99* (Manchester: Manchester University Press, 1980), pp. 180, 181; D. Cammack, *The Rand at War, 1899–1902: The Witwatersrand and the Anglo-Boer War* (London: James Currey, 1990), pp. 17–18; Barlow, 'The Clouded Face of Truth', p. 109.
37. *Today's News Today*, p. 57.
38. C. Dugmore, 'From pro-Boer to Jingo: An Analysis of Small Town English-language Newspapers on the Rand before the Outbreak of War in 1899', *South African Historical Journal*, 41 (November 1999): 262–5; Wilks, *For the Love of Natal*, p. 112.
39. F. J. Dormer, *Vengeance as a Policy in Afrikanderland: A Plea for a New Departure* (London, James Nisbet, 1901), p. 125.
40. Hobson, *The War in South Africa*, pp. 211, 214–17, 227.
41. Cammack, *The Rand at War*, p. 153; Davenport and Saunders, *South Africa*, pp. 226, 230.
42. A. G. Barlow, *Almost in Confidence* (Cape Town and Johannesburg: Juta, 1952), pp. 67, 83. The *Friend* returned to Barlow's management in 1902.
43. *Today's News Today*, pp. 135, 144–5; Shaw, *The Cape Times*, pp. 9–11; S. and B. Stent, *The Forthright Man*, ed. P. Cartwright (Cape Town: Howard Timmins, 1972), p. 79.
44. Mervis, *The Fourth Estate*, pp. 36, 80, 83; Potter, *The Press as Opposition*, pp. 42–3; *Today's News Today, passim*.

45. *Today's News Today*, pp. 215, 246.
46. Mervis, *The Fourth Estate*, pp. ix, 1, 15, 23, 49.
47. M. Fraser and A. Jeeves, *All that Glittered: Selected Correspondence of Lionel Phillips, 1890–1924* (Cape Town: Oxford University Press, 1977), p. 233; Shaw, *The Cape Times*, pp. 25–6.
48. *The editorship of 'The Argus'* (n.pl.: n.p., 1938), p. [3].
49. See Lambert, 'South African British?' *passim*.
50. Ibid.; *Today's News Today*, pp. 216–17.
51. See J. Lambert, 'Britishness, South Africanism and the First World War', in P. Buckner and D. Francis (eds.), *Rediscovering the British World* (Calgary: University of Calgary Press, 2005).
52. See Lambert, 'South African British?', pp. 217, 219–20 This attempt did much to undermine the support given by the English working class to the Labour Party, which by the 1930s became politically irrelevant.
53. *Cape Times*, 12 October 1918.
54. See Lambert, 'An Identity Threatened', *passim*.
55. For a discussion of the press and the war, see J. Crwys-Williams, *A Country at War, 1939–1945: The Mood of a Nation* (Rivonia: Ashanti Publishing, 1992), *passim*.
56. *Dawie*, pp. 119, 152.
57. *A Short History of the Newspaper Press*, p. 28.
58. Mervis, *The Fourth Estate*, p. 153.
59. *Natal Mercury*, 5 October 1960.
60. See *Sunday Times*, 2 October 1960; *Friend*, 4 October 1960; *Star*, 4 October 1960.
61. Lambert, 'South African British?' pp. 221–2.
62. *Cape Times*, 16 March 1961.
63. Shaw, *The Cape Times*, p. 168.

4
'The Old Pals' Protection Society'? The Colonial Office and the British Press on the Eve of Decolonisation

Joanna Lewis and Philip Murphy

As the 1950s drew to a close, there was a growing awareness on the part of British ministers and officials of the power of the media and the need for 'news management'. As Harold Macmillan noted in his memoirs, by 1959 he and his colleagues fought elections in the company of two new developments: television and opinion polls.[1] Yet there remained a tradition under which civil servants were expected to remain relatively aloof from the world of journalism, and ministers expected a degree of deference from the press. The Colonial Office (CO) in particular was keen to keep its own affairs from the critical scrutiny not only of the media but of Parliament itself, fearing that public disagreements about policy within the metropole would weaken the authority of its personnel in the colonies.[2] In this regard the issues of press coverage and parliamentary scrutiny were closely interlinked. Through the mechanism of parliamentary questions, MPs may well have played a more significant role than journalists in holding the Government to account.[3] Yet a large proportion of those questions were inspired by reports in the press, and ministerial replies could, in turn, encourage further investigations by the media.

The attempt to analyse the role of the press in the process of British decolonisation presents the historian with a number of problems. Much of the interaction between Government and the media necessarily took place 'off the record'. Few of those who managed relations with the press during this period have recorded their experiences.[4] Furthermore, the terms of the debate about decolonisation were complex, and it is not always possible to make a clear distinction between 'liberals' and 'diehards'. The paradoxical nature of British Establishment attitudes towards the Empire and race is perhaps most neatly encapsulated by Harold Nicolson's expression of disgust about the brutality of apartheid in a letter to his son Nigel in January 1960: 'You know how I hate the Negroes. But I hate injustice more...'[5] Earlier, in a letter to his wife, Nicolson had suggested, 'We cannot suppress the darkies by shooting them. In fact the rule of Empire is over, and I fear that the Tories will not face the fact.'[6] Nicolson probably spoke for many among the British elite whose unreconstructed notions of racial superiority coexisted with a growing sense of distaste at the human cost of maintaining imperial control.

What this chapter seeks to do is to map some of the ways in which policy-makers and the media interacted. It takes as its focus events in Kenya and Central Africa during and immediately preceding the 'pivotal' year of 1959, the events of which served to highlight the undercurrent of violence in British colonial rule. In the case of Kenya, the issue that threatened to attract the greatest amount of negative media attention in 1959 was the treatment of Mau Mau suspects in Kenya's detention camps. The so-called Mau Mau uprising had resulted in the Colonial Government declaring a State of Emergency in October 1952. A war against 'terrorists' and the Kikuyu people who supported them was fought, which included a military campaign, mass detention, imprisonment and relocation. Yet the British Government proved remarkably successful both in disguising a number of incidents of maltreatment of Mau Mau suspects, and in encouraging the press to cover stories that put the best possible construction on the actions of the Kenya Government. In the past, ministers and officials in London had been prepared to resort to underhand methods to force into the open stories favourable to the administration in Nairobi. In late 1956, following accusations about conditions in the detention camps levelled by the anti-colonial activist Eileen Fletcher, an all-party Commonwealth Parliamentary Association (CPA) delegation (three Labour and four Tory MPs) left for Kenya under the chairmanship of a Conservative, Sir Thomas Dugdale. On their return, a report was prepared, as usual, for the CPA. When the Secretary of State for the Colonies, Alan Lennox-Boyd, read it, he was thrilled, describing it as 'most excellent'.[7] It claimed to have found no evidence to substantiate the Fletcher allegations. Indeed, the process of rehabilitation and release was narrated as a success story. Even better, the report offered support for the broader CO policy of the move towards 'multi-racial' politics. 'We believe', the delegation concluded, 'the complete end of the colour bar will not long be delayed' thanks to the 'natural flow of goodwill among moderate people of all races'.[8]

Although the report had not been intended for publication, the CO saw considerable benefits in it being so. One official noted that the section on common-roll elections would be particularly helpful to them if widely read, 'in the way that the previous delegation's reports helped to pave the way for Lyttelton' (a reference to the Kenyan constitution of 1954). The colonial attaché at the British embassy in Washington wanted the State Department to see it. 'The Americans', he wrote, were 'very concerned about the multi-racial communities in East and Central Africa'.[9] Such a report would do them and Britain 'a great deal of good'. Broad media coverage of the way in which 'moderates' were apparently all pulling together was a highly attractive prospect to the Kenya Government and the CO at a time when African members were boycotting the newly elected legislative council, thus denying Kenya any claim to have a functioning, multi-racial chamber.[10] It might also help to balance left-wing criticism of the Kenya Government's approach to the Emergency, which had been rekindled by accusations of brutality in the camps.[11] Labour MPs, however, were adamant that the report should not be published. Their reasoning was that the visit had been conceived as a 'goodwill delegation' and not an investigative one. Had there been any suggestion that a report would be published, the Labour composition would have been at a higher level and would have included 'at least one QC'.[12] On getting wind of the initial 'manoeuvring' to get the report published, the Labour MP James Griffiths (a former Secretary of State for the Colonies) was instructed to put a stop to it. 'What Kenya needed', he warned, 'was a thorough going over, not a pat on the back'.

Despite Labour's clear stand on this matter, the report was leaked to the press and, on 1 April, *The Times* published a summary of its findings. The CO denied responsibility. Nevertheless, it must have been highly satisfied with headlines such as '7 MPs Clear Kenya Whites' and suggestions that the report was being suppressed. Labour continued to put the brakes on its publication in the meetings of the CPA, but it had eventually to bow to the inevitable when the executive committee of the UK branch of the CPA finally gave way, thus enabling a press handout from Kenya to run with the heading: 'Improved relations between races'.

As for the allegations of brutality in the Kenyan detention camps, the CO appears to have benefited from a high degree of self-censorship on the part of the press. In 1958, a letter had made a successful bid for freedom from the remote Lokitaung prison, bearing tales of cruel and harsh treatment. It was signed by a number of high-profile prisoners from Mau Mau's 'intelligentsia', including Fred Kubai and Bildad Kaggia.[13] The Movement for Colonial Freedom distributed a copy of the letter to all MPs. Newspaper editors received copies too, and it was published by the *Observer* in early June. Complaints about the prison regime were specific, detailed and entirely plausible. Immediately, other papers ran the story, which now carried an additional development since James Callaghan (the Shadow Colonial Secretary) had taken it up. In a sign of the times, a request simultaneously arrived at the Kenya desk of the CO from Associated Rediffusion, a TV company, which wanted to send Macdonald Hastie to Lokitaung to make a documentary. By 16 June, a rash of letters on Lokitaung had been sent to the CO and the press, and some had appeared in the *Observer*. The authors of the latter included Eileen Fletcher, who pointed out that the original letter proved that, as far as the detention camps in Kenya were concerned, 'there was indeed something to hide'. On 18 June, the press ran the story that the CO was refusing to hold an inquiry. Fenner Brockway had a letter on the subject published in the *Manchester Guardian*. Meanwhile, questions were being prepared in the House of Commons from the usual stalwarts of the anti-colonial Left – the Labour MPs John Stonehouse, Fenner Brockway and Barbara Castle. The editor of the *Observer*, David Astor, requested that he be allowed to send a journalist to the camp. Although the *Daily Telegraph* came to the Government's rescue with the headline 'Smear campaign', there was little let-up in the press. A long editorial in the *New Statesman*'s London Diary for 21 June must have made for sobering reading. Its verdict displayed a cynical but shrewd understanding of what was going on. 'Shocking conditions and atrocities were likely to occur in these camps', the editor opined, and when senior officials heard about them, clearly the '"Old Pals' Protection Society" kicked in'.[14]

Yet the situation proved to be well within the news management capacity of the CO, which had developed over the previous years when dealing with similar scenarios. First, they had advance warning about the letter. The *Daily Mail* had sent them a copy 'on a very personal and confidential basis'. Officials pledged to keep this secret so that they could continue to enjoy 'good relations' with the paper. Almost immediately, a note for the press was drafted with regard to the publication of a letter described as coming from 'very questionable sources'. Using the language of inclusiveness and shared moral high ground, the note was carefully designed to encourage restraint. The letter, according to the CO, had been 'extremely damaging and distressing to the morale of a body of devoted public servants working overseas for the good of all races...' Newspaper editors were urged to counter this with 'the facts' to support 'all those people including yourself, who believe that the great hope of Kenya is the establishment of a non-racial community'.[15] Then came a minor stroke of good luck. Around this time, reviews of a book entitled *The Hunt for Kimathi* appeared in some of the broadsheets, written by Ian Henderson and Philip Goodhart. The latter had been a journalist with the *Daily Telegraph* and the *Sunday Times* and was now a Conservative MP.[16] The book offered a timely return to the image of the Mau Mau fighter as a mad, dreadlocked figure in a leopard-skin throw, straight out of Joseph Conrad's *Heart of Darkness*. There was also more serious help at hand. A sympathetic Conservative MP, Patrick Wall, wanted to ask a number of questions in the House of Commons which he ran past the CO. He was seeking to exonerate the colonial official – Charles Ryland – who had been 'named and shamed' in the Lokitaung letter. Wall demanded to know whether the press had checked the facts.[17]

A week later, a firm rebuttal of the Lokitaung allegations was put together in the *Kenya News* Press Office Handout No. 387. Lennox-Boyd resolutely rejected the charges, and requests to visit the camps were politely but firmly refused. Indeed, the Governor himself sent a detailed and gracious letter to Astor explaining why he felt unable to grant access to the Lokitaung camp even to papers of 'great reputation'.[18] So, by the end of 1958, all that officials were left to deal with were parliamentary pressure from Brockway and Stonehouse, who kept the issue alive, and the request from African-elected members of LegCo, the colony's undemocratic parliament, to visit the camps. Meanwhile, on 19 December, the *Daily Telegraph* published the news that the *Observer* had agreed to pay substantial libel damages to Ryland.

Yet the fallout from Lokitaung continued into 1959 due to the persistence of Stonehouse. He received copies of a statement about abuses in a Kenya prison from a Captain E. Law, who had originally written to Lennox-Boyd with a veiled threat to go to the press. Law's case was covered in the press and accompanied by a photograph depicting a pipe-smoking, congenial-looking Brit. His account of what he saw in Kamiti was similar to earlier accusations. He described the Superintendent, Haig Thomas, as 'the worst sadist I have met including the Nips [Japanese] on the Burma–Siam Railway'.[19] On 6 February, Stonehouse obtained 100 signatures for his motion calling for an inquiry within an hour of its being circulated; these included that of Sir George Benson, chairman of the prison reform group, the Howard Reform League. Both the *Economist* and the *New Statesman* published editorials calling for an independent inquiry.[20] Baring and Lennox-Boyd were concerned about reassuring 'reasonable public opinion in the

UK' – hence their enthusiasm for what became the Fairn Inquiry into the detention camp system.[21] Stonehouse's motion was ultimately rejected by 288 votes to 232.

Meanwhile, pressure mounted on rehabilitation staff to keep up the rate of release of detainees. In early March, following the unsupervised and partial application of the Cowan Plan[22] to a larger than recommended number of hardcore detainees at Hola who would not work, 'man-handling' and 'compelling force' degenerated into a brutal free-for-all: eleven men died and scores were hospitalised.[23] The news initially received surprisingly little coverage in the British press, though Barbara Castle immediately tabled a question in the House of Commons. Yet as a local investigation was being undertaken into the circumstances of the 'incident', newspapers in Britain contained headlines such as 'Kenya Europeans here to stay; Labour MP "impressed with colony"', whilst Kenya's press office boasted of 'British MPs' Confidence in Kenya's Future'.[24] This coincidence was not planned by Whitehall.[25] Nevertheless, the positive headlines had been anticipated by the CO. They related to the visit of the most recent CPA delegation consisting of just two, relatively inexperienced MPs: Paul Williams from the Conservative Party and George Thomas from Labour.[26] As the CO prepared to brief the MPs, officials anticipated that they could be 'used as sounding board to our post-Chequers thoughts' (a reference to a conference on constitutional change in East Africa held in January 1959 at the Prime Minister's official country residence). While they expected the issue of the detention camps would be raised, they noted that, in the past, CPA visits had proved 'useful' for publicity.[27] This one would be no exception, and the timing proved to be perfect.

As further details of the Hola killings entered the public domain over the spring and early summer of 1959, leftwing newspapers blamed the absence of a previous inquiry for the deaths.[28] Elsewhere, sympathy for the Government's line was signalled by the headline: 'No Cover-up Says Lennox-Boyd' (*Daily Mail; News Chronicle*). A rare public criticism of the Government from one of its supporters came from the maverick Tory MP Lord Lambton, who published his views in a prominent article in the *Evening Standard* under the banner 'When Loyalty is not Enough'. A clear attack on Lennox-Boyd urging him to take responsibility (i.e. resign) for Hola, the piece is also significant for illustrating a hard-nosed pragmatism at the root of a growing centre-right disengagement from kith and kin in Africa. Such scandals, a media-savvy Lambton pointed out, were 'a propaganda stick' for the Communists and anti-British elements in Africa; it was rule by good example which carried 'our best hopes for Africa'. Yet, in the short term, the CO was comparatively untouched by negative press coverage. A meeting of officials was held to read the newspapers on the day following the publication of a White Paper on Hola. Their only significant concern was that one newspaper had suggested the name Hola meant 'hell' in Swahilli.

If the detention camps provided the focus for media attention about Kenya in 1959, in the case of Central Africa it was the Nyasaland Emergency that grabbed many of the headlines. In order to understand the way in which press–government relations worked themselves out in the context of Central Africa, it is necessary to say something about ministerial responsibility for the region. Between 1953 and 1963, Southern Rhodesia (Zimbabwe), Northern Rhodesia (Zambia) and Nyasaland (Malawi) formed the Federation of Rhodesia and Nyasaland, better known as the Central African Federation. In deference to the Southern Rhodesian settlers' virtual internal self-government, their territory's affairs were the responsibility of the British Commonwealth Relations Office (CRO), which also dealt with the settler-dominated federal government. Meanwhile, Northern Rhodesia and Nyasaland were overseen by the CO. While the CO displayed some sympathy with African frustrations at their slow rate of political and economic advance under federation, and was increasingly suspicious about the commitment of federal ministers to genuine 'multi-racial partnership', the CRO tended to regard such criticisms as 'defeatism'. Hence, disputes within Central Africa over constitutional reform were mirrored within Whitehall by clashes between the CO and the CRO.

The strains created within Central Africa itself by the African rejection of Federation came to a head on 3 March 1959 when, in response to rising unrest in his territory, the Governor of Nyasaland, Sir Robert Armitage, declared a State of Emergency.[29] This was followed by 1,322 arrests, including those of Dr Hastings Banda and other leading members of the territory's principal nationalist movement, the Nyasaland African Congress. Defending Armitage's actions in the Commons only hours after the Emergency had come into force, Lennox-Boyd claimed that action had been required to prevent a 'massacre' that was being planned by Congress. The parliamentary under-secretary at the CO, Julian Amery, spoke even more chillingly of a 'blood bath', invoking the memory of Mau Mau and claiming that there might have been 'a massacre of Africans, Asians and Europeans on a Kenyan scale'.[30] Yet the report of a commission of inquiry chaired by the High Court judge Lord Devlin, which was published on 22 July, seriously undermined the Government's case for declaring the

Emergency and criticised the authorities' subsequent handling of events. In its most resonant phrase, the report noted that 'Nyasaland is – no doubt temporarily – a police state'.[31]

By 13 July, Lennox-Boyd had seen proofs of the Devlin Report and was able to tell Armitage that it was 'very hostile'.[32] Devlin's talent for stinging epigrams made the report a particularly challenging prospect for the civil service in terms of news management. The head of the CO's information department, O. M. Morris, feared that it would 'create in many people's minds the picture of a colonial administration in the last throes of its desperate fight to keep power (much as Marxists have forecast), planning and executing a cracking down operation on a political party which expressed the nationalist aspirations of the time'.[33] The Government's approach to the release of the Devlin Report has already been examined in some detail and need be touched upon only very briefly here.[34] It decided to delay publication, both to limit the time in which the report could be debated before the parliamentary recess and to give itself the opportunity to frame a response. This response came in the form of a published despatch by Armitage. It did so because the British Government did not wish to appear to be directly critical of a commission it had itself established. Nevertheless, Macmillan was clearly determined that the despatch should be as eye-catchingly epigrammatic as the Devlin Report itself, and he directed that it should, where necessary, subject the commission's findings to 'merciless ridicule'.[35] To this end, a formidable group of ministers and officials was assembled at Chequers on the weekend of 18–19 July to assist in the drafting process. At the same time, the Government successfully persuaded Devlin to remove a summary of conclusions from the report. This move was explicitly designed to deprive journalists of easy access to the main criticisms it contained.[36]

If the Government escaped relatively lightly over the Hola affair, it efforts to blunt press reaction to Devlin proved ineffective. While the political correspondent of *The Times* placed what positive gloss he could on the affair, elsewhere, even in publications on the centre-right of British politics, the reaction was highly critical.[37] In a leading article headed 'Rooted in Dishonour', the *Spectator* (then edited by Ian Gilmour) ridiculed the Government's main lines of defence against Devlin's findings.[38] The *Economist* was equally critical of the Government's refusal to accept the commission's findings, claiming that 'Politics has overridden the appearance of detached justice'.[39] Whether or not the Devlin Report and the subsequent press reaction to it had any direct impact on British policy-makers, it almost certainly helped strengthen the hand of Iain Macleod when, after becoming Colonial Secretary in October 1959, he sought to release Banda and open a dialogue with him.

While the news management surrounding the Devlin Report and the subsequent press reaction are fairly well documented, the broader network of media–governmental relations in 1959 is far less so. For the reasons already mentioned, these relationships were highly complex. The CRO's tendency to react with hostility to criticisms of the Federal Government's policies threatened to stifle debate within Whitehall about the future of the Federation. From the point of view of the CO, therefore, there was value even in media coverage that was broadly critical of the policy of the British Government, in so far as it served to raise difficult and contentious issues. The scepticism expressed by media commentators about the performance of the Federal Government and its willingness to make genuine political concessions to African political aspirations was also widely held within the CO itself. Hence, although the CO was not insensitive to criticism, it served its interests to nurture the media as a space for informed and innovative political debate. Media coverage also undermined the ability of colonial Governors to control the flow of information to London, thus strengthening the hand of the CO in relation to its local representatives. In the case of Nyasaland in 1959, there were growing doubts in London about the competence of Sir Robert Armitage. Hence, indignation at the damage that might be done to the prestige of the Nyasaland Government by press criticism was balanced in the CO by a sense that the media was helping to bring to light genuine failings in Armitage's administration.

The CO's approach to the press at this time was characterised by a policy of 'constructive engagement'. Officials had no illusions about the fact that they had few natural supporters in Fleet Street. Morris suggested that, 'Apart from the *Economist*, and possibly the *Sunday Times*, there is no weekly periodical which, to my mind, presents colonial affairs objectively'.[40] Nevertheless, the CO maintained close links with what it referred to as its 'inner circle' of British journalists specialising in Commonwealth and colonial affairs.[41] Members of the inner circle received regular private briefings by the Secretary of State, and even in the feverish political atmosphere that followed the Nyasaland Emergency, relations between the CO and the press appear to have remained cordial. In May 1959, Oliver Woods of *The Times* (and doyen of Fleet Street's colonial specialists) organised a lunch at which journalists interested in African affairs could discuss the future of the

Federation with the minister of state at the CO, Lord Perth. Despite there having clearly been a considerable amount of scepticism expressed as to the wisdom of the Government's policy, Perth recalled that 'On the whole I got a good deal of sympathy although puzzlement on how to proceed without Banda'.[42] Perhaps surprisingly given his paper's critical attitude towards the Federation, one suggestion that emerged from the lunch was that the CO might assist in organising a tour of Africa for David Astor, the editor of the *Observer*, who had never visited the continent. Perth was keen to pursue this, and there was agreement among officials that this might be 'an educational experience' for Astor.[43] One civil servant noted: 'I do not for a moment think that a visit to Africa by Mr Astor would radically change his paper's line, but it would I think lead to some greater accuracy in presentation, and a better editorial sense of what African problems are.'[44]

This is not to say that officials at the CO were incapable of being goaded by comments in the press. Yet even when contentious issues did arise over the Federation, the responses from the CO generally fell some way short of righteous indignation. On 23 May 1959, the *Economist* published a piece entitled 'Contempt of Justice', which was highly critical of the Nyasaland Government for announcing – in advance of the Devlin Report – that it intended to keep Congress leaders in detention indefinitely. The *Economist* noted that the government bulletin in which the announcement appeared also encouraged its African readers to inform on any of their neighbours they believed to be members of Congress. In a further article entitled 'Nyasa Fairy Tales and Witch Hunts' published two weeks later, the *Economist* went into more detail about the crude methods being employed by the Nyasaland Government to persuade Africans to provide information to the authorities. It noted that the bulletins produced for Africans were 'written in the manner of fairy tales for five-year-olds (presumably because the government realises that the majority of educated Africans are already in gaol)'.[45] One such bulletin quoted in the article instructed its African readers that if they knew of any Congress member who had not yet been arrested, 'you must tell the Boma [Government] so that these wicked people can be arrested and removed from your area'. In effect, both articles neatly anticipated Devlin's jibe that Nyasaland had come to resemble a 'police state'.

J. C. Morgan, the assistant under-secretary at the CO responsible for the intelligence and security department, described the original piece as being 'about as "wrong-headed" as possible'.[46] Among his fellow officials, however, there was a notable lack of outrage at the piece. One of them, P. R. Noakes, doubted whether 'it could be held to be wildly unfair'.[47] In an implied criticism of Armitage, he noted that 'whatever is put out for Africans in Nyasaland is also likely to be read by a great many other people'. His colleague William Gorell Barnes agreed that 'the question I feel bound to ask myself is whether we ought not to ask Sir R. Armitage to be a little more careful'.[48]

As press interest in the activities of the Nyasaland Government increased so did that of Downing Street. On 14 June, the appeal for informers was the subject of an article in *Reynolds News* entitled 'Baby Talk for the New Africa'. Two days later, it was taken up in a letter to *The Times* from Violet Bonham Carter and Lord Hemingford, chairman of the Africa Bureau.[49] Once again, they anticipated the terms of the Devlin Report, describing the Nyasaland Government's approach as 'worthy of any totalitarian state'. The following day, the *Manchester Guardian* reported that members of the Liberal parliamentary party had also condemned the Nyasaland Government's appeal.[50] Another issue raised in the letter from Bonham Carter and Hemingford was a proposed amendment to the Nyasaland Children and Young Persons Ordinance, which would have allowed the use of corporal punishment as a judicial penalty against children as young as seven. This had already formed the basis of a separate complaint to the CO from the honorary director of the Africa Bureau, Michael Scott, after the terms of the Bill to amend the Ordinance had been published in *The Times*.[51] Scott's intervention had prompted a debate within the CO about the wisdom not only of the specific amendment proposed by the Nyasaland Government but of the general principle of using corporal punishment in this way. One official described the practice as 'repugnant to modern world opinion'.[52] Nevertheless, the CO was reluctant to ask Armitage to withdraw his Government's Bill. Instead, it asked him to make changes 'designed to bring it into line with the practice in other Colonial territories'.[53]

Having seen the letter in *The Times* and the report in the *Guardian*, Macmillan requested information on both the issues they had raised. In reply, the CO revealed that in response to its approach to Armitage about the Bill to amend the Children and Young Persons Ordinance, the Governor had decided to withdraw the amendment entirely.[54] As to the appeal for informants, the CO stressed that this had been issued without any reference to the Secretary of State, and that the department had 'frankly felt uncomfortable about it'. It noted, however, that Armitage thought it would have a 'very bad effect' if his Government were to withdraw it. Macmillan was clearly not impressed by the CO's response, describing the position as 'very confused and unsatisfactory'.[55] He met Lennox-Boyd on 22 June and discussed the Government's response to a parliamentary question on the issue of informants. Macmillan appears to have persuaded Lennox-Boyd that the answer 'should be somewhat more expansive' than had originally been agreed.[56]

In the wake of the Devlin Report – which had meticulously picked apart much of the Nyasaland Government's justification for having arrested the Congress leaders – there were calls in the press for Banda to be released. Typical of these was Robin Day's column in the *News Chronicle* on 13 August, headed: 'When will Dr. Banda be invited to Balmoral?' The piece juxtaposed the recent visit to London of the Ghanaian Prime Minister, Kwame Nkrumah, who had himself once been 'a political prisoner under British rule' with the current fate of Banda. It urged the British Government to free Banda and bring him to London for talks. In fact, the CO was also exploring the issue of an overture to Banda as a result of a private intervention from one of its 'inner circle' of journalists, Donald McLachlan, deputy editor of the *Daily Telegraph*. McLachlan might appear an unlikely advocate of compromise and conciliation. He was perhaps best known as the author of an attack on Anthony Eden in the *Telegraph* in January 1956, in which he had accused the then Prime Minister of failing to provide 'the smack of firm government'.[57] Yet in the case of Nyasaland, McLachlan favoured dialogue and suggested to Perth that a British minister might visit Banda.[58] In an initiative aimed at preparing the ground for talks, McLachlan also approached Julian Amery to suggest that Sir Roy Welensky, Prime Minister of the Federation of Rhodesia and Nyasaland, be persuaded to give a speech reassuring Africans that full independence for the Federation as a whole would not be possible until all its constituent parts were independent (implicitly, in the cases of Northern Rhodesia and Nyasaland, under African governments).[59]

Perth thought that the possibility of a rebuff from Banda made the option of a ministerial visit to Banda difficult. He was, however, in favour of smoothing the way for some kind of approach and suggested that an inventory should be made of the various statements issued in recent weeks to reassure African opinion that the Government remained committed to securing constitutional development.[60] Perth was even prepared to contemplate that Banda might be allowed to 'come to this country without strings attached, and then have some of his friends work on him'. At the time, however, the feeling among Perth's officials was that the idea of even an informal approach to

Banda would be premature.[61] The decision to call a general election in October closed the issue. Lennox-Boyd directed that the matter would have to wait until the campaign was over.[62] He did, however, ask his officials to explore the legal feasibility of releasing Banda from detention while at the same time banning him from the Federation.[63] Had the election not intervened, it is possible that McLachlan's initiative might have borne fruit and that the approach to Banda might have been made some months earlier than was ultimately the case.

In the long term, Devlin and Hola may well have played a pivotal role in persuading the Conservative Party to loosen its ties with Africa's white settlers. Managing media coverage of the settler colonies was certainly becoming more time-consuming and politically dangerous. The 'Old Pals' Protection Society' was not entirely moribund, and the CO had a relatively easy ride in terms of the accusations of brutality in the Kenyan camps, culminating in the coverage of Hola. Yet the press treatment of the Nyasaland Emergency suggested that the Government would never again have it so good. Henceforth, colonial administrations would be under intense scrutiny, their actions judged against a growing public anxiety about the legacy of British rule in Africa. Faced with the prospect of more robust press criticism, the CO continued to pursue a policy of 'constructive engagement'. In some respects, particularly in its coverage of events in Central Africa, the doubts expressed in the press about the direction of official policy were shared by ministers and officials. If the press urged a move away from the fiction of 'multiracialism' towards an acceptance of the inevitability of African majority rule, this was a direction in which the CO increasingly wished to be led. The press also had a role to play in 'educating' white settlers about changing attitudes towards Africa within Conservative circles in Britain. As Colin Legum noted, coverage *The Times* and *Telegraph* sent clear signals to the settlers that they needed to be more realistic about what they could expect from London. For them at least, the 'Old Pals' Protection Society' was at an end.

Notes

1. Harold Macmillan, *Pointing the Way, 1959–1961* (London: Macmillan, 1972), p. 7.
2. See, for example, the resistance of the CO to the idea of the establishment of a specialist parliamentary committee on colonial affairs because of fears that its activities might 'exacerbate public opinion in the colonial territories' (Watt to Smart, 24 September 1958, CO 1032/135).
3. See David Goldsworthy, 'Parliamentary Questions on Colonial Affairs: A Retrospective Analysis', *Parliamentary Affairs*, Vol. 23, No. 2 (1970): 141–53.

4. Two notable exceptions are Harold Evans, *Downing Street Diary: The Macmillan Years, 1957–1963* (London: Hodder & Stoughton, 1981); and William Clark, *From Three Worlds: A Memoir* (London, Sidgwick & Jackson, 1986). Despite the title of the former, however, neither considers relations with the press at the time of the Hola and Devlin affairs.
5. Nigel Nicolson (ed.), *Harold Nicolson, Diaries and Letters, 1945–62* (London: Collins, 1968), p. 378.
6. Ibid., p. 369. See discussion in Joanna Lewis, 'Daddy Wouldn't Buy Me a Mau Mau: The British Popular Press and the Demoralisation of Empire', in E. S. Atieno Odhiambo and John Lonsdale (eds.), *Mau Mau and Nationhood* (Oxford: James Curry, 2003).
7. Alan Lennox-Boyd to Sir Thomas Dugdale, 8 March 1957, CO822/1787.
8. Commonwealth Parliamentary Association Report on Kenya, (January 1957), especially paras 114 and 115. Ibid.
9. Williams to Buist, 2 May 1957. Ibid.
10. Cavendish Bentinck to Dugdale, 4 April 1957. Ibid.
11. See Lewis, 'Daddy Wouldn't Buy Me a Mau Mau'; Stephen Howe, *Anticolonialism in British Politics: The Left and the End of Empire, 1918–1964* (Oxford: Oxford University Press, 1993), pp. 200–7.
12. Mathieson to Buist, 11 March 1957, CO 822/1787.
13. See Marshall S. Clough, *Mau Mau Memoirs: History, Memory and Politics* (Boulder, CO: Lynne Rienner, 1998); Caroline Elkins, *Britain's Gulag: The Brutal End of Empire in Kenya* (London: Jonathan Cape, 2005), pp. 334–7.
14. Various newspaper articles, minutes and letters found in CO 822/1701.
15. 'Note for the press', undated, unsigned. Ibid. The contents may have been informally passed on to journalists.
16. For a discussion of Henderson's role in Kimathi's capture, see David Anderson, *Histories of the Hanged: Britain's Dirty War in Kenya and the End of Empire* (London: Weidenfeld & Nicolson, 2005), pp. 286–8.
17. Minute, 13 June 1958. CO 822/1701.
18. Baring to Astor, 26 June 1958. Ibid. In an accompanying note, Baring told the CO he had not used their suggestion to mention comparable UK law since, with the likelihood of Jomo Kenyatta becoming a restricted person rather than prisoner, they would have to control his visitors.
19. Various copies of allegation held on CO 822/1270.
20. Both articles 28 February 1959, CO822/1269.
21. Baring to Lennox-Boyd, 29 April 1959, ibid.
22. The Cowan Plan was a tried-and-tested (and approved) formula for getting recalcitrant detainees to undertake manual work. It required a high ratio of guards (especially white guards) to detainees to supervise the separating and manhandling of detainees to a particular site.
23. For a concise account of this incident, see Keith Kyle, *The Politics of the Independence of Kenya* (Basingstoke: Macmillan, 1999), pp. 95–8.
24. *The Times*, 28 March 1959; Kenya News – No. 194. CO 822/1789.
25. Draft letter, March 1959, ibid.
26. Note, ibid.
27. Draft of note to Baring, 9 February 1959, ibid.
28. *Daily Herald*, 'Mau Mau Men Could Have Been Saved', quoting the verdict of one Labour MP, 8 May 1959.

29. See Colin Baker, *States of Emergency: Crisis in Central Africa, Nyasaland 1959–1960* (London: Tauris, 1997).
30. *Parliamentary Debates* (Commons), 601, 3 March 1959, cols. 290 and 337.
31. Philip Murphy, *Alan Lennox-Boyd: A Biography* (London: Tauris, 1999), p. 217.
32. Lennox-Boyd to Armitage, 13 July 1959, CO 822/1545.
33. Minute by Morris, 17 July 1959, CO 1027/140.
34. See Richard Lamb, *The Macmillan Years 1957–63: The Emerging Truth* (London: John Murray, 1995), pp. 234–44; Murphy, *Alan Lennox-Boyd*, pp. 217–23.
35. Moreton to Macpherson, 14 July 1959, CO 1015/1547.
36. Murphy, *Alan Lennox-Boyd*, p. 217.
37. *The Times*, 27 July 1959.
38. *Spectator*, 31 July 1959.
39. *Economist*, 1 Aug. 1959.
40. Minute by Morris, 5 May 1959, CO 1027/330.
41. The precise composition of the 'inner circle' in 1959 is unclear, although in July 1961 ('Inner circle: list of correspondents attending on November 17 1961', CO 967/404) it included Lionel Fleming, G. T. M. Morgan and Clifford Smith (BBC), Roy Lewis (*The Times*), Reginald Steed (*Daily Telegraph*), Patrick Keatley (*Guardian*), Geoffrey Wakefield (*Daily Mail*), Seagham Maynes (Reuters), Colin Legum (*Observer*), Nicholas Carroll (*Sunday Times*), J. Rogally (*Economist*), Don Taylor (*New Commonwealth*), F. S. Joelson (*East Africa and Rhodesia*) and Richard Kershaw (*Scotsman*).
42. Minute by Perth, 26 May 1959, CO 1027/185.
43. Minute by Morgan, 28 May 1959. Ibid.
44. Minute by Carstairs, 2 June 1959. Ibid.
45. *Economist*, 6 June 1959.
46. Minute by Morgan, 28 May 1959, CO 1015/1543.
47. Minute by Noakes, 4 June 1959. Ibid.
48. Minute by Morgan, 4 June 1959. Ibid.
49. *The Times*, 16 July 1959.
50. *Guardian*, 17 July 1959.
51. Scott to Lennox-Boyd, 2 April 1959, CO 1015/1893.
52. Minute by Terrell, 5 May 1959, CO 1015/1893.
53. Moreton to Bligh, 18 June 1959, PREM 11/2786.
54. Moreton to Bligh, 18 June 1959. Ibid.
55. Minute by Macmillan, 19 June 1959. Ibid.
56. Note for the record by Bligh, 22 June 1959. Ibid. For Lennox-Boyd's replies, see *Parliamentary Debates* (Commons), 608, written answers, 30 June 1959, cols. 27–9.
57. Alistair Horne, *Macmillan, 1894–1956* (London: Macmillan, 1988) pp. 389–90.
58. Minute by Lord Perth, 14 October 1959, CO 1015/1754.
59. Minute by Monson, 14 August 1959. Ibid.
60. Minute by Lord Perth, 4 August 1959. Ibid.
61. Minutes by J C Morgan, 5 and 12 August 1959. Ibid.
62. Minute by Moreton, 11 September 1959. Ibid.
63. Minute by Lennox-Boyd, 11 September 1959. Ibid.

5

The Media and the Exile of Seretse Khama: The Bangwato vs. the British in Bechuanaland, 1948–56

Susan Williams

In 1950, the British Government exiled Seretse Khama from his own country, the British Protectorate of Bechuanaland in southern Africa (which became independent Botswana in 1966). Twenty-eight-year-old Seretse was the acclaimed kgosi (king) of the Bangwato, the largest of the eight nations of Bechuanaland. The reason for his banishment was his marriage in 1948 to Ruth Williams, an English woman – who happened to be white. Seretse was initially exiled for five years by Attlee's Labour Government; in 1952, Churchill's Conservative Government made the exile permanent.

The banishment of Seretse triggered a bitter struggle between two sides – a 'tug of war'.[1] On the one side, there were the Bangwato, who regarded Seretse as their rightful kgosi and Ruth as their mother. Seretse's uncle, Tshekedi Khama, who was the Regent of the tribe, had complained that the marriage was not according to practice and custom, because Seretse had not consulted his elders, but when the marriage was discussed in June 1949 at a massive kgotla (assembly) of more than 10,000 men, a clear consensus was reached that the marriage did not affect Seretse's birthright to be kgosi. Nor did it matter that Ruth was white. Seretse had married the woman of his choice, and 'a woman of one's choice refers equally to all colours, whether white, black, green or yellow in this respect'.[2]

On the other side was the British Government, which, as the colonising power, seemed to hold all the trump cards. But there was one area in which it was decidedly weak: the scrutiny of the media and international public opinion. The exile of Seretse was the most publicised issue of British African policy at the time and was widely condemned. The Commonwealth historian David Goldsworthy has commented that world-wide publicity at once made the issue a test case of the soundness of the Government's attachment to the principle of racial equality. As such it was taken up as a discussion point by the educated elites in almost all colonial territories. The Government did not come out of it well.[3]

With its dimensions of injustice, romance, miscegenation and the colour bar, the story was guaranteed banner headlines all over the world. When Ruth first went to Serowe, the capital of the Bangwato Reserve, in 1949, journalists flocked to the village from Britain, the US and South Africa. Some of them were 'straight out of *Scoop* [a reference to Evelyn Waugh's novel], and nearly all pretty grisly', complained the Resident Commissioner of Bechuanaland.[4] A reporter from the British *Daily Express* said that even as Seretse drove his wife to Serowe after her arrival in the territory, 'a small aeroplane prowled over the brick-red track, and a cameraman hung out vertiginously, eager for pictures of the most talked-of couple in the world'.[5] In the middle of Ruth's first night, a man in the house where she was staying was woken by a noise and a beam of light shining through his bedroom window. It was the press, who had been hoping to get a photograph of Ruth and Seretse in bed together.[6] The little wooden post office became the hub of the village. There was so much traffic over the single telegraph line to the outside world that extra operators had to be sent down from Salisbury, the capital of Southern Rhodesia, 500 miles to the north.[7]

Just six months after Ruth's arrival in Bechuanaland, Seretse was brought to London by the British Government – under false pretences, as Winston Churchill pointed out[8] – and then banished. The Government tried to present the exile to the public in a positive light, but it was hampered by the very reason for the exile – direct and heavy pressure from the Union of South Africa and from Southern Rhodesia, neither of which wanted a prominent mixed marriage on the other side of their border. In May 1948, only a few months before the Khamas' marriage, South Africa's white minority had voted into power Dr Malan's Afrikaner National Party, on an election platform of apartheid. South Africa had powerful leverage over Britain: it had uranium, which Britain was negotiating for; it could withdraw from the Commonwealth; and there had been a longstanding threat that South Africa might seek to implement its legal claim to annex Bechuanaland and also Swaziland and Basutoland (later Lesotho), two other British Protectorates in the region.

The British Government was aware that if people knew about the instrumental role of South Africa there would be a storm of criticism from all sides, so it resolved to insist, falsely, that South Africa had had nothing to do with its policy. When Patrick Gordon Walker, Secretary of State for Commonwealth Relations, defended the Government's decision to exile Seretse in the House of Commons on 8 March 1950, he flatly lied:

> we have had no communication from the Government of the Union [of South Africa] nor have we made any communication to them. There have been no representations and no consultation in this matter.[9]

This lie was repeated again and again – in the Bangwato Reserve in Bechuanaland, in the House of Commons and in the House of Lords, and in statements given to the media.

But very few people in Bechuanaland, the UK or anywhere else believed the story that South Africa had not been involved. The affair was seen as another Munich, except that this time it was South Africa that was being appeased.[10] Even people who said they objected to miscegenation believed the Government to be guilty of an injustice. 'If the Bamangwato* do not object to a white consort and the prospect of a half-breed succession', argued *The Times* in a leader, 'it would not seem to be for the imperial Government, pledged before the nations to respect the equal rights of all races, to overrule them in their own domestic concerns.' It believed the Government's lie that no attempt had been made by the Union to exert any influence on the decision. But it was under no illusions that the British decision had not been taken to appease South Africa. 'The truth is', it pointed out, 'that British Africa is divided between one great independent State which believes in the colour bar and a number of smaller States in which the colour bar is repudiated.' This was tragic for the Commonwealth – 'but it cannot', argued *The Times*, 'be for ever evaded'.[11]

Throughout the Commonwealth and the Empire, the British Government was roundly condemned. Krishna Menon, India's High Commissioner in London, went to see Gordon Walker to tell him that in the view of the Indian Government the exile of Seretse was not in the interest of Commonwealth relations.[12] In the Ceylon Parliament, a tabled question announced that the British action would 'rouse the opposition of all coloured people against the Commonwealth'.[13] In Kingston, Jamaica, all political parties combined to express their objection and to warn that the British Government was at risk of losing the support of 'countless millions of colonial people'.[14] Citizens of Trinidad

---

*The British used the form 'Bamangwato' rather than the more correct 'Bangwato'.

pledged to support Seretse.[15] Sacks of letters and telegrams of complaint were sent to London – to the Commonwealth Relations Office (CRO), to the Colonial Office and to the Prime Minister. Even in the US, where 30 out of the 48 states had legislation prohibiting mixed marriage, there was strong criticism, especially from liberals and from the African-American community.

The only support for the British Government came from the white communities of South Africa and Southern Rhodesia, as well as white settlers in Kenya and other British colonies. Millions of South African whites had watched in horror as Ruth joined her husband in Serowe in 1949; South African newspapers were full of disgust about 'chocolate babies';[16] and the Nationalist newspaper *Die Burger* warned, 'Our colour problem will be detrimentally influenced if Seretse Khama and his white wife are permitted to assume the Chieftainship.'[17]

The strategy of the British Government

Almost as soon as Seretse had married Ruth, the British Government sought to prevent him from taking up the chieftainship of the Bangwato. In November 1949, in the period leading up to his enforced exile, they set up a judicial inquiry in Bechuanaland, in order to buy time. The inquiry was presided over by Sir Walter Harragin, the Chief Justice, and had two stated aims: to decide whether the kgotla at which Seretse Khama had been acclaimed as Chief was properly convened; and to determine whether Seretse was 'a fit and proper person to discharge the functions of chief'.[18] The Harragin Report gave the 'right' answer: Seretse should not be recognised as kgosi. But it gave the 'wrong' – though true – reason: the hostility and the demands of South Africa and Southern Rhodesia. It accepted that the June kgotla had adequately expressed the views of the Bangwato and it stated firmly that Seretse was fit to rule:

> Though a typical African in build and features, he has assimilated, to a great extent, the manners and thoughts of an Oxford undergraduate. He speaks English well and is obviously quick to appreciate, even if he may not agree with, the European point of view. Thus he was an easy witness to examine, he immediately understood the questions and answered them without hesitation, clearly and fairly.

'We have no hesitation,' the Report went on,

in finding that, but for his unfortunate marriage, his prospects of success as a Chief are as bright as those of any native in Africa... provided that he shows himself to be as good a judge in the choice of his advisors as he is in other matters.[19]

These conclusions were a disaster for the British Government, from the point of view of public opinion. The Harragin Report contains 'so much explosive material', wrote Gordon Walker in dismay in a note to Attlee, that it would be better not to publish it. Attlee agreed[20] and the report was shelved.

After Seretse's exile had been announced in March 1950, the Government produced a White Paper to explain its decision. Its key justification was the existence of a 'dynastic feud' between Seretse and his uncle, Tshekedi. Only by removing Seretse, argued the White Paper, would it be possible to remove 'the danger which recognition would cause to the unity and well-being of the tribe and the administration of the Protectorate'.[21] Jan Smuts, leader of South Africa's United Party, in whom the British Government placed great faith, had recommended this excuse. 'I believe', he said, that 'the feud between Tshekedi and the Seretse factions is [a] plausible excuse which the British Government may have for banishing both from the Territory.'[22]

It was true that Tshekedi disapproved of Seretse's marriage, which had led to friction between the two men. But uncle and nephew had made a number of successful efforts at reconciliation. These were greeted with dismay by the British administration, because they exposed the mendacity of the Government's cover story. Sir Percivale Liesching, the Permanent Under-Secretary of State for Commonwealth Relations, wrote in October 1950 to Sir Evelyn Baring, the British High Commissioner in South Africa, to warn him that Tshekedi 'may be tempted into a combination with Seretse that would be fatal to our plans'.[23] It was essential for the Government to maintain the story that Tshekedi and Seretse were implacable enemies, otherwise, there was no justification for Seretse's exile. Tshekedi fell into the trap. He publicly ruptured his reconciliation with Seretse and told journalists that he had taken this decision after several conferences with Sir Evelyn Baring; he added that he could see no end to the dynastic feud.[24] His choice of the words 'dynastic feud' was resonant of the White Paper and gave a sense of inevitable and ceaseless quarrelling between the two men. It was exactly what Baring and Liesching wanted.

Another spin put on Seretse's exile was that it would help to introduce the formation of democratic councils by diminishing the rule of the dikgosi (kings). It was 'fully in accordance with His Majesty's Government's policy today', Gordon Walker told the House of Commons in March 1950, 'of affording the people of the African territories for which they are responsible, a fuller say and more direct participation in the conduct of their affairs'.[25] This was met with derision by the Bangwato, since they had reached an overwhelming decision to designate Seretse as kgosi in their kgotla, their own democratic assembly. In any case, the British were now governing the Bangwato through direct rule, which was hardly democratic.

Another strand of the Government's strategy was to discredit Ruth. '[The] [o]nly policy now', said Gordon Walker, after a visit to Bechuanaland at the end of 1950, is 'to allow [an] anti-Ruth feeling to develop'.[26] Efforts to plant such a sentiment in the press were assisted by reporters who did not approve of the Khamas' marriage. 'One of our strongest taboos, particularly to a girl of Ruth's class', wrote Fyfe Robertson in *Picture Post*, 'is the marriage of a white girl and a black man.' There was a view that Ruth *must* be 'cheap', or she would not have married someone who was black. Noel Monks, correspondent for the *Daily Mail*, went to considerable trouble to point out this was not true. 'You can't help admiring her,' he said. 'She's not ... a tart, she's a respectable girl with ideals.'[27]

Some of the press cooperated with Gordon Walker. In the spring of 1950 a note from the *Daily Mirror* told him that 'Our people consider Ruth is no longer "news" ' – so would not go ahead with an article entitled, 'Chuck it, Ruth!' The opinion had been put forward, he was told, that 'if we ran a "slammer" on her now, it might have the effect of raising her from the dead!' Gordon Walker was reassured. He wrote in pencil on the note, 'I hope you are right about Ruth no longer being news – she may yet be again.' Then, revealing his readiness to back a smear campaign, he said, 'Let's keep the "black" in reserve.'[28] Fyfe Robertson, even though he was somewhat critical of the British Government's handling of the Seretse affair,[29] thought it was his duty to check with the CRO before finalising his feature for publication. After his return to the UK from Serowe, he made two visits to the CRO, one of them to talk to Gordon Walker.[30]

In Africa, too, under the driving energy of Sir Evelyn Baring, the British administration sought to influence the press – not only the so-called 'European' press, but also the 'native' press. All the leading vernacular papers in southern Africa were published by 'Associated Bantu Newspapers', an umbrella group based in Johannesburg and heavily controlled by its editorial director, B. G. Paver. One of the newspapers published by the group was *Naledi Ya Batswana*, which was aimed at readers in Bechuanaland. Paver was keen to help Sir Evelyn and assured him that the leader columns of his newspapers would toe the British line.[31] 'Whatever small assistance may have been rendered,' he told the High Commissioner,

> has been given gladly in the interests of the fundamentals to which we subscribe. That is no more than part of my job. Throughout the war years and in the difficult yet stimulating times in which we live, the work of the Bantu Press in South Africa, touching as it does the best interests of Governments and governed, is taken very much for granted.[32]

Paver offered Baring his assessment of attitudes in the region. 'There is a strong feeling', he said, 'that the South African and Rhodesian Governments influenced the decision. The reaction to this is to forget Seretse's own part in the affair and his deliberate challenge to both White and Black sentiment in Southern Africa.'[33]

Only one of the Bantu press papers did not cooperate. 'Our associated paper *Umthunywa* published a leader attacking the British Government', explained Paver to Baring, 'but I consider that this is of no special significance, for *Umthunywa* is run by a private printer who is inclined to leave his leaders to a rather wild and woolly African editor.' He added reassuringly, 'When we have the capital, we shall take over this paper.'[34]

Fighting back: the use of the media by the Bangwato

The Bangwato had few means of fighting against the British decision. They did what they could: they employed the tactic of passive resistance, on the model initiated in Johannesburg by Gandhi in 1906, and refused to pay taxes or cooperate with the administration. They used the law: Seretse and the tribe employed a Mafiking lawyer, Percy Fraenkel, to defend their case.

But their most effective weapon was their use of the media to influence international public opinion – thereby exploiting the Government's only real weakness. This was a weapon that had already been used to great advantage in the past by the Khama family, in their dealings with the British. When Kgosi Khama III of the Bangwato, Kgosi Sebele of the Bakwena and Kgosi Bathoen of the Bangwaketse came to England in 1895 to protest against Cecil Rhodes' plans to colonise their land, they made use of the press to influence public opinion. The success of their protest led Rhodes to comment, 'It is humiliating to be utterly beaten by three niggers.'[35] Tshekedi Khama, too, made adroit use of public opinion when he was deposed by the British in 1933 for flogging a white man. He was re-instated as Regent within three weeks.[36]

Most people in Bechuanaland at this time did not have access to any kind of media. *Naledi ya Batswana* was published in Setswana, the language of the Protectorate, but many people were illiterate. There were few radios in the territory and even if people had access to the BBC Overseas Service, for example, they would need to know English in order to understand it. There were no cinemas. Any films that were brought to a village by the administration had been carefully selected for a particular purpose, such as spreading information about measures to combat foot and mouth disease. For the most part, discussions and announcements at the kgotla were the only source of information and it took days, sometimes weeks, for news to spread through the scattered villages.

But the elite of the Bangwato Reserve, who had received a high level of education at schools in South Africa and who were relatively wealthy, *did* have access to newspapers and radio and they understood how to use the media to their advantage. They cooperated with visiting journalists and invited them to listen to their discussions at the kgotla. They helped sympathetic photographers like the liberal American Margaret Bourke-White to present *their* point of view. The leaders of the Bangwato communicated by post from Bechuanaland with influential people in London, notably the Labour MPs Fenner Brockway, Anthony Wedgwood Benn and Jennie Lee, who fed to the press the information they were sent. In late 1955, for example, Peto Sekgoma, a senior member of the Royal Family and one of Seretse's uncles, sent Brockway a copy of a letter complaining to the Bechuanaland Police about the treatment of Seretse's supporters. He reported the case of a man who had been tied by a trek chain to lion traps over several days and also flogged. He complained, too, that women and children were being publicly flogged in the kgotla.[37] Thanks to Brockway's efforts, it was not long before this information appeared in the newspapers and was also raised in the House of Commons.[38]

After Seretse's exile had been made permanent in April 1952, a delegation of six leading men from the Bangwato Reserve arrived in London to plead with the Government to change its mind. It was a desperate measure, paid for with money collected by an impoverished people. They were met by a battery of press representatives and newsreel cameramen.[39]

'To London Airport come six men of the Bamangwato tribe to plead for the return of Seretse Khama as their Chief,' reported Pathé News, showing the men descending the steps of the airliner that had brought them to the UK. 'It has been decided that neither Seretse nor his uncle Tshekedi should be Chief of the Bamangwatos,' added the newsreel. 'But these visitors will be heard, though no change is expected.'[40] John Redfern, the *Daily Express* correspondent who had been sympathetically following the story ever since Ruth's arrival in Serowe in 1949, was one of the waiting journalists. He observed that the visitors were dressed in light-coloured, snap-brim hats – 'and worried faces'.[41]

The CRO played down the visit of the delegation and were dismissive. 'What with slow speaking and interpreting,' wrote one official to another, 'this is a dreary prospect for the S[ecretary] of S[tate].'[42] But the public, by contrast, were largely sympathetic. As Jennie Lee stated to the House of Commons after their departure, 'Many of us were impressed by the members of the delegation to this country. They seemed responsible and, in fact, distinguished men.'[43] Their visit led to many reports in the press and questions in Parliament. They returned to Bechuanaland empty-handed, in the sense that the banning order had not been rescinded, but they had pushed the issue into the mainstream of British politics and international opinion.

Seretse Khama's decision to use the media

Seretse was shocked when the Commonwealth Secretary told him in March 1950 of the Government's decision to banish him. He had been in London for three weeks and throughout this period he had followed orders from the Government and refused to speak to journalists. But now, indignant and angry, he issued a statement – to tell the press that he had been tricked. 'I am seeing you', he told reporters, 'because I consider that I have been double-crossed.'[44] The Government, he added, proposed to introduce direct rule,

> a form of government that is pretty foreign to the people. I think they are doing themselves more harm than good. This they are doing without consulting the tribe at all. They are going to announce it without asking the tribe's opinion.

'My people did not want me to come to England,' he added, sadly. 'They foresaw the position that has now arisen.'[45]

This made front-page news the next day all over the world. Gordon Walker was furious: 'He thus got 40 hours' start on me,' he fumed in his diary, 'and it took me several weeks to catch up.'[46] He was forced to report immediately on the banishment to the House of Commons, a task he had hoped to postpone for several days. He was badly in need of time because there was a serious risk of revolt over the issue from the Government's own benches. He met Leif Egeland, the South African High Commissioner in London, to reassure him there would be no U-turn. Seretse's 'premature disclosure to the Press', reported Egeland the next day to the External Affairs Minister in Pretoria, was 'extremely embarrassing', but would not lead to any weakening of the Government's attitude.[47]

But Gordon Walker's embarrassment was not the only outcome of Seretse's press conference. The other – and instant – outcome was that the exile was announced on the wireless on the BBC Overseas Service. Ruth was sitting in her house in Serowe when the news of Seretse's banishment was broadcast.[48] The fact that she and some others in the Bangwato Reserve found out immediately about the banishment put local officials at a major disadvantage. The administration was preparing for a kgotla at which Sir Evelyn Baring would announce formally to the assembled Bangwato the terms of Seretse's exile. But now the scope for managing their reaction had been reduced. Even more importantly, from the point of view of the administration, there was less time to prepare for coverage by the press. The massed ranks of the international press in Serowe were generally hostile to the Government. Nicholas Monsarrat, the UK information officer in South Africa (and an aspiring author who was about to make his name with the publication of *The Cruel Sea* in 1951), was sent to Serowe to do everything he could – in the way of meals and alcohol – to persuade journalists to write favourable reports.[49] Meanwhile, the leaders of the Bangwato – taking up the baton passed to them by Seretse – were seeking to publicise the injustice against them. Peto Segkoma told the press that the tribe was boycotting Baring's kgotla, a decision that had been taken at a meeting of leading members of the tribe, which had also been attended by their lawyer, Percy Fraenkel.[50]

Baring flew from Pretoria to Mafiking, on his way to the kgotla. But just before he left Mafiking on the night train for Bechuanaland, urgent news arrived from Serowe about the plan for the boycott. Baring did not take this seriously, but the alarm bells grew louder. There were a number of journalists on the same train, who said that they too had heard rumours of a boycott. Then, when the train finally steamed into the village of Palapye, the nearest station to Serowe, the District Commissioner was waiting to report that the headmen of the Bangwato had told him they were going to boycott the kgotla.[51] Baring ignored these warnings too. But when he was driven to Serowe, he saw no sign of the thousands of people he was expecting to attend the kgotla. The kgotla ground was deserted, except for the press and about 25 European spectators sitting under a tree. 'There were no Africans,' observed an amused John Redfern, the *Daily Express* reporter. 'Sir Evelyn had travelled 1,000 miles to speak to the Bamangwato and the Bamangwato were missing.'

Just five minutes before the High Commissioner was due to arrive at the kgotla ground, Monsarrat hurried to one of the few telephones in Serowe: 'There is no one here. Better tell HE [His Excellency] not to come.'[52] It was a humiliation. The High Commissioner had waited to enter the kgotla ground in his white uniform and sword, crowned with the tall cocked hat and white feathers, and with his Star of St Michael and St George on his chest,[53] but his finery now looked absurd. 'The boycott of the kgotla,' wrote Monsarrat, 'was, in its context, an atrocious personal insult'. He felt personally humiliated. 'The white uniform, white helmet, medals and sword which I had donned for the great occasion,' he complained, 'seemed ridiculous.'[54]

Baring still had to deliver the terms of the parliamentary statement on Seretse's banishment. He arranged for a written instruction by the District Commissioner to be delivered to 24 senior men, asking them to appear before him. Not one of the recipients obeyed. 'Only if we are handcuffed and carried will we go to the kgotla,' said one headman to *The Times*.[55] As a last resort, Baring gave a press conference, at which Monsarrat plied the press men and photographers with drinks. But, said one of the local officials, 'It was not a happy experience. The press were in a destructive mood, for they all sided with Seretse, and questioned Baring with cheerful contempt verging on open hostility.'[56] Baring left in failure for Cape Town.[57]

His humiliation was reported across the Empire and the world. It had been a 'Blunder in the Name of Expediency', was the judgement of the leader in the London *Evening Standard*.[58] The failed meeting was 'one of the biggest flops in Britain's recent colonial history,' observed the American magazine *Life*, which illustrated an article entitled 'Nobody Came to the Meeting' with photographs of the deserted kgotla ground.[59] There was even a photograph of policemen sweeping away the white lines that had been drawn on the ground for the High Commissioner.

Most of the press were fickle. They did not hang around after the boycott of the kgotla and so failed to report the subsequent campaign of passive resistance.[60] But they did cover the High Commissioner's humiliation in detail. 'Never before, in British Africa', wrote Monks of the *Daily Mail*, 'had the Crown's representative been so insulted. The repercussions of the "empty *kgotla*" were felt right throughout British Africa.'[61]

In his book *Ornamentalism, How the British Saw Their Empire*, David Cannadine has described the ways in which the British cultivated a culture of the British Empire. The book is illustrated with images of British imperial status, such as Lord Curzon contemplating his first tiger shot in India as viceroy.[62] How very different was the image of the failed kgotla in Serowe. It was not a symbol of imperial power, but of a diminution of that power: of the 'wind of change' blowing through the continent of Africa, which was identified just a few years later by Harold Macmillan in a landmark speech to the South African parliament.[63]

Exploiting the media spotlight

Almost immediately after the exile of Seretse in March 1950, his friends and supporters in the UK set up the Seretse Khama Fighting Committee. It did valuable work, arranging protest rallies at Trafalgar Square and sending petitions to the CRO. But it was largely a fringe organisation and had little impact on mainstream public opinion. What was needed, thought Fenner Brockway, the veteran anti-colonial campaigner, was an all-party committee with members from across the political spectrum and from the fields of education, arts, religion and sport. A committee of this sort, he believed, would work as a broad-based pressure group and put the injustice against Seretse and Ruth Khama firmly into the media spotlight.[64]

The outcome of these plans was the creation in 1952 of the Council for the Defence of Seretse Khama and the Protectorates. Brockway was chairman and the vice-chairman was the Liberal MP Joe Grimond; the treasurer was the Labour MP Anthony Wedgwood Benn. Members ranged from John Collins, Canon of St Paul's Cathedral, to the cinematographer Frank Byers, the cricketer Learie Constantine, the sprinter MacDonald Bailey, the actors Alec Guiness and Sybil Thorndike, the writer Sir Compton Mackenzie, Kingsley Martin, then editor of the *New Statesman*, and the playwright and Labour politician Benn Levy. The Council was not intended to replace the Fighting Committee, which continued its work, but to bring Seretse's case more into the public eye. Officials at the CRO watched the formation of this new committee with dismay. 'The organisation chiefly concerned hitherto,' observed one, 'has been the Seretse Khama Campaign [Fighting] Committee, which has been a small affair under Communist influence.' But the new council, he realised, was 'clearly intended to be a much more influential body with a wider basis'.[65]

Illustration 1 Seretse and Ruth Khama, with baby Seretse Khama Ian and three-year-old Jacqueline, London, 1953.

The council stayed in constant communication with the Khama family: Seretse, Ruth and their daughter Jacqueline, who had been born in Serowe in 1950. On 10 March 1953, when the Khamas' second child and first son, Ian, was just 12 days old, Brockway called a press conference of the Council for the Defence of Seretse Khama. Cables were read from leading members of the Bangwato tribe, pledging loyalty to Seretse and his son. It was known 'all round the Ngwato tribe', said one telegram, 'that the 4th Khama is born. Again WE humbly request the Government to return our Chief Seretse and family back... We can never change our opinion.'[66] Another cable congratulated both Chief Seretse Khama and Ruth Khama for having a baby boy whose only name is Khama – *Pula! Pula! Pula!** We ask that he and the family come and live amongst us. We want to nurse him ourselves...We, the Bangwato, Seretse's people, want that child here.[67]

The telegrams pleaded for justice: 'We are like sheep in a jungle and there being attacked by a leopard.'[68] These messages were quoted in the British broadsheets, giving a voice to the views of the Bangwato people.[69]

On 23 March 1954, Brockway presented to Parliament a petition from the council, demanding that Seretse be allowed to return to his country and be recognised as Chief.[70] It bore 10,800 signatures and was supported by well-known people including the playwright Christopher Fry, the artist Augustus John, the philosopher Bertrand Russell, the novelist Ethel Mannin, the actor Michael Redgrave and A. J. Cummings of the *News Chronicle*.[71]

In April 1954, the Council for the Defence of Sereste Khama and the Seretse Khama Fighting Committee amalgamated with over 300 other organisations to form a new organisation, the Movement for Colonial Freedom. Brockway, the chairman and founder, hoped this would bring an end to the many little councils, each dealing with a single colonial issue. 'Now', wrote Wedgwood Benn with satisfaction to a fellow member of the Movement, 'we have a chance to be really effective!'[72] The campaign had its own offices in Regent's Park Road, London and a high profile. It made sure that the issue of Seretse and Ruth Khama rarely left the headlines.

The end of exile

In 1956, Seretse and Ruth and their two children were finally allowed to return to Bechuanaland. One important reason for this reversal in government policy was Seretse's continued interest to the media and public opinion.[73] The Government could no longer afford to be seen as appeasers of South Africa for, by 1956, the Nationalist Party had made substantial headway in the implementation of its policy of apartheid and had earned the opprobrium of the world. After his return, Seretse

---

* *Pula* means 'rain'. It is one of the most important words in Setswana and is also used to give greetings. *Pula!* is a shared cry of enthusiasm and pleasure at formal and informal gatherings.

remained a private citizen, because his people's wish for him to be installed as kgosi was refused by the British Government. But in 1965 he was elected as the country's first Prime Minister and, in 1966, he became the first President of newly independent Botswana.

David Goldsworthy has described the Seretse affair as the 'first major confrontation of Britain's liberal policy with southern African white racialism'.[74] However, it was a confrontation that never began. Overwhelmingly, the British Government chose to collude with racialism rather than confront it. The historian Ronald Hyam has argued that the Government had no choice but to adopt this policy. 'All in all', he writes, 'the British government probably did not exaggerate the threat to [Bechuanaland] from South Africa. To that extent its sacrifice of Seretse, against the wishes of the Bangwato, can be broadly vindicated on geopolitical grounds.'[75]

Whether or not the South African threat would have been realised is a matter for conjecture. But the fact remains that South Africa did not annex Bechuanaland following Seretse's return. In any case, it is arguable that the sacrifice of Seretse should be *condemned* on 'geopolitical grounds'. Given the high profile of the Seretse affair and the full attention of the media, the British Government in the late 1940s was handed a unique opportunity to influence values and beliefs in support of racial justice. This opportunity was lost. But if it had allowed – and energetically supported – Seretse to live in Bechuanaland as Kgosi, with his white wife, in the glare of the media spotlight, it would have demonstrated a clear commitment to a non-racial society. This would have provided a valuable and instructive contrast with the developing apartheid state of South Africa. As Fenner Brockway in August 1956 argued to the House of Commons:

If we are to influence the Union of South Africa it would be by making those Protectorates [including Bechuanaland] models of racial equality and of educational, social and political advance.

It is a tragedy that, instead of Bechuanaland appearing like that to the rest of Africa, it has become a symbol of the colour bar because of our treatment of Seretse and Ruth Khama ...[76]

Notes

1. Personal communication by Naledi Khama, Serowe, 13 November 2004.
2. Record of the proceedings at Judicial Enquiry re Seretse Khama [November 1949], vols 1–14, TNA: PRO, DO 35/4123.

3. David Goldsworthy, *Colonial Issues in British Politics 1945–1961: From 'Colonial Development' to 'Wind of Change'* (Oxford: Clarendon Press, 1971), p. 23.
4. Anthony Sillery, 'Working Backwards', n.d., Rhodes House Library, Oxford University, Mss Afr r 207
5. John Redfern, *Ruth and Seretse* (London: Victor Gollancz, 1955), p. 11.
6. Michael Dutfield, *A Marriage of Inconvenience. The Persecution of Seretse and Ruth Khama* (London: Unwin Hyman, 1990), p. 117.
7. Noel Monks, *Eyewitness* (London: Frederick Muller, [1956]), p. 267.
8. *Hansard*, 8 March 1950.
9. Ibid.
10. Tibbetts to US Department of State, 20 March 1950, National Archives and Records Administration, Washington, Rg 59, Decimal File, Box 4897.
11. *The Times*, 9 March 1950.
12. Record of conversation between Secretary of State and Krishna Menon, 15 March 1950, The National Archives of the UK (TNA): Public Record Office, London, UK (PRO) DO 35/4120.
13. *The Times*, 13 March 1950.
14. Reuter, 28 March 1950, National Archives of South Africa (NASA) BLO PS 2/5A.
15. Resolution of the West Indian Political Forum, 13 March 1950, NASA BLO PS 2/5A.
16. *Die Transvaler*, 27 September 1956.
17. Quoted in *Recorder*, 3 September 1949.
18. Harragin Report, 1 December 1949, TNA: PRO PREM 8/1308, Part 1, 120180.
19. Judicial Inquiry Re Seretse Khama, CRO, [November 1949], TNA: PRO DO 35/4123.
20. Gordon Walker to Attlee, 7 March 1950, with additional note by Attlee, 7 March 1950, TNA: PRO PREM 8/1308.
21. Commonwealth Relations Office, 'Bechuanaland Protectorate. Succession to the Chieftainship of the Bamangwato Tribe', March 1950, HMSO, Cmd. 7193.
22. Smuts to Churchill, 16 March 1950, Churchill Archives Centre, Cambridge, 02/101.
23. Liesching to Baring, 27 October 1950, TNA: PRO DO 35/4131.
24. *Rand Daily Mail*, 13 November 1950.
25. *Hansard*, 8 March 1950.
26. Gordon Walker to Liesching, 3 February 1951, TNA: PRO CO 537/7222.
27. Quoted from Monks by Monsarrat, in Monsarrat to Clark, 17 April 1950, TNA: PRO DO 119/1293.
28. Note to Gordon Walker from Fetter Lane, initials undecipherable, 18 April 1950; undated [April 1950] note by Gordon Walker, TNA: PRO DO 121/57.
29. *Picture Post*, 29 April 1950.
30. Joyce to Baxter, 17 April 1950, TNA: PRO DO 35/4121.
31. Paver to Baring, 24 April 1950, TNA: PRO DO 119/1293.
32. Paver to Baring, 24 April 1950, TNA: PRO DO 119/1293.
33. Paver to Baring, 6 April 1950, TNA: PRO DO 119/1292.
34. Paver to Baring, 6 April 1950, TNA: PRO DO 119/1292.
35. Quoted in Neil Parsons, *King Khama, Emperor Joe and the Great White Queen: Victorian Britain through African Eyes* (Chicago: University of Chicago Press, 1998), p. 9.

36. See Michael Crowder, *The Flogging of Phineas McIntosh: A Tale of Colonial Folly and Injustice, Bechuanaland 1933* (New Haven, CT: Yale University Press, 1988).
37. Peto Sekgoma to Officer Commanding BP Police, 28 November 1955, TNA: PRO DO 119/1344.
38. Brockway to Dodds-Parker, 14 December 1955, TNA: PRO DO 119/1344.
39. SAPA-Reuter, 10 April 1952, TNA: PRO DO 119/1307.
40. Pathé News, 'In Support of Seretse', 14 April 1952.
41. Redfern, *Ruth and Seretse*, p. 195.
42. Baxter to Clark, 19 April 1952, TNA: PRO DO 35/4143.
43. British High Commission, South Africa, to CRO, 7 June 1952, TNA: PRO CO 1015/359.
44. *Die Burger*, 7 March 1950.
45. Quoted in Julian Mockford, *Seretse Khama and the Bamangwato* (London: Staples Press, 1950), p. 4.
46. Diary entry for 2 April 1950, *Patrick Gordon Walker. Political Diaries 1932–1971*, ed. Robert Pearce (London: The Historians Press, 1991), p. 188.
47. Egeland to Forsyth, 8 March 1950, NASA PM vol 1/4/21, 1/15.
48. Monks, *Eyewitness*, p. 280.
49. Monsarrat to Clark, 14 March 1950, TNA: PRO DO 119/1290.
50. *Cape Times*, 11 March 1950.
51. *The Times*, 13 March 1950.
52. Monks, *Eyewitness*, p. 281.
53. Uniform described by Charles Douglas-Home, *Evelyn Baring: The Last Proconsul* (London: Collins, 1978), pp. 120–1.
54. Nicholas Monsarrat, *Life is a Four-Letter Word*. Vol. II, *Breaking Out* (London: Cassell, 1970), pp. 271–3.
55. *The Times*, 14 March 1950.
56. Michael Fairlie, *No Time Like the Past* (Edinburgh: Pentland Press, 1972), p. 147.
57. Baring to Gordon Walker, 13 March 1950, TNA: PRO DO 119/1290.
58. *Evening Standard*, 15 March 1950.
59. *Life*, 28 April 1950.
60. Fairlie, *No Time Like the Past*, p. 147.
61. Monks, *Eyewitness*, p. 282.
62. See David Cannadine, *Ornamentalism, How the British Saw Their Empire* (London: Penguin, 2001).
63. Speech to South African Parliament by Harold Macmillan, Cape Town, 3 February 1960.
64. Brockway to Benn Levy, 18 June 1952, University of Sussex Archives and Special Collections, UK (USASC) Benn Levy Papers (BLP) 6/8.
65. Bickford to Baxter, 22 September 1952, TNA: PRO DO 35/4469.
66. Quoted in Memorandum of the Council for the Defence of Seretse Khama, September 1953, USASC BLP 6/9.
67. Quoted in Memorandum of the Council for the Defence of Seretse Khama, September 1953, USASC BLP 6/9.
68. Quoted in Memorandum of the Council for the Defence of Seretse Khama, September 1953, USASC BLP 6/9.
69. For example, *Daily Herald*, 11 March 1953.

70. Telegram from Secretary of State, London, to High Commissioner, Cape Town, 24 March 1954, TNA: PRO DO 119/1340.
71. Quoted in John Lewis, *Lord Hailsham: A Life* (London: Jonathan Cape, 1997), p. 144.
72. Wedgwood Benn to Benn Levy, n.d. [1954], USASC BLP 6/9.
73. See Susan Williams, *Colour Bar: The Triumph of Seretse Khama over British Imperialism and Apartheid South Africa for the Love of His Wife and His Nation* (London: Penguin, 2006).
74. David Goldsworthy, *Colonial Issues in British Politics 1945–1961* (Oxford: Clarendon Press, 1971), p. 160.
75. Ronald Hyam, 'The Political Consequences of Seretse Khama: Britain, the Bangwato and South Africa', *Historical Journal* 29, 4 (1987): 947.
76. *Hansard*, 1 August 1956.

6
Ernest Jones' Mutiny: *The People's Paper*, English Popular Politics and the Indian Rebellion 1857–58

Tim Pratt

The Indian Mutiny of 1857–58[1] was relayed to the British parliament, press and people through a modernising communications network that brought Indian affairs to the imperial metropole more rapidly than ever before. This network, and the information that flowed through it, was constituted by a mixture of public and private investment, expertise and knowledge. The imperial governing authorities had developed the newly instituted Indian telegraph system, enabling the very latest information to be transmitted to Britain in a matter of hours, whilst private shipping companies had developed an 'overland' route that enabled mails carrying private correspondence and official documents to reach Britain in little more than a month, information that fleshed out the skeletal details provided via the wires. Although the means of transmitting news from India was either recently implemented or improved, much of the material constituting it thus remained of a largely similar character to the period preceding these innovations.[2]

Government and press refined and exploited these developments with a degree of interdependence. *The Times* stood in the vanguard of Fleet Street organs in this respect. Its correspondents in Bombay and Calcutta gathered, collated and evaluated news, opinion and rumour from local sources across the subcontinent, wired the headlines to Britain immediately (issues of cost and practicality precluded transmission of more material in this fashion) and forwarded substantive material in the mails. This was so effective that *The Times'* ability to gather Indian information and disseminate it within Britain frequently outstripped that of the government itself, let alone the rest of the press. Fortunately for the incumbent Palmerston ministry, the politically Peelite *Times* had aligned itself behind his political standard by 1857.

The government and *The Times* thus tacitly informed and supported one another's authority and expertise in the Indian sphere at this fraught time.[3]

The information transmitted in this fashion during 1857–8, especially the shocking accounts of murder and defilement of Britons by Indian insurgents, has commonly been seen as having united the country in following and supporting the dramatic counter-insurgency operation,[4] restricted political dissent whilst the 'national crisis' was resolved,[5] and helped shape and harden perceptions of an essential British racial, martial and cultural supremacy over its imperial subjects in the longer term. Although historians have acknowledged that elements of imperial policy and administration attracted criticism in the imperial metropole as a result of the rebellion,[6] the possibility that the rebels were actively supported in their struggle has been almost completely ignored.

This chapter seeks to redress this lacuna through analysis of the depiction of the Indian Mutiny in *The People's Paper*, a weekly newspaper run and edited by Ernest Jones, arguably the most prominent leader of the late Chartist movement. The first section will show how Jones used his narration of the course of the Mutiny to advocate the revival of the Chartist cause and advance his credentials as the man best fitted to lead the movement. Rather than joining the chorus of horrified condemnation of the Indian insurgents, Jones actively sought to identify the causes of the rebels and Chartism by attempting to elide the political, racial and cultural differences between the British and Indians being highlighted in parliament and the mainstream press, instead stressing the linkages between their respective causes.

The second section will show how the fluidity of the nineteenth-century newspaper as a text, and indeed the concept of 'news' itself, helped Jones manipulate the information available to him on imperial and foreign affairs to advance his position and attempt to discredit those of his political rivals. In addition, I show that in many ways the modern components of the imperial communications newsgathering network aided Jones in this enterprise, and that ultimately it was the faltering of the rebellion, Jones' precarious financial position and the power of the unsubstantiated atrocity narratives reaching the British press via the more traditional route of the personal mails that undermined the efficacy of a radical interlinking of the causes of sweeping domestic and imperial political reform.

Narrating the Mutiny? Revolt in India and the cause of British political reform

The first news of revolt in India reached Britain a matter of days after its outbreak at Meerut on 10 May 1857, and immediately became subject to a debate over its origins and character. In parliament, the Conservative Party configured the rising as a national revolt against liberal reforms enacted during the preceding quarter-century, which had abandoned respect for traditional laws and customs, offending 'the principle of Nationality' on which British control of India was founded.[7] Palmerston's government, supported by *The Times*, denied this interpretation and stressed its purely military character.[8] The submissive, irrational and divided peoples of India could not mount such a rising. The Mutiny was purely among excitable sepoys, and would be easily crushed.[9] A speedy resolution to the crisis was predicted against such adversaries, with the maintenance and strengthening of British rule the inevitable outcome.[10] If there was a criticism to be made of Indian policy, it was that Indian society was inherently unfit to enjoy properly the advantages bestowed on them by the British ruling genius.

The interpretation of the Indian Mutiny expounded by Ernest Jones directly opposed that of *The Times*, representing the Mutiny as a national rising rather than a purely military affair, and anticipated the downfall of British rule in India.[11] The coincidence of the outbreak with British military weakness in the region caused by hostilities with China and Persia showed agency and rationality on the part of the rebels.[12] By mid-July, Jones had grown bolder in ascribing to the Mutiny a patriotic character.[13] Although the revolt was still largely within the army, 'one success of the insurgent, or hesitation of the usurping force, may fan the fires of war, from Burmah to Bombay, from Calcutta to Madras'.[14] This confidence increased as August brought news of the concentration of rebel forces around Delhi, the ancient capital of 'Hindostan', which Jones saw as indicative of a 'steady pursuit of their magnificent object, national independance' [sic].[15] A litany of social grievances affecting every section of Indian society would soon ensure a national revolution. *The Times* could not be more wrong in its confident assertion that 'time will tell in our favour'. Rather, the rising would gain more support across the subcontinent. Only bickering or 'unexpected imbecility of conduct' among the insurgents could check the success of the rebellion.[16]

Jones' interpretation of the Mutiny was not advanced as an anti-patriotic diatribe. Rather, it was part of a broader narrative of the coming of democracy across the world. This meta-narrative was constructed on essentially European foundations, unsurprising given Jones' close involvement with internationalist socialist movements earlier in the decade,[17] and the considerable popular enthusiasm manifested for the European liberal nationalist cause in England since 1848. However, the Mutiny brought India from the margins to the centre of this master-narrative as Jones increasingly recognised Indian affairs as offering a powerful vehicle for articulating his political views to the disenfranchised classes of England.[18]

Initially, Jones chose to advance the cause of domestic political reform by stressing how the loss of India due to chronic mismanagement by the ruling order would be ruinous for the livelihoods of English working men.[19] However, from July onwards a series of articles and features began to push the Indian Mutiny to centre stage in this narrative. Tellingly, this development coincided with the quickening pace of Jones' efforts to reassert control over the domestic reform movement through organisation of a conference to decide on the future course of action to be pursued by the Chartist movement. Further details of the conference were outlined in the 'Current Notes' section of the 11 July issue of *The People's Paper*, accompanied by the exhortation to:

> make this Conference an efficient one; throw bickering and jealousy to the wind, unite in this great hour...France is awakening, Italy and Spain are heaving, India is in arms, you see the great hour is approaching by these signs.[20]

Jones also began to configure India and the rebellion in an increasingly European image. An article on the condition of 'Hindostan' was published in serial format through July, describing her peoples and the oppressive conditions of British rule. This drew heavily on the same melodramatic tropes and imagery routinely deployed to describe the dispossession and repression of the peoples of England and Europe by cruel, debauched and corrupt usurping regimes.[21] By early September Jones' representation of the Indian people and the rebellion had shifted further to dissolve the bonds of patriotism that could prevent the disenfranchised classes of England from identifying with the insurgents and their cause. What might be termed an orientalist depiction of the variety of peoples of India given in his July articles on 'Hindostan',[22] emphasising their bewildering variety, difference and otherness (among the peoples of the subcontinent, as well as between Briton and 'Indian') was replaced by an emphasis on the 'Hindhu' [sic] as the true people of

India, who had endured and survived successive Muslim invasions, yet had seen their independence robbed from them in the space of 100 years under 'a foreign tribe, the pedlars of the earth, the merchant-robbers of Leadenshall-Street'.[23] The resonances here with popular narratives locating the true English nation in the Anglo-Saxon people, dispossessed and repressed under the Norman yoke, are marked, with Jones refracting the image of India and her people through the prism of English popular political culture to dissolve boundaries of race and religion, asserting the justice of the rising.[24] The revolt was thus a cause as just as any of the European movements, and the English people were exhorted to support and identify with their 'Hindu brethren'. The rebels in India fought for the principles of liberty and national independence, and their success would strike a blow against oligarchy and tyranny in the imperial centre.[25]

From August 1857 onwards, Jones was confronted with the challenge of maintaining the credibility of his Mutiny narrative in the face of evidence of the faltering fortunes of the insurgents and eyewitness accounts of atrocities committed on the imperial British body. Having implicitly yoked the prospect of successful domestic reform to the progress of the revolt, Jones needed to sustain the momentum of his entwined narrative. Jones thus responded to *The Times'* triumphal accounts of the recapture of Delhi in October[26] by stressing the continuing spread of the revolt in order to depict a burgeoning, active movement, and attempted to rebut the power of the atrocity stories that became central to *The Times'* coverage[27] by pointing to diverse evidence suggesting the brutality of British rule in India had influenced the actions of the rebels.[28]

However, with *The Times* consistently backing calls to postpone discussion of proposals for domestic political reform in deference to the resolution of imperial affairs in the limited time available for the parliamentary session,[29] Jones also used the rebels' failings as examples of the perils to be avoided by the reawakening Chartist movement. The Chartists had to redouble their efforts to revive the movement. Concerted political action was required to convince the government to put forward reform proposals for which the people could 'work harmoniously together'.[30] The experience of the Indian insurgents now offered important negative examples to their Chartist 'brethren'. The lack of unity Jones had predicted as being the factor most likely to thwart the success of the rising was, by September, portrayed as underlying the inability of the rebels to smash the overstretched imperial forces, despite their overwhelming numerical superiority:

Instead of one grand general rising in all quarters, which would have utterly overwhelmed all resistance, only a part of Bengal rises...Bombay waits till Bengal has been fighting and bleeding for months, then it begins to rise.[31]

Moreover, subjugated peoples such as the Sikhs and the 'Ghoorkas' [*sic*] were blinded by their petty animosities against the 'Hindhu', and fought on the side of the British despite being 'crushed beneath the self-same yoke'.[32]

Just as the Indian rebels had been cast in the image of the dispossessed people of England to inspire support for their cause, Jones now reversed the analogy to urge the Chartists into concerted political action in the imperial centre. British democracy had its own Sikhs and 'Ghoorkas', those 'who back up the oppressor, because they hate their brethren more than they hate the foe',[33] a thinly veiled reference to Jones' rivals for the leadership of the Chartist movement who had softened their stance over the nature and extent of reform required, and parliamentary and middle-class reformers whose limited proposals would merely serve to bolster the ramparts of 'Corruption Castle' against Chartist insurgents. However, with a list of those localities still uncommitted to sending delegates to the forthcoming conference printed in an adjacent column, there could be no doubt about those to whom Jones now referred:

We also have our Madrases and Bombays in British Democracy. Districts or localities that stand aloof, and watch or wait to see how the struggle turns...when by their united energetic action they would raise such a gale as would blow each dark and antiquated wrong off the surface of the land.[34]

To avoid these perils, Jones made it clear that a strong, far-sighted leader was necessary to organise the domestic reform movement. Jones' fitness to lead the Chartist movement was openly being called into question by rivals, and his narration and analysis of events in India was crucial in his efforts to reassert his credentials for this position.[35] As both sides of the conflict in India failed to make the most of their perceived advantages in the field, and the national press grew increasingly condemnatory of the blunders made in the tactics and administration of the imperial armed forces, Jones drew examples from both Indian and British sides of the battle for the subcontinent to illustrate his arguments for the absolute necessity of strong leadership in the struggle for

domestic reform. British anxieties over the stalling counter-insurgency
were the product of the 'want of a proper head' for the Indian army.[36]
The problem for the rebel forces and the British reformers ran parallel to
one another, with one crucial difference: whilst the rebels badly needed
a leader, 'here it is the enthusiastic troops that are wanted for the
leader!'[37]

These exhortations to the Chartists to unite under Jones' generalship
reached a crescendo during November and December 1857, coinciding
with his abandonment of the full Charter as a political aim, instead
urging participation in a unified reform movement with the middle
classes with only universal suffrage and the repeal of property qualifica-
tions for MPs as objectives. With hopes for a 'successful' outcome to the
Indian rebellion fading, and Jones ostensibly reneging on political
principles he had so vociferously expounded up to this point, Indian
affairs slipped back to the periphery of his reformist political narrative.
Jones' new political stance was justified by the prescient leader's ominous
forecast of the true, metropolitan significance of the reinforcements
levied for Indian service by crown and government:

> Under cover of the Indian war an immense army is being estab-
> lished. If we are beaten in India, and lose it, the army will not be
> reduced, but the force . . . will be quartered at home. If we conquer in
> India, the pretence will be advanced that a vast force is needed to
> prevent future outbreaks – *and that force will be stationed in England
> not in Hindostan.*[38]

With the new army installations ringing the capital, the time was not
one 'in which to quarrel with any section of the community that we
believe to be honest and friendly'.[39] Although conceding four points of
the Charter for the sake of unity, in the long term their new allies
would be converted to full endorsement of its provisions. These concessions were measures to unify and strengthen the army of reform against
its oligarchic rival, and were indicative of the virility of Jones' generalship, not compromise and submissiveness.

From December 1857 onwards the grand narrative of the coming of
democracy, driven by the impetus of revolutionary forces in India and
Britain, slowly came apart. Jones grudgingly accepted that the imperial
regime would maintain an imperial foothold in India for some time to
come[40] and thus turned his attention to participation in the debate over
the measures of reform necessary to 'secure' India for the future benefit
of England and her people, unsurprisingly arguing that reform of the

domestic political system was the necessary precursor to instituting a just system of rule in the subcontinent.

The vitality and urgency had largely drained from Jones' narrative of the Mutiny by this stage. Serious financial problems reduced the amount of effort and space Jones could devote to such in-depth commentaries, and it no longer represented an effective vehicle for narrating his political interests. The sense of action and purpose generated by the prospect of a concerted attempt to overthrow the imperial order could no longer be maintained, while the disappointing turnout and course of debate at his reform conference in February 1858 frustrated the domestic ambitions he had yoked to his narration of the Mutiny. After the conference there was little need to prolong the analogy between the rebels and the people of England, which had become progressively more difficult to maintain as the chances of their success diminished. The Indian Mutiny had been an effective motif, as Jones could construct and manipulate bonds of identity between the reform movement and both sides in the conflict to suit his purposes, but the storms emerging over the question of political refugees from the European mainland offered far greater potential for mobilising popular protest against the government in 1858, not least because the vexed issue of race no longer had to be addressed.[41]

Constituting the news: 'Indian' information and metropolitan agendas

Despite his subsequent political and financial troubles, Jones' most recent biographer has identified the Mutiny as marking a high point in his political fortunes for the credibility his interpretation of Indian affairs brought him in reforming circles.[42] It would thus seem that Jones' Mutiny narrative had a considerable 'throw' or purchase,[43] and the means by which this was realised are worthy of serious consideration. In the remainder of this chapter I shall thus examine how the fluid structure and nature of 'news' as a concept and newspapers as texts in the mid-nineteenth century assisted Jones in his efforts to construct an image of himself as a prescient, expert analyst of Indian and military affairs, eminently fitted to leadership of a domestic political reform movement.

The nature of the flow of news emanating from India to Britain via the only partly modernised imperial communications network aided Jones' cause considerably. The first news reaching Britain from India in May 1857 came via terse telegraphs and official dispatches, providing skeletal details and none of the 'eyewitness' accounts that were subsequently so powerful in mobilising national opinion behind the counter-insurgency. This was a function of the imperial telegraph system's newness, with the high rates for dispatches and low carrying capacities prohibiting detailed communiqués, while the network's vulnerability to rebel assault exacerbated such information shortages in the longer term. The effect of this was that the government, its opposition, *The Times* and Jones (indeed, the whole nation) were all effectively reduced to speculation on the causes and nature of the outbreak and its likely duration until further telegraphs, or fuller information contained in the ship-borne mails, reached Britain. As we have seen, Jones' prediction of a bloody, protracted and expansive rebellion, although undoubtedly propounded through a large measure of self-interested political calculation, proved far nearer the mark than the rapid and efficient suppression of a directionless rising predicted by the Palmerston ministry and *The Times*. In the early stages of the revolt Jones was thus able to emphasise his seeming prescience as further news confirmed the spread of the rising and undermined the credibility of the establishment narrative, allowing him leeway to attribute malign motives to the government and its Fleet Street allies in misleading the British public.

With *The Times* pioneering the gathering of Indian information for a British audience the contemporary popular press simply fed from its table, freely copying or pirating its news in order to present events in India to their readers, seemingly with no fresh or exclusive news from the subcontinent to challenge its narrative of the revolt.[44] However, Jones also proved himself to be capable of subverting *The Times'* imperial communications network for his own ends. Jones used his editorials to highlight evidence from *The Times'* two Indian correspondents that contradicted its core narrative of the Mutiny. For example, in the wake of the British recapture of Delhi, Jones triumphantly reported that *The Times* echoed his earlier prognosis that its fall had not weakened the power of the insurrection.[45] However, this view had not been extracted from a leading article, but a communication from the Calcutta correspondent of *The Times* from 16 November.[46] A leader in the following day's edition had been at pains to dismiss this as indicative of resentment on the part of the region's Anglo-Indian population at the nature of British governance on the subcontinent, and instructed its readers to look to news from Bombay for a picture of the Mutiny undistorted by sectional grievances and jealousies.[47] Jones thus effectively used his editorial privilege to re-present and re-read *The*

Times' coverage of the Mutiny within the pages of his own organ to bolster his narrative of Indian events.

The fact that the mid-nineteenth-century newspaper was a fluid and open text, with ample scope for its readership to play an active role in constructing and giving meaning to news narrative through, for example, the selection of which articles to read, and in which order,[48]gave Jones scope to influence the narrative thus constructed through a number of devices. Leading articles in newspapers such as *The Times* had no headlines in this period, yet Jones deployed headings such as 'The Indian Revolution'[49] and 'The Patriot War in India'[50] in an attempt to draw the reader into the text and frame his/her reading of what followed. Jones also tried to shape the way in which his readership linked articles by directing their attention from his leading articles to other sections where his arguments would find support, for example to news and opinion extracted from foreign and national newspapers. This was important, as the need to fill pages with material lifted from other press organs meant *The People's Paper*, like most of its contemporaries, was unlikely to form an ideologically coherent text when read as a whole.[51]

With the nature of the conflict in India making the role of war correspondent pioneered by W. H. Russell in the Crimea largely impossible, detailed accounts of the rebellion gleaned from personal letters sent to Britain from soldiers and members of the Anglo-Indian community assumed great importance. The experience of the eyewitness was still held as the arbiter of true representations of the Mutiny, and the terse communiqués reaching Britain from India could not fulfil this function.[52] Ostensibly intended for a personal rather than a national audience, they were replete with a mixture of tales of fortitude, heroism and bravery in the field, and melodramatic, harrowing narratives of suffering at the hands of the insurgents.[53] The picture of the rebels as wild, irrational savages driven by rapine and plunder they appeared to affirm fed and buttressed *The Times'* version of the Mutiny, while the familiar language and tone in which they narrated the conflict readily invited the reader to share in the triumphs and horrors they depicted in a way the abstract accounts of troop manoeuvres could not achieve.

Jones could not escape the impact of these accounts, not only because of the huge currency they obtained in British culture in late 1857, but also because his own organ reprinted many when filling its pages with material lifted from other press sources. The claim to truth of many of these letters was highly dubious, with many actually creating or recounting rumours of atrocities and indignities in an unquestioning fashion, and judged to have no certifiable foundations in truth by subsequent enquiry.[54] However, the thirst for information from the source of the conflict saw these reprinted uncritically in the Anglo-Indian and British press, impressing the public with the truth of their accounts.

However, the issue of their veracity was largely left unquestioned by Jones, no doubt deterred by the paucity of available evidence contradicting them so soon after the outbreak of the revolt and the extreme sensitivity of their subject matter. Instead, he mined them for evidence that the British outdid the Indians in brutality and savagery. Passages in letters vowing bloody vengeance on the rebels were thus highlighted, with Jones alleging them to be inspired by bloodthirsty calls for revenge emanating from parliament and *The Times*. Britain thus risked casting herself out of 'the pale of civilised nations'.[55]

Jones also printed accounts from authoritative sources of atrocities committed overseas by British soldiers and administrators to bolster his argument. Under the title 'Who Are The Torturers?' a litany of mass murder, torture and defilement perpetrated by British troops on the native population of Ireland was published on 17 October 1857, many of the crimes bearing uncanny similarities to those recounted in the Indian mails, including the language used to describe them.[56] By drawing on these diverse examples of British barbarism, the idea that Britain could only be a benevolent master whose charges thus had no conceivable excuse for their shocking conduct was dismissed.[57] Jones also repeatedly emphasised how his evidence for the injustices he described came from the highest military and civil authorities, allowing him to 'convict the criminals out of their own mouths'.[58] Indeed, the article 'Who is the Torturer' told how atrocities recorded against the Indian populace had been brought to the attention of the House of Commons in June 1857; thus misrule could not be denied. Such a corrupt and tyrannical imperial polity thus required thoroughgoing reform.

Of course, the true expert seeing the linkages between Indian and British reform and capable of rectifying the injustices of misrule was Jones himself, and *The People's Paper* was an important vehicle for reminding (or informing) Jones' readership of these qualities. Having been established both as a vehicle for promoting Jones' political thought and his financial position,[59] *The People's Paper* frequently carried transcripts and extracts from his speeches, poetry and essays, and advertisements for future events and currently available publications. The popularity of his poetry had been central to Jones' rise to prominence in the Chartist movement.[60] When the first page of every issue of *The People's Paper* from August 1857 until the end of October that year carried an advertisement for his poem 'The Revolt of Hindostan; or The New World' immediately above the 'Current Notes' section, accompanied by favourable reviews and a note explaining the circumstances in which it had been written, the drive to reaffirm his credentials as a radical political leader and a prescient analyst of Indian and military affairs, and to bolster his precarious finances, coalesced. As the note proclaimed:

> The above poem was written with the Author's blood, when denied the use of pen, ink, and paper, while confined during 1848 and 1849 in a solitary cell on the Silent System, in Westminster Prison; and, though composed nine years ago, contains a prophecy of this present Revolt in Hindostan, correct even in many of the minutest details.[61]

An extract from this work was printed on the leader page on 24 October, showing how the tribulations currently facing one of the heroic leaders of the counter-insurgency (and engaging the attention of a national press increasingly critical of the government's handling of the counter-insurgency operation), were among these details:

> This Britain felt, till pride of wealth and birth
> Were forced by danger to give way to worth;
> A veteran soldier for her leader chose,
> By public service worn, and private woes;
> But where one quick, strong will alone could save,
> A timid council's guiding thraldom gave.[62]

The admixture of political critique, poetic romanticism and self-promotion evident in these interlinking quotations encapsulate much of how Jones deployed his editorship of *The People's Paper* to advance his cause. His identification of Sir Colin Campbell as a worthy hero, and the implication that the reform movement in Britain would do well not to ignore their own 'veteran soldier' by falling prey to 'timid council', exemplify his proclivity to switch between identification with rebel or counter-insurgent as the likelihood of a successful rebellion receded and the controversies surrounding the mismanaged British operation gave him an equally powerful narrative motif for advancing his own interests. The weekly restatement of his impeccable credentials as a radical leader, mobilising powerful tropes of self-sacrifice and suffering for the cause that became the basis of a personality cult after his death,[63] tapped into long-established rituals and rhetoric deployed by Chartist leaders (and their political antecedents) to claim the right to speak for and lead the people against the established political order.[64] His self-proclaimed powers of prescience, constantly affirmed by his seeming ability to predict the course of events in India more accurately than the political establishment for much of 1857, were taken to near-mystical levels by his claim to have foreseen events of the Mutiny nine years in advance, although the mundane truth that 'The New World' had been written to warn America against the perils of imperialism (and almost certainly with ink, pen and paper) was elided.[65]

Jones' temporary rise to the forefront of the movement for domestic political reform in late 1857 on the back of his reading of Indian affairs was thus bolstered by the fluidity of the nineteenth-century newspaper as a text and 'news' as a concept. With *The Times* having a stranglehold on the provision of synchronic news from the seat of the conflict, a knowing exploitation of the form of the newspaper was essential to undermining the validity of its narrative when no alternative sources of such information were available. Jones thus continually used his editor-ship of *The People's Paper* to reconstitute and re-read *The Times'* narrative of the Mutiny in order to undermine its credibility, simultane-ously creating and exposing inconsistencies, and pointing to alternative readings of the evidence it arrayed that compromised its validity. Jones ranged widely across geographical and temporal boundaries to support his depiction of imperial culpability in the outbreak, and cited the authority of crown and government (not to mention his own 'proven' perceptiveness) to support his case. The coalition between press and government seemingly emerging in the field of imperial communica-tions and Indian affairs thus did not present an insurmountable barrier to the advancement of his position.

Conclusion

This chapter has sought to make two important points about the reception of the Indian Mutiny in Britain during 1857 and 1858. First, I have shown that the radical 'Englishness' that had proved flexible enough for European radicals such as the Italian Giuseppe Mazzini and the Hungarain Lajos Kossuth to be appropriated into (or portray themselves within) could also accommodate the Indian insurgents as comrades and exemplars to British reformers,[66] across boundaries of race, religion and culture which much of the existing historiography appears to have tacitly accepted as being impermeable. Of course, this identification was contingent, ambiguous and opportunistic. Jones called for English reformers to identify with both rebels and counter-insurgents according to whichever cause best illustrated his own concerns, and these concerns appear always to have been paramount. Jones' participation in the lampooning of 'negrophist' barristers at the mess of the Northern Circuit at the height of the General Eyre controversy in March 1867 reinforces suspicions that freedom for India was above all a convenient vehicle for Jones' own metropolitan political narrative, and not a conviction based on a belief in racial or cultural equality.[67]

Second, scholars of the press and its relationship to British politics and culture should treat with caution statements from contemporaries and latter-day scholars alike that the genesis of 'modern' communications networks instituted an authoritarian control over the news, hence taming and domesticating the Empire as a theme in metropolitan politics. Was the imperial communications system conveying news from India to Britain in 1857–8 'modern'? Was it even a system? As we have seen, the most modern feature of the system, the telegraph, in many ways aided Jones far more than his establishment rivals in the press and politics, the paucity of information it carried creating the conditions where both were forced into speculation on the causes and course of the Mutiny until further news could be assimilated, with Jones consistently seeming the more astute commentator in its early months. The flexibility of 'news' and 'newspapers' as ideas and entities in the mid-nineteenth century further aided Jones. Indeed, it could be argued that the long-standing channels of Indian information utilised by the press – namely gossip, rumour and private communication – ultimately played the key role in mobilising British sentiment against the insurgency. The dissemination and use of imperial information from the media in British politics, culture and society is thus an area where much further research needs to be done.

Notes

1. My predominant usage of the term 'Indian Mutiny' reflects how the uprising of 1857 was conceptualised within contemporary British discourse and culture. It can be argued that revolt, rebellion and rising would be more valid terms for characterising the nature and course of events in India, and I also use these terms within my text.
2. D. Peers and D. Finkelstein, ' "A Great System of Circulation": Introducing India to the Nineteenth Century Media', in D. Peers and D. Finkelstein (eds.), *Negotiating India in the Nineteenth Century Media*, (Basingstoke: Macmillan, 2000), p. 7.

3. G. Dawson, *Soldier Heroes: British Adventure, Empire and the Imagining of Masculinities* (London: Routledge, 1994), pp. 86–8.
4. Ibid., pp. 79–145.
5. K. T. Hoppen, *The Mid-Victorian Generation 1846–1886* (Oxford: Oxford University Press, 1998), pp. 167–94.
6. See E. Palmegiano, 'The Indian Mutiny and the Mid-Victorian Press', *Journal of Newspaper and Periodical History*, 7 (London, 1991): 3–11; L. Peters, ' "Double-dyed Traitors and Infernal Villains": *Illustrated London News, Household Words*, Charles Dickens and the Indian Rebellion', in Peers and Finkelstein (eds.), *Negotiating India*, pp. 110–34.
7. T. R. Metcalf, *The Aftermath of Revolt: India, 1857–1870* (Princeton, NJ: Princeton University Press, 1965), pp. 72–3.
8. Ibid., pp. 73–4.
9. *The Times* (hereafter *TT*), 10 June 1857, p. 8.
10. *TT*, 30 June 1857, p. 9.
11. 'Omen from India', *The People's Paper* (hereafter *PP*), 16 May 1857.
12. 'Indian Discontent', *PP*, 23 May 1857. There is no evidence the rebel leaders took this into account when launching their rising.
13. 'The Patriot War in India', *PP*, 11 July 1857.
14. 'The British Empire', *PP*, 18 July 1857.
15. 'India', *PP*, 1 August 1857.
16. Ibid.
17. M. Finn, *After Chartism: Nation and Class in English Radical Politics, 1848–1874* (Cambridge: Cambridge University Press, 1993), pp. 137–41.
18. Jones' calls for democratic reform in Britain were usually addressed to the English, rather than British, people.
19. 'Where Shall We Get Our Cotton?', *PP*, 27 June 1857.
20. 'Current Notes', *PP*, 11 July 1857.
21. See the reports of the Fourth and Fifth 'Political Soirées' serialised in *The People's Paper* throughout January and February 1857.
22. 'Hindostan', *PP*, 4 July 1857.
23. 'The Indian War', *PP*, 5 August 1857.
24. Christopher Hill, 'The Norman Yoke', in his *Puritans and Revolutionaries: Studies in Interpretation of the English Revolution of the Seventeenth Century* (London: Panther, 1968), pp. 58–125.
25. 'The Indian Struggle', *PP*, 5 September 1857.
26. *TT*, 27 October 1857, p. 8.
27. *TT*, 29 August 1857, p. 8.
28. 'The Indian War', *PP*, 8 August 1857; 'The Indian Revolution', *PP*, 21 November 1857.
29. See, for example, *TT*, 9 November 1857, p. 6.
30. 'To The Chartists!', *PP*, 3 October 1857.
31. 'Indian Insurrection and British Democracy', *PP*, 26 September 1857.
32. Ibid.
33. Ibid.
34. Ibid.
35. 'Personal Leadership', *PP*, 5 September 1857.
36. Ibid.
37. 'Indian Insurrection and British Democracy'.

38. 'To The Chartists', *PP*, 7 November 1857.
39. Ibid.
40. 'How to Secure India', *PP*, 2 January 1858.
41. B. Porter, *The Refugee Question in Mid-Victorian Politics* (Cambridge: Cambridge University Press, 1979).
42. M. Taylor, *Ernest Jones, Chartism, and the Romance of Politics 1819–69* (Oxford: Oxford University Press, 2003), pp. 181–3.
43. Peter Mandler has recently identified a reckless analysis of texts without careful consideration of their reception, or 'throw', as a major 'problem' with what has been termed 'the New Cultural History'. P. Mandler, 'The Problem with Cultural History', *Cultural and Social History*, 1 (London: Arnold, 2004), pp. 94–117.
44. Dawson, *Soldier Heroes*, pp. 84–6.
45. 'The Indian Revolution', *PP*, 21 November 1857.
46. *TT*, 16 November 1857, p. 7.
47. *TT*, 17 November 1857, p. 6.
48. M. Beetham, 'Towards a Theory of the Periodical as a Publishing Genre', and A. Humphreys, 'Popular Narrative and Political Discourse in Reynolds Weekly Newspaper', both in L. Brake, A. Jones and L. Madden (eds.), *Investigating Victorian Journalism* (London: Macmillan, 1990), pp. 19–32 and pp. 33–47.
49. *PP*, 21 November 1857.
50. *PP*, 11 July 1857.
51. Beetham, 'Towards a Theory of the Periodical', p. 24.
52. Andrew Barry, 'Lines of Communication and Spaces of Rule', in Andrew Barry, Thomas Osborne and Nikolas Rose (eds.), *Foucault and Political Reason: Liberalism, Neo-Liberalism and Rationalities of Government* (London: UCL Press, 1996), p. 131.
53. Dawson, *Soldier Heroes*, pp. 79–110.
54. Ibid.
55. 'The Indian Revolution', *PP*, 21 November 1857.
56. 'Who Are the Torturers?', *PP*, 17 October 1857.
57. 'Who is the Torturer?', *PP*, 12 September 1857.
58. 'Hindostan', *PP*, 25 July 1857.
59. Taylor, *Ernest Jones*, pp. 130–42.
60. Ibid., p. 78.
61. See, for example, *PP*, 5 September 1857.
62. 'Sir Colin Campbell', *PP*, 24 October 1857.
63. Ibid., p. 6.
64. J. Belchem and J. Epstein, 'The Nineteeenth-Century Gentleman Leader Revisited', *Social History*, 22 (London: Routledge, 1997): 174–93.
65. Taylor, *Ernest Jones*, pp. 142–50.
66. Finn, *After Chartism*, pp. 60–180.
67. Taylor, *Ernest Jones*, pp. 207–9.

7

Writing to the Defence of Empire: Winston Churchill's Press Campaign against Constitutional Reform in India, 1929–1935

Ian St John

It was while touring North America in the autumn of 1929 that Churchill heard of the Viceroy, Lord Irwin's, declaration that the goal of British policy in India was the granting of self-governing Dominion status within the Empire. Churchill was outraged at what he took to be the hoisting of the white flag of surrender in India. He was not alone. On 1 November, the day after Irwin's announcement, the *Daily Mail* attacked the Conservative leader, Stanley Baldwin, for his willingness to endorse the initiative without consulting his Cabinet colleagues. In the Commons later that day Baldwin responded to the *Mail*'s allegation, declaring that 'every statement of fact and every implication of fact contained in that article is untrue, and in my opinion gravely injurious to the public interest, not only in this country, but throughout the Empire'.[1] But the *Mail* was not to be deflected and, on 16 November, carried an article by Churchill in which he denounced Irwin's declaration as 'criminally mischievous'. Dominion status could not be accorded to a nation in which 60 million persons were 'untouchables', the political class represented only a tiny fraction of the population, and racial and religious antagonisms meant that 'the withdrawal of British protection would mean the immediate resumption of mediaeval wars'.

The events of these few weeks epitomised what was to be played out over the next six years. Unsympathetic observers found Churchill 'wild on the subject of India', and he himself reflected that it was a 'question one cares about far more than office, or party or friendships'.[2] To press his views he headed a campaign that would alienate him from the Conservative leadership, exclude him from the National Government and compromise his critique of Britain's foreign policy. The campaign was fought across a broad front. But from the beginning the press in general occupied a strategic role.

Matters of motive

Given that Churchill's personal experience of India was limited, focused on military aspects and the polo field, and was a long time distant, why did he choose, in 1929, to make India the governing passion of his political career? Leading Conservatives were in no doubt that India represented an issue on which he hoped to appeal to the Conservative backbenchers, berate the Labour and later National Governments, and clear the way for his elevation to the premiership. Samuel Hoare, who as Secretary of State for India bore the brunt of Churchill's attacks, was especially cynical. 'Winston', he declared as late as 1935, 'is out to make the maximum trouble. He is determined to smash the National Government and believes that India is a good battering ram.'[3] Several historians have endorsed varieties of this opportunistic interpretation. For Ball, Churchill was a politician looking for an issue to revive his career; Alan Clark writes that he scented 'personal advantage'; while according to Middlemas and Barnes, he found in India 'fresh material for a crusade against the leadership'.[4] Bridge concludes that 'the issue afforded him the opportunity to establish himself as an alternative leader to Baldwin...'[5]

Churchill was certainly impatient at finding himself on the opposition benches and did little to disguise the fact that the premiership was the remaining object of his ambition. 'Only one goal still attracts me', he wrote to his wife in August 1929, 'and if that were barred I should quit the dreary field for pastures new.'[6] In this context India was a promising card to play. Imperial issues resonated with the Tories, and with Baldwin pledging Conservative support for the Irwin–Labour Government initiative, Churchill expected a backbench rebellion. Did not Hoare admit that 'scarcely anyone' in the party liked the Declaration?[7] In addition, with Churchill at odds with the majority of Baldwin's critics on the issue of protective tariffs, India provided shared ground for a leadership bid. Churchill was too ambitious a politician to take up India if it had appeared a doomed cause that would marginalise him politically. Quite the reverse: 'India', he declared in 1930, 'is going to become increasingly the greatest problem of British politics and may well be the fighting line between the parties.'[8] He felt sure that he was on the right side of the line, enthusing in 1931 that:

> the whole spirit of the Conservative Party is with me, and that much of their dissatisfaction with [Baldwin] turns itself into favour with me...Every speech that I have made and step that I have taken, has been well received beyond all expectations...Anything may happen now if opinion has time to develop...[9]

In this hope he was encouraged by supporters like the press magnate Lord Rothermere, who wrote: 'You have really got your foot this time on the ladder that quite soon leads to the Premiership.'[10]

Yet to say that Churchill expected to gain personally from the Indian controversy does not explain why he focused so intensely on *this* question, or why he maintained his engagement when it was so evidently *damaging* his position. All the evidence points to the fact that the fate of British rule in India struck an extremely sensitive nerve. He had gone, commented Baldwin in December 1930, 'quite mad about India', and shortly afterwards Churchill acknowledged in a letter to Baldwin, 'I care more about this business than anything else in public life.'[11]

Partly, no doubt, discussion of the fate of India reawakened memories of his own Indian days. 'He has become once more', reflected Baldwin, 'the subaltern of Hussars of 96.' Yet his nostalgia was for more than his own youth; it was for the imperial world order that had set the parameters of his career as a soldier, journalist and politician. Churchill grew to maturity at a time when Britain's global power was at its height and never lost his Victorian certainty that the Empire was a force for progress in the world. Similarly, he never doubted that India, besides being a source of economic strength, prestige and manpower, was the fulcrum on which the imperial system turned. Its loss 'would mark and consummate the downfall of the British Empire',[12] compared to which the 'loss of Ireland' was 'petty'.

So, Churchill was passionate about India because he was passionate about British power in an increasingly threatening world. Events since 1914 had shattered any belief he had previously entertained concerning the inevitability of progress on Whiggish lines. The whole trend of post-war history was towards the construction of great empires by regimes that had turned their back on democracy and free trade. Against this backdrop it was incomprehensible that Britain should dismantle the greatest empire the world had known, providing, thereby, fodder for other less scrupulous powers – and all in the name of an increasingly discredited model of democracy.

As such, India threw into relief the psychology of British power. Did the governing elite have the resolve and self-belief to keep what Britain had secured? Or was the country to retreat in the face of opposition? If strong leadership were provided over India, he confidently believed, not only would Gandhism be crushed and British rule secured for generations to come, but the spirit of empire would 'arise in its old strength'.[13] India, then, was a test of British will and destiny; 'the greatest question Englishmen have had to settle' since the war. Churchill was stirred by it for *these* reasons, and it was for precisely these reasons that it threw into question Baldwin's leadership of the Conservative Party. For everything suggested that Baldwin did not have the fighting spirit to uphold Britain's interests. Unless the Conservative backbenchers could force Baldwin to resist the Indian reform proposals, or make way for someone who would, then the party would be complicit in a fatal event.[14]

Methods of opposition

The Conservative front bench supported the India policies of Irwin and the Labour Government. Indeed, from 1931, with the formation of the National Government, the Conservatives were directly involved in their promotion, with a Conservative, Samuel Hoare, Secretary of State for India. Baldwin and Hoare concurred with Irwin that a gradual extension in the participation of Indians in their own Government was inevitable. It was implicit in the whole ethos of British rule in India since the nineteenth century, and the process had taken a significant stride forward with the Government of India Act of 1919, which had introduced the 'dyarchy' system of shared British–Indian Government at provincial level. Given the corresponding advance of Indian nationalism under Congress, it was inconceivable that Britain could reverse or even stymie the process. The challenge was to manipulate it so as to ensure that the substance of Britain's Indian interests were upheld as long as possible.

The solution that emerged was a dual one. First, Irwin hoped, by announcing a long-term commitment to grant full self-government, to convince Indian opinion of Britain's goodwill and persuade moderate nationalists to work with the British in the short to medium term.[15] The Irwin Declaration, in other words, was a public relations exercise devised to divide the Indian opposition and rebuild trust in the Raj. Second, in the light of the discussions at the first Round Table Conference of 1930,

Hoare saw the possibility of recruiting the princes to an all-India federal system. This would check the radicalism of Congress and mean that Britain could safely concede a degree of power at the centre.

It was a subtle exercise in *realpolitik* and one which, leading Conservatives believed, precisely suited the needs of a country struggling to maintain its extensive imperial commitments in a context of growing strain on resources. Yet to Churchill such acceptance of imperial decline was anathema, as was the duplicity inherent in the Irwin–Hoare strategy. As he remarked to a follower of Gandhi's in 1934:

> I believe in truth...I have no use for those people who say to the Indians, 'This is a wonderful constitution to lead you to the desired goal, etc.', and then say to others, 'This is all right, we have got it all safely tied up. Don't be anxious, the Indians will not be able to do anything.' I hate that kind of thing.[16]

It followed that if Churchill were to block Indian reform he would have to combat not merely the policies of Irwin and the Labour Government, but of his own party hierarchy. And of course, from 1931, with the formation of the National Government, all these distinctions blurred: Conservative, Labour and Liberal Cabinet ministers, the India Office, his party leader, successive Viceroys – all were in his sights. But the odds were stacked against him. For good reason Churchill commented to Irwin, 'you will start with the big battalions on your side',[17] and for similarly good reasons he sought alternative avenues of opposition, of which the press was most important.

The role of the press

The press occupied a central place in the anti-reform campaign. 'Without the help of this powerful press', commented Churchill to the Secretary of the Indian Empire Society (IES) in 1931, 'we can do nothing'.[18] With the combination of cross-party agreement and massive government majorities, the Fourth Estate was the only national forum in which supporters of more traditional approaches to Imperial Government could make their opinions felt – especially given the BBC's consistent refusal, until 1935, to allow Churchill access to the wireless to broadcast his views on India. In addition, the inter-war period was the hey-day of the press lords – of proprietors of papers with circulations running into millions and who sought to deploy the popularity of their papers in the service of their political ambitions. Churchill was on good terms with the two greatest press lords – Rothermere and Beaverbrook – both of whom were contemptuous of Baldwin and were already campaigning for a more vigorous programme of imperial consolidation. Thirdly, Churchill had a longstanding interest in the uses of newspaper journalism. From the beginning of his career he had sought publicity for his actions by writing about them, understanding, comments Charmley, that in an age of the popular franchise it was the 'office boys' who read the *Daily Mail* who had the vote.[19] Subsequent events had only deepened his sense of the power of the press:

> No institution has gained more in power in the twentieth century than the Press...While Parliamentary institutions have grown steadily weaker, the newspapers have become stronger and the Press has blithely consented to fill the gap caused by the subsidence of the House of Commons...[20]

Though he did not view these developments without disquiet, Churchill was too realistic a politician not to respond to them. After all, he wrote around 800 press articles over his lifetime and was described by the veteran pressman Herbert Sidebotham in 1932 as 'the greatest living journalist'.[21] Churchill's written style exactly suited the requirements of modern journalism: 'It is succinct', said Beaverbrook, 'it is interesting, and it appeals to the audience. What a leader writer Mr Churchill would have made!'[22] It was inevitable that Churchill should make extensive use of his pen – or, more accurately, the services of his dictation secretary – in the struggle against Irwinism in India.

There were several ways in which Churchill used the press in his campaign on India. Most obviously, its pages provided a platform from which he and his allies could expound their views and try to reach the wider public. By far the most important outlet for Churchill in this regard was the *Daily Mail*. The pioneer mass circulation daily, the *Mail* still enjoyed in the early 1930s the largest readership of any newspaper. Since 1922 it had been owned by Northcliffe's brother, Lord Rothermere, a man of domineering personality who was determined to deploy the power afforded by his paper's circulation to advance his various political obsessions. These proved a decidedly mixed bag. His hatred of socialism saw the *Mail* contribute to Labour's 1924 election defeat with the Zinoviev letter. Baldwin's failure to demonstrate sufficient gratitude only confirmed Rothermere in his mounting contempt for the Conservative leader. Rothermere's championship of 'Justice for Hungary' in the 1920s almost saw him elevated to the throne of that country.[23] In 1929 he threw his not inconsiderable weight behind two campaigns: Beaverbrook's crusade for an imperial tariff; and Churchill's fight to save India. It was the latter that meant more to him.

By the 1930s Rothermere found gloom and decay wherever he looked and India was no exception. British power, under the feeble leadership of Irwin, Baldwin and MacDonald, was on the fast track to dissolution. For India the result would be civil war, while for Britain it would mean 'bankruptcy and revolution'.[24] The deluge was approaching and Rothermere saw Churchill as the only person who could avert it. Accordingly, Rothermere gave strong support to Churchill, sending messages of encouragement from his residences on the continent and placing his papers at his disposal. 'I hope you will go straight forward in your Indian campaign', he wrote from Monte Carlo. 'Do not allow any of your old colleagues to restrain you. Unless our people understand India and its essential necessity to us, England will disappear in an economic collapse of inconceivable gravity. I have told all my papers to give you plenty of publicity, and you will have as much as you want.'[25] From San Remo he urged: 'You have a superb chance. Be untiring and unfaltering. Chuck holidays and live laborious days.'[26] Well might Churchill comment, 'Rothermere writes or telegraphs every other day avowing undying fidelity.'[27]

In the weeks following Irwin's declaration the *Mail* gave extensive coverage to Indian affairs, including articles on the 'Peril in India' by such IES stalwarts as Lord Sydenham, Sir Michael O'Dwyer and Sir Reginald Craddock. Strongly worded editorials denounced the 'calamitous consequences' of Irwin's initiative, which would include the introduction of a prohibitive tariff on British goods and the repudiation of the national debt of India. 'The shock would be such that it would take us a generation to recover...'[28]

Churchill's first article appeared as part of the 'Peril in India' series on 16 November, with the same issue including an editorial calling for Churchill to replace the 'invertebrate' Irwin as Viceroy. Over the next months and years the paper was the staple outlet for Churchill's articles on India, with such titles as 'The Real Issue in India', 'India may still be saved from Disaster' and 'The Priceless legacy of Warren Hastings'. Churchill realised the importance of the *Mail*'s backing and did his best to retain Rothermere's notoriously fickle interest. Without the strongest support from the *Mail*, Baldwin, he told the proprietor, 'with *The Times* at his back' would be 'master of the fate of India'.[29] Where the *Morning Post* reached 'the local swells...you deal with the mass of middle-class voters and party men and women' – precisely the people to be won over if the Conservative Associations were to place the necessary pressure on the leadership.[30] In February 1931 Churchill wrote to Rothermere making suggestions for more coverage of the India campaign, including greater attention to his speeches, which were 'just as good reading as any article that I write'. He suggested a meeting with the Assistant Editor, Herbert Wilson, to discuss his plans, adding: 'I am a pretty good journalist; could you not instruct Wilson to pay favourable attention to what I suggest?'[31] A meeting with Wilson was arranged and Rothermere hoped it yielded Churchill what he wanted. Certainly, over the course of the campaign the support of the *Daily Mail* was the key asset the diehards possessed and as late as 1935 Hoare was of the belief that 'the country is bored stiff by Indian reforms. If it was not for the *Daily Mail* and *Morning Post*, the issue would be dead in the constituencies.'[32]

The support of Rothermere brought with it not only the *Mail*, but the rest of his press empire. The *Sunday Despatch*, for instance, was a Rothermere paper that opposed Baldwin's Indian policies, accusing him, in January 1930, of an 'unforgivable blunder' in encouraging Indians to expect Dominion Home Rule.[33] Although the provincial press was declining in importance in the inter-war years, its pages offered another outlet for Churchill's arguments. In London Rothermere's *Evening News* was a prominent ally – running the infamous headline, during the St George's by-election of March 1931: 'Gandhi is watching St George's.' The *Bristol Evening World*, a Rothermere title, gave significant assistance to the campaign of the India Defence League (IDL), providing the loudspeaker system for Churchill's 1935 Bristol speech on India. In February 1931 the paper exalted Churchill for standing out 'alone among Conservative leaders, with enough courage to picture before us the unemployment, bankruptcy and bloodshed which must result from the foolish project of granting Dominion Status'.[34] The *Derby Daily Telegraph* congratulated Churchill for engineering 'a vigorous campaign against our abandonment of India…'[35] The *Newcastle Evening World* similarly claimed for Churchill the support of 'tens of thousands of clear minded persons' who believed that 'weak-willed negotiations with agitators must cease, and firm rule must be substituted for it'.[36] Not without reason did Churchill comment in February 1931 that Rothermere's papers 'in every part of the country are writing eulogistic articles and friendly paragraphs…'[37]

In one respect, however, Rothermere failed to deliver: namely, in the shape of Lord Beaverbrook. The owner of the *Daily Express*, the second mass circulation daily, was concurrently engaged upon his own campaign for imperial protection. In return for supporting Beaverbrook's campaign, Rothermere extracted a promise that the *Express* would go 'all out on India'.[38] Yet this never happened, for Beaverbrook had no emotional attachment to India. The Empire that interested him was that of the white Dominions. Of course, he might have taken up the Indian issue if Churchill had, in return, agreed to back Empire Free Trade. To this end Beaverbrook invited Churchill to dinner in January 1930 and sought to persuade him, pacing the room and 'piling argument on argument and statistic on statistic'.[39] But free trade in food was the one consistent belief in Churchill's shifting career and he was not prepared to compromise on the issue.[40] From 1931 personal factors also played a part in the *Express*'s coolness towards the India campaign. Beaverbrook was a longstanding friend of Samuel Hoare, the new India Secretary, who was an important political contact and whose brother had invested in *Express* shares.[41] Beaverbrook congratulated Hoare on his appointment and ensured that he was not subject to criticism within his papers. Indeed, by 1934 he was commenting, 'I do not disagree with Mr Baldwin over the India issue.'[42]

However, the press was more than an outlet for anti-reform opinion. It was also a vehicle for the conduct of campaign activity. Through its pages meetings were advertised, appeals for funds made and members of the IES recruited. Again, it was the *Daily Mail* that was pivotal. In the lead-up to the IES's important Manchester meeting Churchill reminded its Secretary, Sir Mark Hunter, that 'Lord Rothermere has given directions that his papers are to work up interest in the meeting and support it in every way'. Douglas Crawford, the Foreign Editor of the *Daily Mail*, 'will no doubt do all that is needful'.[43] Hunter replied that he had had meetings with *Mail* staff in Manchester and with Crawford in London. The paper had sent a representative in connection with a special announcement of the meeting: 'He is to send me a typescript of what is proposed should be published and I will send to you for your comments.'[44] To 'seal the bond' of the *Mail*'s cooperation Churchill ensured that Rothermere's son Esmond was invited to speak and arranged that the two should travel up together: 'I will look after you and see that you are not bored.'[45] Prior to the rally the Manchester Constitutional Club organised a dinner at which the local Editor of the *Mail* was one of the eleven guests. Tactfully, Churchill reported favourably on Esmond's performance to his father, praising his 'good voice, easy manner and sentences turned in the best Parliamentary style. I think he is very much inclined to come a long way with this fight.'[46] Rothermere was equally complimentary: 'Congratulations on speech. Go right ahead and you will find I shall give you unlimited support.'

Rothermere urged that the Manchester meeting be speedily followed up by another at the London's Albert Hall. 'Modern electorates forget almost over night. Frequent repetition is the only method by which they can be influenced. An occasional article in the *Daily Mail* does nothing, but repetition does everything.'[47] Again Churchill emphasised to the IES the importance of liaising with the *Mail*, suggesting that the meeting begin by 7.30 pm at the latest 'to favour reporting'. Hunter replied that he had visited the *Daily Mail* office where 'I have been promised every assistance towards making the Albert Hall meeting a success'.[48] Ironically, the *Mail*'s forthright backing for the rally, which coincided with the St George's by-election, was to help undo Churchill's campaign.

Newspapers were also a source of information. Outside of Government, the press's newsgathering system was vital if Churchill and his allies were to counter the version of events promulgated by the India Office. By far the most significant part played by the press in this regard related to the events leading up to Churchill's accusation of a breech of parliamentary privilege in the conduct of the Joint Select Committee's investigation of the Government's White Paper on Indian reform. The allegation was that Hoare and Lord Derby had pressured the Manchester Chamber of Commerce into revising its intended submission to the JSC, which was judged too negative regarding the consequences for Lancashire of the Government's reforms. Churchill was alerted to the story on 31 March 1934 by William McWhirter, Managing Director of Rothermere's papers, who sent him an article the *Mail* was running the next day alleging that a 'wilful, deliberate and unfortunately successful attempt' had been made to 'doctor' evidence presented to the JSC. Churchill discussed the matter with Douglas Crawford, who sent him the relevant documents.[49] Recognising the potential of the issue to strike a blow at Hoare and the reforms, Churchill requested a meeting with the Manchester informants, which Rothermere arranged at the Savoy Hotel in London on 8 April. At the meeting Churchill declared that 'once the secret is out ... the press will immediately take it up, and keep on with it. What will then happen will be an uproar.'[50] Hoare had to admit that Churchill's attack in the Commons was 'all very well stage managed ... all the press had been carefully prepared by him' – so carefully in fact that 'he sent a verbatim copy' of the speech to the press while delivering another in the House: 'it had the kind of dramatic effect that he and his friends desired. All the busybodies were running about the lobby saying that it was a very serious affair and that it would certainly lead to my resignation if it did not break up the whole government.'[51] It *was* a serious affair, though it failed to topple the Secretary of State or the Bill, the charges being – unsurprisingly – rejected by a Committee of Privileges that included the Prime Minister MacDonald and Baldwin. Still, it delayed the work of the JSC for nearly two months, and the irritation engendered amongst the Government's ranks was reflected in an editorial in *The Times* which commented that 'Judgement', was never Churchill's 'strongest quality' and his angry rejection of the Committee's findings only confirmed 'that the latest charge of a breech of privilege belonged to the same class of reckless assaults on the whole India policy of successive governments'.[52]

The final contribution of the press to Churchill's India campaign was the least regarded at first and yet proved the most productive of results. This was the impact on Indian opinion. The whole purpose of the Irwin Declaration and subsequent Government of India Bill was to convince Indian opinion of British good faith and liberal intentions. The public utterances of British politicians were therefore the very stuff on which the Government's Indian strategy was founded, and the chief guide to Britain's real intentions towards India was accordingly the British press – not only directly, but indirectly since, as Kaul shows, the Indian press extensively utilised and commented on the copy of British papers.[53] In India Churchill was a well-known figure and his voice was taken to be the authentic expression of the British imperial viewpoint. Edward Russell, Assistant Editor of the *Morning Post*, was impressed by the 'awe in which he is held among Indian politicians and the Indian Press ... he is regarded as a kind of "bogey man", and they all seem frightened to death of his influence in British politics'.[54]

In this context Churchill's speeches, patronising, rich with invective and oozing contempt for the educated *babu*, were devastating to the whole Irwinite–Hoare agenda. In Churchill's hands Gandhi was reduced to a 'malignant subversive fanatic', 'a seditious Middle Temple lawyer ... posing as a fakir of a type well-known in the East'.[55] He had no qualms about stating that Indians were incapable of governing themselves and that Britain should act on the assumption that their rule would last indefinitely. Such statements seemed to one supporter of the reforms 'deliberately framed to upset Indian opinion'.[56] Certainly they were relayed for Indian consumption: 'We have read with deep interest the long *Times of India* cable report' of your speech at the Queen's Hall, wrote one Indian supporter of the Raj. 'I congratulate you upon the bold stand you are making against the further thrust of the western democratic system in India...'[57] Irwin's reaction was less favourable: he later recalled contemplating the 'irretrievable damage' that Reuters reports of diehard speeches in the Commons would do in India, later arguing that they helped discredit the reform project and 'strengthened the demand for independence'.[58]

It gradually became apparent that the key to derailing the Government's strategy was the princes. Initially willing to enter an all-India federation, they began to get cold feet and both sides lobbied hard for their support. In this area Churchill worked with the *Morning Post*. H. A. Gwynne, its Editor, was in close touch with the leading representatives of the princely states via Madhava Rao, the paper's special correspondent in India. Gwynne and Rao organised two missions to India of socially well-connected diehards to try to stiffen the resolve of the princes not to join a federation. Rao was keen that Churchill himself visit India, pointing out that it would have a 'marvellous political effect. It will completely shake up the Government and everyone concerned in India...'[59] Regrettably, Churchill declined the offer and never visited India again. Gwynne related the disappointing news to Rao:

> There are two struggles, one in England and one in India. The English is the paramount one and if we win the princes have nothing to fear. We must concentrate our energy here – and hence cannot always spare people from this country.

Ironically, it was the 'paramount' struggle in England that was lost and the princes who saved the day for the diehards. In February 1935, they assembled in Bombay to consider the federal scheme. Speeches critical of the plan were delivered and a resolution (which Hoare suspected had been drafted by the *Morning Post*) rejecting affiliation to an all-India federation passed. The *Post* passed on to Churchill a report of the secret proceedings and 'within hours', Hoare complained, 'Winston was able to quote in the House extracts from several of the speeches. The House was not unnaturally astonished that whilst he seemed to know everything that was happening, I seemed to know nothing.'[60] Churchill and his allies were jubilant at the princes' decision, recognising that it wrecked the federal scheme.[61] It was, indeed, the one victory of their campaign – though the degree to which they themselves were responsible has been debated. While it suited Hoare and Irwin to place the blame for this outcome on Churchill and the diehards, Bridge has argued that it was Congress who 'defeated the 1935 Act', frightening away the princes by their strong showing in the 1937 provincial elections.[62] Whatever the reason, Churchill would have settled for the outcome.

Deficiencies in Churchill's press campaign

Notwithstanding this belated achievement, Churchill's India campaign yielded meagre results. While he and the diehards rallied sections of backbench opinion, it was never enough to alter Indian policy significantly; though denouncing the reforms, they were generally seen as failing to articulate a convincing alternative; and however successful in rousing the anger of activists, they were unable to inconvenience the leadership to any degree. The most important factor in this disappointing outcome was the balance of political forces. When Churchill began his campaign in 1929 he was resisting the policy of a Labour Government. After 1931 he found himself opposed to a Conservative-dominated coalition with unprecedented majorities. India was never able to produce the kind of political earthquake necessary to reconfigure this balance of forces.

Even so, aspects of Churchill's deployment of the press contributed to this outcome. First, there was the matter of the *type* of press he used. Churchill focused his energies on the mass circulation press, and especially the *Daily Mail*. There were good reasons for this. Rothermere was a personal friend who put his press empire at Churchill's disposal. This was no mean gift – the *Mail* reached a massive audience and Churchill had always had a greater affinity with the popular press for which he provided 'good copy'. Personal considerations were also present. In 1929 Churchill's finances received a dual blow from the loss of government office and the Wall Street crash: quite simply, he needed the money popular journalism generated. Hence the importance of the kind of deal he made with the *Mail* in 1931 under which he was to be paid £7,800 for writing an article a week for a year.[63]

Still, there were problems in utilising the popular press to oppose the Indian reforms. The mass circulation papers were simply not influential in shaping the details of the India debate. Their main strength was their claim to embody public opinion, yet this was hardly a plausible boast in the context of India which, as an issue, failed to engage with a general reading public. Indian policy had always been made by a closed circle of experts. The *Mail* never pretended to be part of this select coterie and the attempt by Churchill and Rothermere to bludgeon their way into the debate was disabled by the belief that their fulminations were heavier on indignation than popular pressure. When Lord Linlithgow, Chairman of the JSC on Indian reform, wrote to Churchill that 'The Indian problem does *not* interest the mass of voters in this country', Churchill could only counter: 'It interests profoundly all those loyal, strong faithful forces upon which the might of Britain depends...'[64] In an age when the might of Britain was transparently on the ebb tide, that was really the problem.

Though Churchill's journalistic style was admirably suited to its context, it highlights a deeper weakness in the conduct of his India campaign: namely, his pronouncements were too confrontational and one-dimensional – couched, as Hoare complained, in the language of 'headlines and platform slogans'.[65] Although Churchill paid lip-service to the need to implement the Simon Commission report, he did little to disguise his belief that the entire exercise in power-sharing was a mistake. This was an unrealistic response which left Churchill marginalised. This was exemplified by his refusal to serve on the JSC, a decision deprecated by the former *Telegraph* proprietor Lord Burnham. Gwynne, too, believed that Churchill should have accepted the invitation in order to cross-examine the government case and then 'produce a minority report that would run up and down the country like a flame in dry grass'.[66] When Churchill appeared before the Committee, his lack of detailed knowledge of India or the bill was exposed.

As a corollary, Churchill failed to secure the support of the more serious political press. A range of factors was at work here. By far the most influential paper in Indian reporting was *The Times*. Unfortunately, under Geoffrey Dawson's editorship, that paper was not only an enthusiastic proponent of the reforms, but harboured a hatred for Churchill, whom Dawson considered a 'traitor' to his party.[67] Dawson was a close friend of Irwin's who, as a member of the Round Table group, helped formulate the 'dyarchy' plan for India and fully supported the strategy of responding to Indian nationalism with carefully judged concessions, thereby making him, in Churchill's opinion, one of the 'fuglemen of Imperial surrender'. Dawson visited India in early 1929 and it was during long conversations with the Viceroy that the idea of a series of Round Table meetings to discuss India's future was agreed.[68] In Britain he set himself to 'give a lead to public opinion' over the reforms and 'stiffen poor Baldwin', who 'has been going through great difficulties with his party.'[69] He planned a special 'India Number' of *The Times* (which appeared on 18 February 1930) and visited Baldwin over 100 times during the 1930s – assisting him in drafting his India speeches.[70] Churchill was regularly attacked in *The Times* as an 'unrepresentative extremist', an unreconstructed subaltern of the 1890s, whose speeches were 'almost as remote from reality as the orator himself'. The India campaign, reflected *The Times* journalist Colin

Coote, marked 'the real beginning of the dislike – amounting to a vendetta – of *The Times* newspaper against him'.[71] Well might Irwin write to Dawson: 'All your contributions have been quite admirable and no words can say how grateful I am to you for having assisted people to retain or regain their sanity.'[72]

Of the other more serious political papers, the Liberal *News Chronicle* was naturally averse to Churchill's whole stance, as was the *Manchester Guardian*, while the other leading provincial paper, the *Yorkshire Post*, supported the Conservative Party leadership. Churchill might have hoped for backing from the *Daily Telegraph* – which was publishing extracts from his biography of *Marlborough* as well as articles on European affairs – and approached its proprietor, Lord Camrose, to this end. Unfortunately, Camrose was a supporter of Baldwin and owed his elevation to the peerage in 1929 to the Conservative leader.[73] Far from wishing to help Churchill's campaign, he admitted that 'we differ in politics today' and was involved in discussions with Davidson and Baldwin concerning the foundation of a new London evening paper to counter the impact of Rothermere's *Evening News* and Beaverbrook's *Evening Standard*.[74] The *Observer* was another disappointment. Garvin, the Editor, was both a critic of Baldwin and a longstanding friend of Churchill's and pressed for his inclusion in the National Government. Yet despite these auspicious omens, Garvin decided to back Hoare's Federal strategy.[75] Thus, of the political papers, Churchill's only consistent support came from the *Morning Post*, a paper destined to disappear and of which it was said, with some reason, that no cause was truly lost until the *Morning Post* supported it.

Churchill himself must assume a share of the responsibility for failing to win greater press backing. His bombastic style meant that, while he might inspire existing supporters, he lacked the finesse to secure new ones amidst a sophisticated audience of journalists and editors. During a dinner with Churchill in 1933 Victor Cazalet found him 'passionate about India', saying, 'he felt like cutting people and hating them as he had never hated before in his life', to which Cazalet replied, 'the way to convert doubters was not to brand them as traitors but to produce sound reasons why his scheme as more likely to hold India for the Empire than that of the Government'.[76] This Churchill never did.

Of course, the Government was itself not passive in the matter of media management. The Conservative leadership utilised its own press contacts to bolster support for its policy. J. C. C. Davidson, the party chairman till 1931, was active to this end, priming the *Telegraph* and

Guardian in advance of the publication of the White Paper – which was, said Hoare, 'better received than I expected'. It was Davidson also who was deputed to win over the editor of the *Yorkshire Post*, while Hoare was able to call on the loyalty of Beaverbrook's *Express*. When the report of the JSC endorsing the White Paper was presented to the Commons, Hoare was happy to remark that 'our press was very helpful'. Of the 26 principal London and provincial papers, 22 endorsed its findings.[77]

In fact, the Government went beyond simply seeking to influence leading journalists. Unnerved by the extent of the IDL propaganda it decided to counter with its own campaigning organisation. This was the Union of Britain and India (UBI), formed in 1933 at the initiation of Hoare, Davidson and R. A. Butler (Under Secretary for India), which operated in conjunction with the India Office and was funded by Conservative Central Office. Francis Villiers, President of the European Association of India, headed the organisation, his services gaining him a knighthood in 1936.[78] Sir Alfred Watson, till 1933 the Editor of the Indian *Statesman*, was also involved. The UBI organised speaker meetings and arranged a stream of pro-White Paper publications, beginning with Sir John Thompson's *The White Paper*. Hoare assured the Viceroy, Lord Willingdon, that they were leaving nothing to chance between the first and second readings of the India Bill and that the UBI was 'going on with its campaign'.[79]

However, the most important deficiency of Churchill's press campaign owed little to India or even Churchill *per se*. The essential problem was that Churchill was associating in his campaign with the popular press at a time when its leading proprietors, Rothermere and Beaverbrook, were already engaged in a bitter feud with Baldwin and the Conservative leadership. Their motives were mixed, often personal, and not relevant to this chapter. What is important is that they shared a contempt for Baldwin's leadership and wished to displace him – possibly in favour of Beaverbrook himself. In 1929 they agreed to use as their pretext the demand for an imperial customs area – what Beaverbrook called Empire Free Trade – in which the bonds of empire would be strengthened and British industry encouraged by the erection of a tariff on non-empire goods. A national campaign to this end was launched which, in 1930, was taken one step further with the formation of a United Empire Party to fight by-elections against Conservative candidates.

This campaign, running parallel to the fight over Indian reform, caused Churchill great difficulties. He did not approve of its goal of a tariff barrier around the Empire, which he believed would 'hand over

South America to the Yanks, split the Empire for ever, and shatter the Conservative party into smithereens'.[80] Nor did he approve of the formation of a rival party and the policy of running candidates against Conservatives who opposed tariff reform. But most important was the fact that the antics of the press barons actually consolidated Baldwin's position. Rank-and-file Tories hated the vulgar populism of the 'gutter press', and when to this was added the ultimate Tory crime of disloyalty to party, the result was a rejection of Rothermere and Beaverbrook's pretensions to power. However unpopular Baldwin may have been within the Conservative Party, most Conservatives were not prepared to be seen moving against him at the behest of some plutocratic press lords. As Beaverbrook came to recognise, the 'hostility of the Tory party to Rothermere and myself' means that anything 'we curse...however wrong and distasteful', is guaranteed to win the blessings of the 'rank and file'.[81]

Beaverbrook might take mischievous pleasure from this state of affairs, but for Churchill it was deeply problematic. Rothermere was his chief backer, yet his association with the *Mail* was also his greatest liability for it meant that he was implicated in the press baron's fierce struggle with Baldwin. 'Up till now,' observed his friend Freddie Guest in 1932, 'you have been regarded as either a *Daily Mail* or a *Daily Express* spearhead to punch the National Government and perhaps more particularly to punch Mr Baldwin.'[82] Surely, by his willingness to work with men like Rothermere and Beaverbrook, who wished to overthrow Baldwin, he was only confirming that his motivation was not to save India but to boost his career.

All this may have been acceptable if Rothermere and Beaverbrook had achieved their ends. But Baldwin, with his instinctive grasp of Conservative sensibilities, was able to turn the flank of his opponents and fight them on the ground, not of policy or leadership, but of the ethics of newspapermen aspiring to manipulate the political process. He selected, as the occasion of his counter-attack, the St George's by-election in 1931, where the Conservative candidate was facing stiff opposition from an Empire Free Trader and anti-Indian reformer, Sir Ernest Petter. At the Queen's Hall on 17 March he made one of the most important speeches of his career. The issue, Baldwin declared, was not who should lead the Tory Party or what should be its policy. The question was where should power lie – with the Conservative Party and parliament or with the 'engines of propaganda' conducted by Rothermere and Beaverbrook, which pursued their ends with falsehoods and misrepresentations, and aimed at 'power without responsibility – the prerogative of the harlot through the ages'? It was a stroke of genius. By raising the principle of press intervention he hit many birds with one stone: he won the loyalty of conventional Conservatives, who had always resented the boastful conduct of bumptious press men; he deflected criticism away from his own conduct to the principles of political legitimacy; he divided the press, with most editors keen to disassociate their papers from 'harlot' rivals; he punctured the pretensions of the self-regarding press lords (causing Beaverbrook to abandon his campaign); and he discredited Churchill's chief outlet and, by association, his campaign in general. From this blow Churchill's India campaign never really recovered. From an offensive that could possibly carry him to the premiership it became an exercise in diehard resistance, with all the marks of thwarted ambition and bloody-minded attachment to obsolete cause.

Why, ultimately, did Churchill's campaign yield such minimal results? The fundamental issue was one of credibility. Churchill quite simply was not trusted. His political career as a Conservative who turned Liberal then Conservative, his role in granting independence to Southern Ireland, his denunciation of Dyer in the 1919 Jallianwallah Bagh debates and his transparent desire for office, all failed to convince the bulk of Conservative MPs and party members that his opposition to Indian reform was motivated by a genuine concern for British interests rather than a wish to advance his career. 'His voice', commented Beaverbrook, 'lacks that note of sincerity for which the country looks.'[83] His press campaign could not overcome this basic deficiency. Quite the contrary: by bringing him into close contact with the irascible Rothermere and the Yellow Press, it exacerbated it. By the end, even IDL colleagues such as Lord Salisbury were coming to regard Churchill as a liability. To quote Beaverbrook again:

> The weakness in this Indian issue is that Winston Churchill is making it his ladder for the moment. Churchill has the habit of breaking the rungs of any ladder he puts his foot on.[84]

Conclusion

The press occupied a pivotal position in the political drama of 1929 to 1935. It was seen, simultaneously, as a means by which Churchill could advance his career and an issue through which Baldwin could save his. In the event it was the latter who prevailed in the sense that Churchill did not forward his career – rather it went backwards; he did not defeat the Indian reform proposals and the strategy of conciliating nationalist forces they represented; and Baldwin was able to scapegoat the press barons and rehabilitate his standing within the Conservative Party. Yet it does not follow that Churchill's press campaign was a complete failure. He and his colleagues had raised the profile of the Indian issue from its usual doldrums and kept up sustained pressure on the Government. Most important, press coverage in Britain impacted negatively upon opinion in India – a matter of ultimately decisive importance given that the whole point of the Irwin Declaration and subsequent reforms was to persuade Indians that they had gained more than they in reality had. This battle for the Indian mind was lost by the Government: Congress was not appeased, the moderates made little headway and the princes stayed out of the projected Federation. Thus, while the battle against the reforms was lost in Britain, it was won in India, where it truly mattered. Several factors were at work here. But Churchill's campaign and deployment of the press played a part and for this reason: at least these were not, for Churchill, wholly wasted years.

Notes

1. Quoted in K. Middlemas and J. Barnes, *Baldwin: A Biography* (London: Weidenfeld and Nicolson, 1969), p. 541.
2. Quoted in J. Charmley, *Churchill: the End of Glory* (London: BCA, 1993), p. 258.
3. Hoare to Willingdon 10 March 1935, ibid., p. 1112.
4. A. Clark, *The Tories: The Conservatives and the Nation State 1922–1997* (London: Weidenfeld and Nicolson, 1998); Middlemas and Barnes, *Baldwin*, p. 580.
5. C. Bridge, *Holding India to the Empire: The British Conservative Party and the 1935 Constitution* (London: Oriental University Press, 1986), p. 61.
6. Churchill to Clementine Churchill, 27 August 1929, *CCV*, p. 61.
7. Hoare to Irwin, 13 November 1929, ibid., p. 111.
8. Churchill to A. Bailey, 27 August 1930, Churchill Papers (CP), Char 2/69.
9. Churchill to Clementine Churchill, 26 February 1931, *CCV*, pp. 280–3.
10. Rothermere to Churchill, 31 January 1931, CP.
11. Churchill to Baldwin, 24 September 1930, ibid., p. 90.
12. Quoted in Bridge, *Holding India*, p. 62.
13. Churchill, Speech at the Carlton Club, 25 May 1932, *CCV*, p. 435.
14. Churchill to H. A. Gwynne, 1 May 1933, ibid., p. 589.
15. See Bridge, *Holding India*.
16. Mira Slade, Memorandum, *CCV*, p. 919.
17. Churchill to Irwin, 24 March 1931, CP, Char 2/180A.
18. Churchill to Sir Mark Hunter, 9 January 1931, CP, Char 2/180A.
19. Charmley, *Churchill*, pp. 20–1.
20. Churchill, speech at the Newspaper Press Fund Dinner, 29 April 1931, in Rhodes-James (ed.), *Speeches*, p. 5024.

21. H. Sidebotham to Churchill, 16 December 1932, *CCV*, p. 506.
22. K. Young, *Churchill and Beaverbrook: A Study in Friendship and Politics* (London: Eyre and Spottiswoode, 1966), p. 94.
23. For this, see P. Anderson, 'Patriotism under Pressure: Lord Rothermere and British Foreign Policy', in G. Peele and C. Cook (eds), *The Politics of Reappraisal 1918–1939* (London: Macmillan, 1975).
24. Rothermere to Churchill, 3 February 1931, CP, Char 2/180A.
25. Rothermere to Churchill, 29 January 1931, ibid.
26. Rothermere to Churchill, February 1931, ibid.
27. Churchill to R. Churchill, February 1931, *CCV*.
28. *Daily Mail*, 5 November 1929.
29. Churchill to Rothermere, 3 February 1931, *CCV*, p. 259.
30. Churchill to Rothermere, 3 May 1933, ibid., p. 592.
31. Churchill to Rothermere, 3 February 1931, ibid., pp. 258–9.
32. Hoare to Lord Brabourne, 4 March 1935, ibid., p. 1100.
33. Middlemas and Barnes, *Baldwin*, p. 560.
34. *Bristol Evening World* 3 February 1931.
35. *Derby Daily Telegraph*, 2 February 1931; 5 February 1931.
36. *Newcastle Evening World*, 6 February 1931.
37. Churchill to Clementine Churchill, 26 February 1931, *CCV*, p. 281.
38. Rothermere to Churchill, 31 January 1931, CP, Char 2/190.
39. Harold Nicholson's Diary, 23 January 1930, *CCV*, p. 137.
40. A. Chisholm and M. Davie, *Lord Beaverbrook: A Life* (New York: Alfred Knopf, 1993), p. 292.
41. S. Koss, *The Rise and Fall of the Political Press in Britain* (London: Fontana Press, 1990 edition), p. 905.
42. Quoted in A. J. P. Taylor, *Beaverbrook* (London: Hamish Hamilton, 1972), p. 337.
43. Churchill to Hunter, 4 and 9 January 1931, CP, Char 2/180A.
44. Hunter to Churchill, 10 January 1931, ibid.
45. Churchill to E. Harmsworth, 12 January 1931, ibid.
46. Churchill to Rothermere, 3 February 1931, ibid.
47. Rothermere to Churchill, 3 February 1931, ibid.
48. Hunter to Churchill, 16 February 1931, ibid.
49. Gilbert, *Prophet of Truth*, p. 512.
50. Ibid., p. 514.
51. Hoare to Sir George Stanley, 10 May 1934, *CCV*, p. 788.
52. *The Times*, 14 June 1934.
53. C. Kaul, *Reporting the Raj: The British Press and India 1880–1922* (Manchester: Manchester University Press, 2003).
54. E. Russell to P. Donner, 18 July 1934, *CCV*, p. 829.
55. Churchill, speech before West Essex Conservative Association, 23 February 1931, in Rhodes-James (ed.), *Speeches*, p. 4985.
56. Gilbert, *Prophet of Truth*, p. 369.
57. J. Bhagwanlal Durkal to Churchill, 9 December 1934, CP, Char 2/225.
58. Earl Halifax, *Fulness of Days* (Collins, London, 1957), p. 123.
59. Rao to Gwynne, 15 September 1934, ibid., Char 2/225.
60. Hoare to Willingdon, 1 March 1935, *CCV*, pp. 1092–3.
61. Churchill to Clementine Churchill, 2 March 1935, ibid., p. 1097.

62. Bridge, *Holding India*, p. 151.
63. B. Bracken to Churchill, 22 August 1931, *CCV*, p. 350.
64. Linlithgow to Churchill, 1 May 1933; Churchill to Linlithgow, 2 May 1933, ibid., pp. 589–91.
65. Hoare to Willingdon, 19 May 1933, ibid., p. 604.
66. Gwynne to Churchill, 4 April 1933, CP, Char 2/193.
67. Dawson to Baldwin, 6 May 1933, *CCV*, p. 594.
68. Bridge, *Holding India*, p. 28.
69. G. Dawson to Irwin, 5 March 1931, *CCV*, p. 291.
70. Ibid., p. 292.
71. C. Coote, *Editorial: The Memoirs of Colin Coote* (London: Eyre and Spottiswode, 1965), p. 162.
72. Cf. *The History of The Times*, Vol. IV, Part II 1912–48 (London: Times Publishing, 1952), pp. 869–70.
73. Koss, *Rise and Fall of Political Press*, pp. 518–19.
74. Middlemas and Barnes, *Baldwin*, pp. 592–3.
75. D. Ayerst, *Garvin of the Observer* (London: Croom Helm, 1985), p. 223.
76. V. Cazalet, Diary, 19 April 1933, *CCV*, p. 579.
77. Ibid., p. 124
78. Ibid., p. 481.
79. Hoare to Willingdon, 19 December 1934, *CCV*, p. 967.
80. Harold Nicholson Diary, 6 July 1930, ibid., p. 168.
81. Koss, *Rise and Fall of Political Press*, p. 888.
82. F. Guest to Churchill, 14 December 1932, CP, Char 2/184.
83. Taylor, *Beaverbrook*, p. 302.
84. Ibid., p. 327.

8
India, the Imperial Press Conferences and the Empire Press Union: The Diplomacy of News in the Politics of Empire, 1909–1946

Chandrika Kaul

The quinquennial Imperial Press Conferences, which began in London in June 1909, together with their progeny, the Empire Press Union (EPU), were indicative of a growing recognition by the press of its strategic position within the Empire. The Conference was the brainchild of the journalist Harry Brittain, later Conservative MP for Acton, and reflected an appreciation of the growing role of the press, not only within Britain, but in all parts of her far-flung Empire, and a conviction that it was desirable to bring into personal contact 'those who are charged with the conduct of the great organs of public opinion'.[1] A conference bringing together in the 'Mother Country' the press of the British Empire could only encourage 'inter-Empire knowledge and understanding'.[2] The idea was accorded a positive reception by the British press, with both Fleet Street and the major provincial papers sinking their differences and remembering 'only their community of interest'[3] – the welcoming reception being attended by around 600 media men representing all shades of political opinion. This was also reflected in the composition of the organising committee, which included, on the Liberal wing, the editors C. P. Scott of the *Manchester Guardian*, Alfred Spender of the *Westminster Gazette* and Robert Donald of the *Daily Chronicle*, while the Conservative press was represented by Lords Northcliffe, Burnham and Arthur Pearson, proprietors of the *Daily Mail, Daily Telegraph* and *Daily Express* respectively, and Arthur H. Gwynne, editor of the *Morning Post*. Emphasis was placed on the economic, military and social advances of the host country and extensive tours and lavish hospitality were an integral part of the proceedings, which lasted from 7 to 26 June. 'It was one continuous round of work, enlivened by festivities', reminisced the Indian delegate, Surendranath Banerjea.[4] In the process, representatives of the 'Fourth Estate' found themselves coming into close contact with military departments like the army and navy, the Houses of Parliament and town councils, as well as provincial and national newspaper associations, universities, industrialists and even the Royal Family. A list of the politicians who attended functions in connection with the First Conference attests to the status it enjoyed within governing circles: the Prime Minister Herbert Asquith, Sir Arthur Balfour, Lord Curzon, Earl Cromer, Viscount Grey, Viscount Haldane, Viscount Morley and the Earl of Rosebery. Subsequent conferences in the Dominions followed a similar template and were organised by the press and media institutions of the host country (often with substantial government logistical support), which issued a quota of invitations to the press of the Empire and undertook all the expenses.

To carry on the work of the Imperial Press Conference on a more regular basis, the EPU was established as a permanent organisation, with its headquarters in London and branches, or sections, throughout the Empire and Dominions. In the words of its First Chairman, Lord Burnham, it was set up to promote 'better understanding, mutual help, and common efficiency in the whole newspaper Press of our far-flung Commonwealth'.[5] Its governing body comprised a Council with nominated members from the sections according to a predetermined allocation of seats or votes. In 1922 the overseas sections consisted of:

> Commonwealth of Australia (including British New Guinea, Fiji, the British Islands of Polynesia and mandatory territory); Dominion of Canada; Dominion of Newfoundland; Empire of India and Ceylon; Straits Settlements, Federated Malay States, and Hong Kong and Far East; Dominion of New Zealand (including mandatory territory); Union of South Africa and Rhodesia; East Africa; West Africa; West Indies and British Guiana; such other country or group of countries within the British Commonwealth of Nations as the Council may approve.[6]

The Council had the power to elect as an Associate or Honorary Life Member 'any person who has rendered distinguished service to Empire journalism'.[7] Being a non-governmental organization, it was funded largely through patronage and donations from press magnates and media associations, as well as from annual membership subscriptions.

Members and associates resident in the UK paid the following rates in 1922:

> Proprietors of or representatives of Morning Newspapers £10, of Evening Newspapers £7, of Federations and Societies representing newspapers and periodicals including trade and technical journals and of news agencies £10, of London National weeklies and of trade and technical journals £5, of Provincial weeklies £3, Associates £3.[8]

The EPU helped to facilitate interaction between the journalists of the Empire, arrange for the convening of regular conferences, increase access to official and parliamentary news in London for overseas journalists, lobby vigorously to reduce press cable rates and raise the profile of a host of issues affecting the press, such as freedom of information, postal charges, wireless costs, broadcasting, intra-Empire air services, libel laws and censorship, as well matters of imperial interest like migration and empire security and trade.

Donald, chairing the Second Conference in Ottawa in 1920, claimed that the EPU was the 'chief organ' of pro-imperial 'propaganda' within the British Empire. Its influence 'extends far beyond the newspapers which it represents, into the remotest corners of the Dominions, Colonies and dependencies'. In spreading information about the 'Mother Country' it had, claimed Donald, 'helped to mould and guide public opinion in all parts of the Empire'.[9] Such sentiments were predicated on a firm and continuing belief on the part of the organising committee and EPU office-holders in the British imperial enterprise in the context of the inter-war years.

This was well illustrated a decade later by the passion informing the inaugural speech of the proprietor of *The Times* and Unionist MP John Jacob Astor, on taking over the chairmanship of the EPU:

> I am told that the word 'Empire' is out of fashion. With us, the Empire is not a fashion, but a faith, and our faith is quite undiminished.... The strength and solidarity of our Commonwealth of Nations rests upon public feeling and upon the functions of this body to organise public opinion throughout the Empire for the common good in the true British fashion of independence, and interdependence.[10]

Illustration 2   The Hon. Major John Jacob Astor, chairman of the EPU.

India and the EPU

At the centre of this British imperial system was India. The strategic and economic importance of India to the Empire is well known. Yet India also occupied a correspondingly important position within the Empire's media and communication system. As discussed in *Reporting the Raj*, leading British national papers, and of course Reuters, maintained correspondents and bureaux in the subcontinent, and India figured prominently in the London press.[11] But India had also taken up the idea of the newspaper with alacrity: by 1905 over 1,500 newspapers and periodicals were being published annually in English and the vernaculars, and a thriving journalism culture was widespread access in the subcontinent. India, then, for reasons of strategy, politics and the dynamics of the press itself, had a strong *prima facie* case to be represented at the Imperial Press Conferences. Yet it was also, unlike the Dominions, an evidently dependent colony and one whose relationship with Britain and the rest of the Empire was being tested by the increasingly vociferous, and mass, demands for self-government – demands which were themselves advanced through the medium of a partisan Indian nationalist press. India's engagement with the Conferences and the EPU was therefore charged with political significance from the start.

The focus of this chapter is on the three Conferences held in London during 1909, 1930 and 1946, as well as wider aspects of Indian involvement with the EPU. The key issues for analysis include: the nature and context of India's participation; the relationship between India's journalistic representation and the politics of imperial government; the significance of India's participation; and the consequences, for the press and also politically, of Indian involvement.

The strategic importance of India

The Empire's telegraph and cable system had India as a focal point. Indeed, India had provided the major impetus to the pioneering developments in underwater cable technology which were initiated in the early nineteenth century in Calcutta on the River Hugli. In addition, key routes to other imperial centres passed through India and Ceylon. Thus, for instance, the cable route connecting Britain to Singapore and Hong Kong proceeded via Madras and southern India, and then carried on to connect with Australia. Any issues relating to the price and availability of cable services within the Empire as a whole necessarily involved the subcontinent. A similarly pivotal role was apparent with the advent of air travel in the twentieth century. The first imperial airmail service in 1929 linked London to Karachi, and by 1930 was continuing to Delhi. By the 1940s, the route was appropriately termed the 'Tiger' and took 27 hours for a one-way flight. The earliest air routes to Australia followed the chain across the subcontinent to Calcutta and Rangoon. Yet, perhaps most significant was India's symbolic importance. It was the most populous part of the Empire and home to substantial economic interests. It had a thriving and active journalistic tradition conducted primarily in English. Indian coverage was increasingly seen as important to leading metropolitan papers – it was prestigious, it attracted the services of foremost journalists and it was widely seen as an example of the press's imperial service. Quite simply, India had to be included if the Conferences were to represent legitimately an imperial information community.

The EPU Council had, accordingly, welcomed Indian participation from the beginning. In his inaugural speech at the First Conference, Lord Rosebery was at pains to stress the need for the EPU to instruct the British democracy 'as to the right method of governing and guiding that ancient civiliation of India'.[12] Further, the principle of press equality within the Empire was early acknowledged. While feting a group of visiting Indian journalists during the First World War,[13] Burnham claimed that the EPU represented an important stage in the growth, not only of the press but also of the British Commonwealth. To the sound of cheers he declared: 'The Empire Press Union knew no distinction of race, religion, or colour. It embraced within its folds newspapers of all opinions.'[14]

The nature of Indian involvement

Although the EPU was formed to encourage the sharing of information within the Empire, it quite quickly became a forum for the articulation of Dominion and colonial media interests. What were the Indian interests and how effectively were they represented within the Conference framework?

The size of the India, Burma and Ceylon contingent at the Conferences varied between seven and twelve per conference. For example in 1909, there were seven representatives, who were, in the words of the leader of the delegation Stanley Reed, 'a happy family...fortified by the trumpet voice of Surendranath Bannerji'.[15] Reed was editor of the conservative *Times of India*, a widely respected Anglo-Indian daily which nevertheless took a spirited independent stance on issues of imperial politics and economy as well as the activities of opposition parties, like the Indian National Congress and the Muslim League. Viceroys like Curzon and Linlithgow held it in high esteem, claiming it served a critical public in India. Reed returned to Britain in the inter-war years, was elected a Conservative MP, spoke frequently on Indian issues in Parliament and continued to represent India on the EPU Council in London. In the 1940s, his successor, Frank Low, was to play a similar role *vis-à-vis* the EPU, as well as being the chief India correspondent of the London *Times*. Both were knighted for their services to journalism. Others at the First Conference included Everard Digby of the *Indian News*, G. M. Chesney from the *Pioneer*, A. E. Lawson of the *Madras Mail*,

F. Crosbie Roles representing the *Times of Ceylon*, and J. Stuart of the *Rangoon Gazette*.

Until the 1930s, the India section was drawn predominantly from British journalists working on the large, Anglo-Indian press. Several of these journalists represented the conservative and pro-government newspapers, such as the *Pioneer*, the *Madras Mail*, the *Englishman*, the *Civil and Military Gazette* and the *Fauji Akhbar*. As the *Pioneer* remarked, 'An Anglo-Indian journalist is an Englishman first and a journalist afterwards'.[16] Yet there were also prominent delegates from the more independent and critical wing of Anglo-Indian journalism. Arthur Moore, chairman of the Indian EPU in the inter-war years, was editor of the Calcutta daily the *Statesman*, a Liberal newspaper long noted for its outspoken critique of official policies, 'standing far in advance politically both of established Imperial authority and of the bulk of local British opinion'.[17] Its founder-proprietor Robert Knight had been unsparing in his denunciation of official policies regarding, for instance, frontier policy or the famine of 1877, and was among the British sympathisers who in 1885 had helped found the Indian National Congress. His successors followed in his footsteps, while at the same time making the *Statesman* a commercial success with a large circulation among Indians and joint publication in Calcutta and Delhi. William C. Wordsworth, senior assistant editor of the paper, and another Conference delegate, was an Oxford-educated Fellow of Calcutta University, president of Presidency College and member of Council of the Bengal Sanskrit Association.

Although their involvement was at first limited, we witness over the period 1909–46 the emergence of a distinct Indian presence, a presence that, quite significantly, also reflected journalistic traditions critical of British rule. In 1909, this was represented by the impressive figure of Banerjea, an English-educated former Indian Civil Service man. Besides being a moderate politician and erstwhile President of the Congress, he was also proprietor-editor of the *Bengalee*, an influential nationalist weekly. At the Conference in 1930, it was K. C. Roy, a member of the Legislative Assembly and representative of the Associated Press of India (API), who was the sole Indian delegate. The API news agency served effectively two masters – its Indian clientele and the Government of India, with which it maintained good relations and which helped subsidise its operations. Officials were keen to continue with this system as it provided them with an avenue to gauge Indian sensibilities, despite the fact that the API was regularly critical of British policy and gave prominence to the activities of nationalists.

By the time of the 1946 Conference, however, there was a marked rise in the numbers of Indians as well as a shift in the complexion of the papers they represented, with 50 per cent of the contingent now comprising representatives of radical nationalist papers. The Indian press, both English and vernacular, was a prominent vehicle for the articulation of national, anti-imperial sentiment and provided a rare forum for political participation under the Raj. The 1946 delegation quite clearly reflected the changing balance of political forces in India and the growing self-confidence among the indigenous press. Now there were only two British members: the leader of the delegation, Frank Low, and A. A. Hayles of the *Madras Mail*. The Indians comprised Devadas Gandhi, the son of Mahatama Gandhi, representing the *Hindustan Times* (Delhi), Tushar Kanti Ghosh of the *Amrita Bazaar Patrika* (Calcutta and Allahabad), S. Sadanand of the *Free Press Journal* (Bombay), and H. A. J. Hulugalle, editor of the *Ceylon Observer*, the only English-language daily on the island. At only half an anna a copy, the *Free Press Journal* (established in 1930) was an inexpensive nationalist paper which featured telegrams of the now defunct nationalist news agency, *Free Press of India*, which had been 'the clearing house of news of a nationalist view' from all parts of India, Burma and London.[18] With the promulgation of the 1930 Press Ordinance, there was fear that publication of its telegrams would lead to proceedings against it (as indeed had been the case with a number of newspapers and journals), leading to its amalgamation with the *Journal*. Tushar Kanti Ghosh was editor of the *Amrita Bazaar Patrika*, a flagship Indian newspaper founded in 1868 by his father, Sisir Kumar Ghosh, who had been an ardent nationalist and religious reformer.

Tushar Kanti was himself also president of the All India Newspaper Editors' Conference. Under him the *Patrika* began simultaneous publication in Calcutta and Allahabad (being the only Indian-owned paper to do so), as well as employing a chartered plane for early distribution. The *Patrika* had realised the commercial potential for an Indian-run paper, without giving up its ardent nationalist position.

An equally striking shift in the character of Indian representation occurred in the membership of the EPU Council in London, which by 1946 consisted predominantly of metropolitan-based Indian journalists with an anti-imperial track record. Such a presence was facilitated by the fact that the number of Indian papers with London offices grew rapidly, from eight in 1901 to 47 in 1914 and 63 by 1921. In 1945–46 these included, for instance, T. Basu and S. Kabadi, representing the *Patrika, Hindustan Standard* and *Bombay Chronicle*, K. S. Shelvankar of the *Hindu*, D. V. Talmankar and J. M. Deb of the *Kesari* and H. S. L. Polak and D. Anand

Illustration 3   Tushar Kanti Ghosh, editor of the *Amrita Bazaar Patrika*.

of the *Leader*. The *Chronicle*'s opposition credentials had been well displayed, for instance, in its vociferous attacks on the official handling of the Amritsar massacre in 1919, which had led to the deportation of its editor, B. G. Horniman, from India – the only instance in the twentieth century when the Raj had felt compelled to expel a British subject.[19] The *Kesari*, founded by the nationalist Bal Gangadhar Tilak, was the voice of traditional Marathi opposition in the west of the country, and was matched in its nationalist fervour by the English-language *Leader*, established in the United Provinces in the north. The South African Polak was a vociferous champion of the Indian cause and a devoted follower of Gandhi. The *Hindu*, from its inception, had established institutional links with the Indian National Congress and provincial politics in the Madras Presidency in the south. The *Hindustan Times* was established by the Akali political intelligentsia of the Punjab as a vehicle for the articulation of national as well as specific regional grievances. Thus, in terms of national profile and geographic spread at least, the subcontinent was well represented in the Conference/EPU forum.

From humble beginnings before the Great War, by the 1930s and 1940s an equally significant shift was taking place in the composition of the Indian branch of the EPU. As Moore noted, in the early years, 'Outside India not much was known of newspapers in India other than those owned by British proprietors.'[20] The early Indian EPU was constituted entirely from these papers. At that stage it had no office or secretary and no funds of its own, for while members paid a small subscription, this was to the central organisation in London. It functioned mainly as a sounding board for the five yearly conferences. In 1930, however, 'the desirability of an Indian attending the Conference was strongly felt', and by arrangement through Reuters, Roy, as noted above, attended the Conference. The Indian section functioned primarily from the Calcutta office of the *Statesman*, whose successive editors, Alfred Watson and Arthur Moore, also served as chairmen of the EPU. They advised its members on a range of issues including copyright, cable and wireless communications, and airmail. Importantly, they also made representations to the Government of India and, through the London Council, to the British Government on other more general issues, such as broadcast timings, advertisers' broadcasts and newsprint duties. In 1936, the section made, in the words of Moore, 'our most notable advance', with the decision to publish a monthly 'India, Burma and Ceylon News-Bulletin' for distribution throughout the Empire. Both British-owned and Indian newspapers and correspondents contributed to this monthly for over three years until the outbreak of the Second World War. Though publication was resumed on a quarterly basis in 1940, it was intermittent during these years due to spiralling costs and newsprint shortage, and while regular publication was intended to be resumed after the war, Independence in 1947 put pay to this venture.

Thus though dominated by Anglo-Indian papers in the initial years, the Indian EPU slowly began to attract Indian nationalist papers, bridging the traditional chasm between these two press establishments. Of great importance was the realisation on the part of leading Anglo-Indian journalists of the need to involve the growing Indian press establishment for the EPU to be truly representative. This was exemplified by the strenuous endeavours of Moore, who was able to entice such leading opposition papers as the *Hindu, Kesari, Amrita Bazaar Patrika, Leader, Hindustan Times, Tribune, Bombay Chronicle* and *Bombay Free Press Journal* into the EPU fold. He was also convinced that the Indian EPU needed a resident Indian journalist as its chairman and was instrumental in ensuring that his successor in 1943 was K. Shrinivasan, editor of the *Hindu*. This was 'a matter of great satisfaction to me personally', wrote

Moore. 'A free association of this kind seems to me likely to prove of the utmost value in the great years of decision which lies immediately ahead.'[21] Significantly, then, the EPU, despite the initial imperial ethos of its founders, evolved in practice to accommodate the increasingly vociferous Indian perspective. Nationalist papers, far from breaking to form a new institution, elected to remain within the EPU fold – a development symptomatic of the continuities which characterised the transfer of power in India more generally.

Thus, the Imperial Conferences and the EPU allowed the worlds of Fleet Street, Anglo-India and the Indian press to coalesce to an unprecedented degree and the consequent networks of information, opinion and influence impacted one on the other. Given the nature of the EPU as a forum for the advocacy of communication interests it was important that the Indian delegations at the Conferences be able to speak with one voice, and this was indeed often the case. However, the relationship between India and the EPU was always complex. First, as a dependent empire, Indian interests did not always coincide with British imperial interests, and this became more frequently the case as larger numbers of Indian-nationalist journalists participated in the organisation. Second, India's representation and interests could never be considered independently of the politics of information control and nationalist agitation within the subcontinent.

The politics of Indian involvement

The Conferences and EPU were founded on the idea of a shared culture of free news reporting across the Empire. Of course, all governments restrict access to information in various ways. But in the self-governing Dominions press freedom was vigorously upheld and, if restrictions were undertaken on a limited scale, they were the result of autonomous government policy. The difference in India was that the Government was part of the imperial system of control, which explicitly restricted access to information and the reporting of news. There was, therefore, a significant problematic in India's relationship to the Conferences/EPU which increased over time.

The London Conferences coincided with important political developments *vis-à-vis* India which heightened her visibility on the international stage. The 1909 Conference convened in the wake of the inauguration of the Morley-Minto Reforms, which appeared to concede more constitutional responsibility to Indians. Yet the following years also witnessed severe press restrictions, including a revised and more powerful Press

Act (1910) and the Seditious Meetings Act. This pattern was to repeat itself in 1930, when the Conference was held in the aftermath of the launch of a successful civil disobedience campaign led by Gandhi and the Indian National Congress, which was also accompanied by widespread publicity in the Western press. The Government of India, in an attempt to limit the damage from adverse propaganda, instituted the 1931 Indian Press Emergency Powers Act and other punitive measures. Ironically, this repression was juxtaposed with detailed negotiations to institute a federal system for India with marked increase in power-sharing – efforts eventually embodied in the Government of India Act 1935. Finally, in 1946, the Conference met in the dying days of the Raj when the prospect of British withdrawal was imminent.

With regard to the relationship between the Conferences, EPU and the Government of India there were two main variables at work. First, the Government *within* India had a long-established tradition of controlling the press through punitive legislation embodied in successive Press Acts, censorship and emergency powers. Not surprisingly it was sceptical of the value of Indian press participation in the EPU and did nothing to facilitate the development of the EPU structure within India. The Conference discussions and motions as well as EPU-sponsored initiatives relating to the freedom of the press were politically sensitive issues within India. This was revealed by the official response to proposals to hold a Conference in the subcontinent in 1936–37. In London, the India Office had made concerted efforts, particularly from the First World War onwards, to organise official machinery to cater for imperial propaganda and publicity in the West and in the United States. The main institutional innovation in 1921 had been the creation of an Information Office.[22] The information officer in the 1930s was Hugh MacGregor, who had formerly covered India for *The Times*. MacGregor was keen to exploit the potential for India publicity that such an event would create. As he astutely noted, 'The occasion would offer an altogether exceptional opportunity of interesting the world in India and so improving India world relations commercially as well as politically.' It would, further, have 'a political value by placing India in the same level as the other Dominions and also by more closely associating the Indian press with British standards'.[23]

The perspective in New Delhi, however, was quite the reverse. A. H. Joyce in the Information Department was keen to distance the Government: the Indian-owned press was ill-organised, he argued, and there was 'no guarantee of co-operation with the English-owned section... The Indian-owned press might use the occasion of such a conference for a renewed attack on the Press Act.' The Director of Public Information, I. M. Stephens, was even more forthright in voicing the Government's fears: the 'chief risk' was that the Conference delegates 'would be nobbled by extreme nationalists here, who might be expected to enlarge upon the difference between the amount of freedom enjoyed by the press in India and in other parts of the Empire'.[24] In other words, while London was more concerned with the global image of India, the Government in India was preoccupied by the risks of nationalist agitation.

Second, the India Office had, from the beginning, taken an interest in the Conferences, with the Liberal Secretary of State John Morley addressing its first meeting. At the 1930 Conference, which met against a backdrop of intensified mass agitation in the subcontinent, the Labour Secretary of State for India, William Wedgwood Benn, was moved to take an overtly political stance in the inaugural speech. Indians, he claimed, 'rightly ask – that for Indians, as for inhabitants of all other parts of the Empire, there should be the recognition of equality of status, and nothing is more helpful in consolidating the points of union between the different parts of the Empire than an acknowledgement of this equal standing'.[25] While upholding the British insistence on maintaining law and order, he reiterated the underlying 'fundamental principle' of the British: 'in India, as in the Dominions, the object of Government is to direct its policy in the interests of its own people... Indian issues are decided in the Indian interest.'[26] 'Force' was no remedy for the Indian situation, and Wedgwood Benn argued, instead, that 'the real sanction of Government is public opinion and it must depend upon that great force in India as it does elsewhere'.[27]

This political balancing act was complicated by the extent and character of the nationalist movement. As is apparent, the growth of anti-colonial agitation in India posed a basic challenge to the EPU model of imperial co-operation in the sphere of media and communication. The campaigns of the Congress raised the question of the future of India within the Empire and highlighted the oppression and censorship operated by the Raj. This challenge to the ideals of imperial unity found a forum within the Conferences/EPU. 1930 and 1946 witnessed a growing number of Indian journalists critical of British hegemony and increasingly articulating a nationalist perspective. Significantly, the EPU took up the issue of censorship in India and the use of coercive powers by the state at its first annual conference in 1936 (an innovation aimed at supplementing the five yearly meetings), coming, as it did, on the heels of the Government of India Act 1935 and increasing disquiet in nationalist and press circles at the frequent recourse to emergency powers exercised by the Indian Government from the early 1930s. The EPU president, Astor, liaised directly with the Secretary of State, the Marquess of Zetland, and the Conference passed a resolution that any government censorship 'should be in accord with definite, reasonable and known rules, and that as little room as possible should be left for interpretation by individual officials', and argued that 'the most useful form of censorship in any circumstances is free co-operation between officials and newspaper Press...'.[28] (Astor took a keen personal interest in the subcontinent, an interest stimulated by his experience as ADC to the Viceroy from 1911 to 1914 and reinforced by a visit to India in 1936.) Similarly, at its fourth annual conference in London in 1939, the EPU resolution, after hearing reports from India and the Dominions, noted its 'alarm' at the number and gravity of instances of encroachment by legislation and otherwise on the freedom of the press, and 'affirm[ed] this freedom to be an inseparable part of the liberty of the individual and vital to the survival of Government by the people'.[29] However, a potential clash between the EPU and the Indian Government over this issue was nullified by the outbreak of the Second World War, which transformed the environment of reporting across the Empire.

Outcomes and significance of Indian involvement

Illustration 4   The Conference at work, 1946.

Indian participation gave the EPU legitimacy and helped to convey an impression of imperial solidarity in the press sphere. As the veteran journalist and editor of the *Review of Reviews*, W. T. Stead, noted in 1909, the presence of Banerjea 'saved the assembly from being a mere sectional representation of the white-skinned minority of the subjects of the King';[30] it also helped raise the profile of the news media within the Empire. The Conferences more specifically provided a rare forum for Indian journalists to raise concerns and grievances on an international stage. For instance, Banerjea argued that times were critical for India, with the spread of political violence and the inauguration of the Morley-Minto constitutional reforms. It was, therefore, of great importance that the British understood the situation within India, and this in turn implied the ready accessibility of cheap news. 'If we had cheap cablegrams, the false, misleading telegrams regarding Indian affairs would not be sent to this country. They would be wired back for confirmation and correction.'[31] Roy took a more direct stance in 1930, utilising the favourable opening provided by the Secretary of State's address to argue that: 'all we want is fairness and equality of treatment'.[32] Roy also maintained that while Reuters supplied the bulk of foreign news to India, 'There is no gainsaying the fact that the news we receive is of a pro-British character.' He demanded that a fuller and more comprehensive service covering other parts of Asia and the Commonwealth be supplied to India.[33]

The thorny issues of press freedom, government censorship and political control were raised more forcibly at the 1946 Conference. Ghosh, speaking as editor of one of the most politically influential Indian papers, and supported by S. Sadanand of the *Free Press Journal*, contended that they 'enjoyed hardly any freedom of the Press during any crisis'.[34] Citing the example of the Bengal famine of 1943, Ghosh claimed that newspapers had anticipated what was coming and warned the Government on a daily basis of the impending peril: 'The Government did not heed us but passed an order telling us we must not refer to the food situation at all. We were even asked not to refer to this order, thus preventing us from continuing our editorials on the food situation. So we had to stop writing these editorials and we had no means of telling our readers why.'[35] He also claimed that messages which had been passed by censors in Britain were routinely held up in India. In addition, distortions of Indian events were allowed to go unchallenged because they were not allowed to be contradicted by the Indian press. His demand for a strong resolution urging freedom of the press in India was adopted by the Conference.

In terms of the EPU impact on Indian journalism, the importance of communication systems for the promotion of imperial solidarity was emphasised as a key objective of the EPU.[36] There was widespread support for rate reductions due to the 'paramount importance' of reducing the cost and improving the telegraph links between the various parts of the Empire.[37] From the start, the Indian delegation played a prominent role in this process and with considerable success. In 1909, it led the way in demanding cheaper cable communications, and formulated the official resolution adopted by the Conference. Reed argued that the conditions under which India was 'kept in telegraphic touch with the outer world can only be described as grotesque'.[38] The press rate to India was the same as that charged to Australia, which was double the distance from Britain. The price ratio between press and private cablegrams to India at between 9 and 10 pence and two pence was one and a half times the cost in any other part of the British Empire:

> In every other part of the world news is considered of so much public importance that it is entitled to a specially cheap rate...[but] the picture of India, represented in large sections of the English Press, sometimes cannot be recognised as the land we live in...that is not only an enormous inconvenience, but a serious Imperial menace... May I ask how you are going to guide the [British] democracy on the affairs of India at one shilling a word?[39]

The case for cheaper communications was articulated within the imperial idiom – i.e. while the reduction in costs would undoubtedly facilitate access by the press to overseas news, it was imperative for a stronger empire. While common action for imperial defence was indeed crucial, 'we place freer telegraphic action first because it is absolutely essential to the success of every scheme for common Imperial action. You cannot build up a durable Empire on ignorance'.[40]

These Conferences and the EPU undoubtedly played a leading role in maintaining pressure on the authorities. Between 1909 and 1923 the standard press rate for India fell by 67 per cent. The penny-per-word cable rate was finally achieved under the impact of the Second World War. In addition, the benefits from the communication revolution via the air mail were actively promoted by the EPU and accrued early to the Indian Empire. In 1930 the Indian airmail carried about 5 per cent of letter mail between Britain and India in both directions. The press made appreciable use of this medium. As the Postmaster General, H. B. Lees-Smith, remarked: 'Indian newspapers are now able to print about a week earlier a good deal of material for which they used to have to wait for the ordinary post.'[41] Such developments made possible both more efficient news collection and an expansion of reporting from the periphery and Indian reporting from Europe.

As we have noted, the Conferences and EPU also helped build bridges between the Indian and Anglo-Indian press establishments. It was believed by the founders of the EPU that the organisation might, in conjunction with the British press, act directly to raise the standard of the Indian press reporting. 'There was room on our side', declared Burnham, 'for giving facilities for a news service to the Indian Press of India, which would enable them to form and educate the great masses of people of all nations and all classes who make up the Indian Empire.'[42] Such formalised and rather patronising arrangements were not implemented, and the importance of the EPU remained, rather, a sphere of social interaction where Indians could mix on terms of equality with their British and Dominion counterparts. Conception of India's equality within the Empire were, indeed, realised at a relatively early stage in the press sphere. This reflected, to an extent, the speed at which Indian journalism matured and became important politically and commercially.

These occasions also gave Indian journalists a rare opportunity to participate on an international stage and to form networks and connections with the wider press community. They were invited to parliamentary and press receptions, attended civic functions and were feted by a variety of political and social organisations and pressure groups, thus helping to raise the profile and prestige of Indian journalism. Banerjea, for example, spoke at various meetings organised by Sir William Wedderburn and the India group in Parliament and British sympathisers like A. O. Hume, Ramsay Macdonald, Sir Henry Cotton, Mr Mackarness, Sir Charles Dilke and W. T. Stead as well as Indian student associations, and the committee of Indian residents presided over by Mr Parekh, who was also involved with *India*, the propaganda journal of the Indian National Congress. Stead wrote in the *Review of Reviews* praising Banerjea's 'lucid intelligence, his marvellous command of English, and his passionate devotion to his native land'.[43] In Manchester, Banerjea had an interview with C. P. Scott, and addressed a public meeting in the Town Hall on behalf of the Conference delegates. In more concrete terms the EPU also helped facilitate the working of the Indian journalist in London, who gained easier and more sustained access to Parliament for India-related events, as well as to the India Office through collaboration with the information officer and the Information Department. As Roy commented at the conclusion of the 1930 Conference, his initial scepticism at the benefits of his participation were misplaced: 'The Conference . . . is a great success, and an eye-opener to me. I am proud to have entered the Conference and to have learned many lessons from many senior journalists.'[44] At this level of individual personal interaction at least, Indian participation was felt to be have been of some value. Yet the case of Roy indicates the wider political issue at stake – namely, the advantage of integrating imperial critics. This, we have seen, the EPU achieved remarkably smoothly in the case of India – the 1946 Conference being less a swan-song for the organisation and more a stage in its transfiguration into the Commonwealth Press Union, which occurred in 1950.

Symbolically, the most important aspect of India's engagement with the Conferences and EPU was that it represented an example of Indians taking their place alongside the representatives of Britain and the Dominions. As such, the EPU prefigured, by several decades, the realisation of India's equality of status as a self-governing state within what was to become known as the Commonwealth of Nations. The logic of the ideal of a free press and an uninhibited interchange of information within the Empire dictated this state of affairs from the beginning. However much the EPU might have seen itself as a partner in the project of imperial consolidation, its character as an autonomous press body meant that it inevitably reproduced, this time on an empire-wide scale, the reciprocal yet problematic relationship between government and the Fourth Estate.

Concluding remarks

India represented a test case for the Conferences and EPU. Founded on an Anglo-Saxon model of liberal press freedom, a model it believed was of universal applicability, the EPU could not but encompass India. Yet, although India was accorded the status of membership of the imperial press family, it remained the awkward relation. For whatever its nominal status, India was a subject colony dominated by British business interests. It was characterised by a stringent press censorship on the one hand, and a growing anti-Empire journalistic and press culture on the other. India's membership was thus a potential source of tension and embarrassment and threatened, always, to raise profounder questions about the nature of imperial rule and political freedoms. However, on the whole these tensions were successfully managed before 1946 and the Conferences and EPU did achieve a certain political profile. However, the basis for this management changed over time. At first, India was primarily represented by British journalists operating within the subcontinent.

The lone Indian in 1909 was a former ICS man and model moderate. Yet, as the forces of Indian politics stirred, as the press expanded and as the British themselves recognised that India must, at some stage, move to self-government, more and radical Indian journalists were represented. With them came objections to censorship and press restrictions within India. The EPU could not discount these criticisms, running as they did counter to its very ideal of a free imperial press union. The leadership of the EPU, especially its chairman, Astor, decided to take up such grievances, which resulted in motions critical of press censorship being passed, and protests lodged with the India Office. Whether this gulf between press and official attitudes would have steadily widened over time, or whether Indian representatives would have broken away from the EPU, is difficult to say as the blizzard of war transfigured the imperial landscape. By 1946 the old Empire was receding, India stood on the threshold of independence, and the EPU was itself shortly to transform into the Commonwealth Press Union, meeting as such for the 1961 Conference, the first in the subcontinent and jointly hosted by India and Pakistan. The almost 40 years between the 1909 and the 1946 London conferences saw a radical redefinition of Britain's relationship with India. These changes were played out on a minor key within the EPU, but, in their own way, they not only reflected the shifting political and economic climate of empire but pointed the way to a relationship, not of rulers and ruled, but of equals.

Acknowledgements

The author would like to acknowledge the financial support she has received for this research project from the British Academy and the Carnegie trust; and technical assistance from Luke Moodley.

Notes

1. Sir Harry Brittain, *Pilgrims and Pioneers* (London, Hutchinson & Co., 1946), p. 200.
2. Ibid., p. 197.
3. W. T. Stead, 'The Editors of the Empire at Home', *Contemporary Review* (London, July 1909), p. 46
4. S. Banerjea, *A Nation in Making* (London: Oxford University Press, 1927), p. 261.
5. Lord Burnham, *India and the Empire*, Institute of Commonwealth Studies London, ICS/121/6/3.
6. *The Empire Press Union Memorandum and Articles of Association and Bye-Laws* (London: Newspaper World Press, 1922), p. 17.

7. Ibid., p. 13.
8. Ibid., p. 14.
9. 'News of Greater Britain', pamphlet, p. 2, ICS/121/6/4.
10. EPU monthly newsletter no. 3, June–July 1929, ICS/121/2/2.
11. Chandrika Kaul, *Reporting the Raj, The British Press and India, c. 1880–1922* (Manchester: Manchester University Press, 2003).
12. As cited in the *Daily Mail*, 7 June 1909.
13. See Kaul, *Reporting the Raj*, Chapter 5.
14. Burnham, *India and the Empire*.
15. S. Reed, *The India I Knew* (London: Odhams Press 1957), p. 39.
16. *Pioneer*, 24 December 1897.
17. I. Stephens, *Monsoon Morning* (London: Benn 1966), p. vi.
18. M. Barns, *The Indian Press* (London, George Allen & Unwin, 1940), p. 374.
19. Kaul, *Reporting the Raj*, Chapter 8.
20. Letter from Moore to the Indian EPU members, 11 February 1943, L/I/1/88, India Office Records, British Library, London.
21. Ibid.
22. Kaul, *Reporting the Raj*, pp. 135–58.
23. H. MacGregor to A. H. Joyce, 15 December 1936, Home Poll, 156/36, National Archives of India (NAI).
24. I. M. Stephens to H. Macgregor, 11 March 1936, Home Poll, 1936, 156/36, NAI.
25. Proceedings 1930 Conference, p. 21, ICS/121/3/3/3.
26. Ibid., pp. 23–4.
27. Ibid.
28. J. J. Astor to Marquess of Zetland, 9 July 1936, Home Poll 161/36, NAI.
29. EPU monthly newsletter, July 1939, ICS 121/2/2.
30. Stead, 'The Editors', p. 48.
31. Ibid., p. 151.
32. Proceedings 1930, p. 26.
33. Ibid., pp. 172–3.
34. Proceedings 1946 Conference, pp. 55–6.
35. Ibid.
36. C. Woodhead, *Press and Empire* (Durban, 1909), p. 11; *Whitaker's Almanac* (London, 1910), pp. 692–3.
37. Ibid.
38. Reed, *India*, p. 41. T. H. Hardman, *A Parliament of the Press* (London: EPU 1909), pp. 40–1.
39. Ibid., pp. 140–1.
40. Reed, *India*, p. 40.
41. Proceedings 1930, p. 29.
42. Burnham, *India and the Empire*.
43. Cited in Banerjea, *Nation in Making*, p. 281.
44. Proceedings 1930, p. 321.

9

'Business as Usual'? British Newsreel Coverage of Indian Independence and Partition, 1947–1948

Philip Woods

Illustration 5   The Mountbattens wave farewell to British troops leaving Bombay, 17 August 1947.

It is surprising that in all the attention that historians have given to India's independence and to the partition of the subcontinent in 1947, little, if any, notice has been paid to the newsreel coverage of those momentous events.[1] Yet the newsreels, perhaps more than any other mass medium, have defined the way in which we see the first major decolonisation of the twentieth century. The images of Nehru speaking to the Indian Constituent Assembly, his famous 'Tryst with Destiny' speech, at midnight on 14 August 1947, and the joyous celebrations of 15 August in New Delhi are etched on the mind.[2] As well as the celebrations, we remember the tragic scenes of mass migration, the miles of pitiful refugees clinging to the few possessions they could carry, and the trains in which so many would-be migrants would be slaughtered in the movement of over ten million refugees across the new boundaries between India and Pakistan. These are all images that come to us from the newsreels. Indeed, immediately after the Second World War when cinema attendance in Britain was at its height, and in the years before television news established itself, the newsreels were a major source by which the public received its images of current events. In addition to the British market, the newsreels had a worldwide audience, largest of which was in the US, but even in India itself these newsreels would have been shown, at least in the city cinemas which took western films.[3]

Five newsreel companies, all subsidiaries of feature film companies, screened their products regularly in British cinemas. Three of the newsreels were ultimately controlled by American companies: Paramount News, Pathé News and Movietone News; the other two, Gaumont-British News and Universal News, were controlled by the British film magnate J. Arthur Rank. For the most part, the newsreel trade recognised the need to concentrate on entertainment and avoid controversy, propaganda or intrusive editorial comment – anything that might offend their audiences. The pre-war newsreels were therefore considered anodyne, covering lightweight events such as sports, society weddings, fashion shows and ship launches.[4] Although this chapter focuses on newsreel coverage of a serious international issue, it has to be remembered that international subject matter generally formed only a minor part of total newsreel footage. The time devoted to international stories was usually short and the fast pace of the narrative meant that it would have been difficult for audiences to analyse in depth the content or bias, even if they were giving it their full attention, which seems unlikely. As a result of the Second World War and its aftermath, newsreel coverage had become more serious and more realistic, but overall the newsreels lacked a clear commitment to addressing the 'burning political and social issues of the day'.[5]

Two editions of newsreels were shown in the cinemas each week. This meant that the newsreels reached a large proportion of the British public, as it was calculated that one third of the population went to the cinema at least once a week, and all cinemas showed newsreels under wartime arrangements which continued until 1950.[6] Though the newsreels had been a popular part of the cinema programme before the Second World War, there is evidence that they lost favour in the early years of the war when the news was almost inevitably grim and the commentaries were more blatantly propagandist. However, they seemed to regain popularity as the tide of war turned and this continued after the war as more competition between the newsreels was restored.[7]

Of the five newsreel companies, only two had originally allocated cameramen to film the independence celebrations in India or Pakistan. Paramount and Movietone used two local Indian cameramen, or 'stringers' as they were known, the brothers Ved and Mohan Parkash, respectively. Louis Mountbatten, a very publicity-conscious Viceroy, was concerned at this low level of newsreel coverage for such an important event and through his press attaché, Alan Campbell-Johnson, asked the Newsreel Association to provide a rota cameraman, who would provide footage to all the newsreel companies. The rota system had started in the Second World War as a means of conserving film stock and cameramen while securing the greatest possible coverage of different fields of war. Although effective, it tended to lead to a certain sameness in the different newsreels, and was not popular with all of the newsreel companies.[8] However, it was widely used in peacetime for filming royal events, and was the only means through which Mountbatten could secure widespread coverage of the events in India at short notice.

On 14 July 1947, just one month before the date set for independence, the Newsreel Association offered the services of the Gaumont-British cameraman John Turner, who had a distinguished record filming with the Royal Navy and in South-East Asia during the Second World War.[9] Mountbatten agreed to give Turner all facilities both in Delhi and on tour, but was adamant that he was not to be attached to his staff – he was 'to publicise India and not the Viceroy'.[10] Later in the month the Newsreel Association agreed to send Peter Lennox of Hearst Metrotone (MGM) as rota cameraman to cover Pakistan, where Mohammed Ali Jinnah and not Mountbatten was to be Governor-General.[11]

Turner finally arrived in India on 10 August 1947, with only four days to prepare for the momentous transfer of power. He was very reliant on co-operation from the men on the spot, the Parkash brothers and Max Desfor, stills photographer with the Associated Press news agency.[12] In addition, there was an American cameraman, Robert Hecox, who was working for MGM's *Metro News*. It was from these western newsreel firms that the world would receive its images of India and Pakistan's independence celebrations. It was unfortunate that there was no Indian newsreel to cover the events: the official Indian newsreel, *Indian News Parade*, which had been set up in the war, had been closed at the end of 1946 because Indian politicians mistrusted its background in providing imperial propaganda. It was not until 1949 that a newsreel was re-established by the Films Division of the Ministry of Information and Broadcasting.[13] However, there were documentary teams in Delhi filming the celebrations from the Indian perspective, most notably that of Dr P. V. Pathy, the pioneer of Indian newsreel and documentary.[14]

In many ways, the story of the pictorial representation of Indian independence revolves around the last Viceroy, Lord Mountbatten, and his wife, Edwina. This was partly because their roles were so important – this was the first time that Britain had voluntarily transferred power to a major colonial possession, and it was important to establish the right image to the world. Independence was not to be seen as a humiliating withdrawal or scuttle, but rather the fulfilment of Britain's mission in India, famously envisaged by Thomas Macaulay in the nineteenth century. The fact that India was being partitioned was to be played down as the unfortunate but unavoidable consequence of deep-seated cultural differences between the Hindu and Muslim communities. The more positive aspect was that Mountbatten was able to persuade both India and Pakistan to remain within the British Commonwealth, which meant that it was much easier to emphasise elements of continuity of relations between the metropolis and the new Dominions.

Another reason that the Mountbattens were so central to the news-reel view of Indian independence was that they were such a glamorous and photogenic couple. Louis Mountbatten had the double attraction of being a cousin to King George VI and a handsome figure, with the presence of a film star. There is no doubt that this increased the interest of the newsreels, especially the American companies.[15] Edwina Mount-batten was glamorous in her own right, a wealthy heiress and socialite of the flapper era who had turned into a social activist and carer in the Second World War and its aftermath.[16] Finally, it should be noted that Mountbatten was much more aware of the importance of the modern media, especially cinema, than his predecessors – he was a film enthu-siast and had his own cinema in the Viceroy's House in New Delhi as well as at Broadlands, his Hampshire home. Whereas the previous Viceroy, General Wavell, had been suspicious of the media and felt uncomfortable in front of the press, Mountbatten positively revelled in the limelight. Right from the start, he made sure the historic events of his Viceroyalty were fully covered by the media. His inauguration as Viceroy was opened up to photographers and newsreel cameramen for the first time. Special facilities were also given to the newsreels for the 3 June announcement of partition of the subcontinent.[17]

The most important events that the newsreel covered were the transfers of power which took place in Karachi on 14 August and in New Delhi on 14 and 15 August. These events were, by their nature, joint productions of the successor states and the imperial power. The two sides took rather different views of how independence should be celebrated. India and Pakistan saw these events as a triumph of their long struggles for national independence and were, therefore, keen to present to the world an image of their national identity in the celebrations.[18] As an example of this, Jim Masselos has shown how, in the rituals of the assumption of power in the Indian Constituent Assembly in New Delhi at 11 pm on 14 August, the indigenous idiom was dominant:

> They were the singing of songs associated with the freedom movement, each standing as quasi-anthems; the presentation of the new National Flag, not by suitably bedecked military men, but symbolically by the women of India; and finally the sounding not of brass wind instruments beloved in British ceremonies but conch shells which related the event to Indian tradition.[19]

The British Paramount newsreel editor cut these scenes in the Constituent Assembly, which were so important to the Indian image of independence. Instead, he started coverage of the Indian celebrations the next morning with the swearing-in of Lord Mountbatten as first Governor-General of India in the Durbar Hall of what was now called Government House.[20]

On 15 August, the first full day of independence, the style of events followed rather more in the British ceremonial tradition, but with many of the old hierarchies and social separation between rulers and ruled abandoned, either deliberately or by force of events. However, it is worth remembering that both the colonial power and the new nations made compromises in these ceremonials to avoid causing offence. A good example is the agreement reached by Mountbatten and Nehru that there should be no events in which the Union Flag was lowered.[21] One of the major themes which the newsreels emphasised was the goodwill shown to the British as they departed. Mountbatten, who had already shown sympathy to nationalist movements in South-East Asia while Commander of SEAC, had made a point of being filmed with

Indian nationalist leaders, thus preparing British audiences for the transfer of power. A good example is his early meeting with Mahatma Gandhi, who in the war years had been imprisoned and subjected to a newsreel blackout. Now, Gandhi was feted by the Mountbattens and, in what has become a famous image, is shown leaning on Edwina Mountbatten's shoulder in a clear image of reconciliation.[22] Gandhi's role as a 'one-man peace force' during the process of partition is recorded by the newsreels in an entirely sympathetic manner.[23]

The newsreels of the celebrations in Karachi on 14 August are, in contrast to the coverage of events in New Delhi, much more formal. This was partly a reflection of the more sober mood of celebrations in the new capital of Pakistan, which had a large Hindu population.[24] However, the media coverage of events was on a smaller scale in Pakistan than in India, and this may have been partly due to weaker media management.[25] Metro News (MGM), which provided the rota cameraman Peter Lennox, pulled out of its British operations in early December 1947, and although Gaumont-British took over his employment, only two other newsreel companies were interested in using his material.[26] Whatever the case, there does seem to be an imbalance in the coverage of the two new Dominions. But with most cameramen based in New Delhi, it was more difficult to film in Pakistan. This however was to have an important impact on the coverage of the disputes between India and Pakistan, especially over Kashmir.

In contrast to the mood of the newsreel coverage of independence celebrations in Pakistan, the material from India was positively euphoric. The technical difficulties of covering the events was great – from the dark interiors of the Constituent Assembly at midnight to the movement of the main protagonists between different parts of Delhi amidst crowds that numbered in hundreds of thousands. Turner was very reliant on the Parkash brothers and their Indian colleagues to show him the different vantage points and to share the filming from various locations. Early in the morning he filmed establishing shots which were designed to set the context for a western audience: pictures of New Delhi's English road names contrasted with the street scenes of India, the roadside barber and cows roaming the streets.[27]

Turner did manage to film Indian politicians and the Mountbattens arriving at the Council House, but the crowd overwhelmed his rostrum so that he could not film the Mountbattens returning to Government House. In the afternoon, Turner filmed them 'in mufti' playing with Indian children at the Roshnara Gardens and handing out sweets, in accordance with Indian custom. This was not the 'impromptu' visit that

Mountbatten claimed it to be, but a photo-opportunity provided by Mountbatten's press attaché to show the more informal side of the celebrations.[28]

In the late afternoon, Mountbatten returned to uniform in order to unfurl the Indian flag in Prince's Park, near to Victory Arch. The crowds were much larger than expected and he could not reach the flag-pole. Even Campbell-Johnson could not have arranged the rainbow that appeared in the sky as the flag rose, and anyway, the newsreels were strictly in black and white.[29] The films were rushed back to London and were shown in cinemas in London on 21 August and in Delhi on 24 August. Mountbatten was apparently impressed with the coverage – 'the excellence of the photography and the competence of the commentary'.[30] Cynics might think that well he might be, such was the centrality of the Mountbattens in the presentation of India's first day as an independent nation. The Indian Prime Minister even had to be rescued from the crowds by Mountbatten's coach. *Filmindia's* comments on the Indian documentary covering these events might well have applied to the western newsreel: it complained that it looked like 'a second marriage procession of the two Mountbattens with thousands of Indians clamouring like monkeys for a ring-side view'.[31] Be that as it may, the newsreel undoubtedly captured the joy of the occasion and the anarchically democratic nature of the birth of the Indian nation.

The next day, 16 August, Nehru addressed a crowd of more than a quarter of a million from the ramparts of the Red Fort in Delhi. This was the precursor to the annual celebrations of Independence Day in Delhi on 15 August. The choice of the site in Old Delhi, the historic capital of the Mughal Empire and the site of the recent Indian National Army trials, was symbolically important for India, but was not covered by the British newsreels. Instead, they showed Mountbatten in Bombay the next day bidding farewell to the first British troops to leave India. Pathé viewers were promised that 'the rest of the British troops will leave India as soon as possible'.[32]

The real stage management of independence had taken place behind the scenes, however. The partition of India, which had been formulated by the distinguished British judge Sir Cyril Radcliffe, inevitably exacerbated communal tensions in the disputed regions of Punjab and Bengal. Mountbatten decided not to spoil the celebrations and to delay publication of the partition boundaries until after independence. British newsreels had already highlighted Hindu–Muslim–Sikh differences as one of the most important problems the new Dominions faced.[33] As the violence flared it was presented as the culmination of centuries of communal differences in the subcontinent. Pathé helpfully pointed out that 'more Indians have been killed in the past month than in all the riots during the past 50 years . . . the East was wistfully saying goodbye to the reign of the British'.[34]

If the commentaries could be facile, the pictures that the cameramen sent home were extraordinary. Even in a post-war world used to large numbers of refugees, the images of the many miles of refugee columns moving across flooded areas of northern India, were poignant in the extreme. Cameramen like John Turner faced the dilemma of how far they could venture from Delhi into the Punjab, where the worst of the massacres were taking place. There were the problems of finding transport, maintaining personal security and being able to get film back to London quickly from inaccessible regions. Turner's one foray across the border into West Pakistan proved fruitless for these reasons. His best film, along with that of Ved Parkash, came from Delhi itself and also from following in the footsteps of Lady Mountbatten in her role in charge of relief operations for the refugees. The Indian Government had asked Mountbatten to chair the Emergency Committee overseeing the crisis. Mountbatten used his wife's wartime experience as Superintendent-in-Chief of the St John's Ambulance Nursing Division and with prisoners of war in South-East Asia, to good effect. Countess Mountbatten chaired the United Council for Relief and Welfare and showed tremendous energy and organisational skill. The newsreels picture her touring the camps and showing direct and physical sympathy with the plight of the refugees.[35]

Delhi, especially Old Delhi, had always had a very large Muslim population. Many fled to Pakistan after Partition, but substantial numbers remained and were joined by refugees seeking safety. In September, Hindu and Sikh attacks on Muslims had forced thousands of Muslims to seek refuge in camps throughout the city. The conditions in the camp were appalling, and there was a tendency to treat the Muslim camps as the responsibility of the Pakistan Government. The newsreels filmed the distribution of rations in one of the camps – they amounted to only one quarter of a chapatti per person – and also refugees queuing for the one standpipe that served thousands of people. Gandhi visited the camps on 13 September and this did lead to some improvements as the Indian Government took responsibility and moved some of the refugees to camps with better facilities. It also persuaded some Muslims that it was safe to return to their homes.[36]

The newsreel cameramen in these situations were perforce journalists as well as cameramen. They had to research the background of the topics, choose locations, shoot the film, write up 'dope-sheet' summaries of what they had shot, including quite detailed stories around their film. Ultimately though, once they had sent their film back to London by air, marked 'Useless if Delayed', the film was entirely in the hands of the newsreel editor who could rearrange the pictures and the story as he saw fit. Commentary and music would be added that could influence the mood and message of the story. Inevitably, the cameramen knew that some of the shots they recorded were too gruesome to be shown in cinemas. The public, however, had become increasingly inured to seeing corpses on screen, and the film of the Delhi riots included quite a few of these, examples perhaps, in the words of the British Paramount commentary, of 'An orgy of Oriental savagery...'.[37]

Covering news events involves a measure of luck as well as judgement. In addition to covering crisis stories, cameramen filmed a good deal of stock footage that their companies could use in the future. For John Turner, this meant travelling to different parts of India, covering diverse items such as a festival in Assam or street scenes in Calcutta.[38] Back in Delhi, he managed to film Mahatma Gandhi at his residence, Birla House, shortly after he had called off his fast to improve Hindu–Muslim relations. Despite the fact that there had been an abortive bomb attack on 20 January 1948, the newsreel cameramen were caught unprepared when Gandhi was assassinated ten days later at a prayer meeting by Nathuram Godse, a Hindu extremist.[39] Turner was in a Delhi cinema at the time, his raw film stock exhausted, so that he had stopped attending at Birla House.[40] Ved Parkash did an outstanding job finding pieces of film stock from friends in Delhi in time for the funeral which, according to Hindu custom, would take place the next day.[41] The resulting newsreel is quite remarkable, considering the uncertainties about film stock, its quantity and quality, the inordinate length (four and a half miles) of the funeral procession and the vast, emotional crowd which pressed in on the cortège. Ved Parkash filmed the early part of the procession as it left Birla House and Turner took over along the route and at the pyre itself. What strikes one today is the way that Mountbatten had again stamped his imprint on this deeply Indian occasion. It was, in effect a military-style funeral, with a naval bodyguard, Mountbatten himself resplendent in naval uniform, and a military vehicle to carry the body of a man who was profoundly pacifist.

It is generally recognised that one of Mountbatten's great achievements as Viceroy had been to cajole most of India's 565 princely states into acceding to one of the new Dominions. The few exceptions, especially the states of Hyderabad and Kashmir, were to cause difficulties in relations between India and Pakistan, nearly leading to outright war. Both crises involved delays caused by the fact that the ruler of each state was of a different religion from the majority of his subjects. Mountbatten's role, and indeed the British position overall, was an awkward one. Mountbatten had been asked to chair a Joint Defence Council by both Dominions, but he was Governor-General of only one of them. British officers continued in commanding roles in both the Indian and Pakistan armies and, indeed, Field-Marshal Auchinleck remained Supreme Commander of the two armies until this arrangement ended on 30 November.

The newsreels had always paid a disproportionate amount of attention to the Indian princely states. This was partly because they were so picturesque, exotic and therefore interesting to western viewers. Kashmir had a particular interest because it was traditionally a place of retreat for the British from the scorching summer heat on the plains of northern India, a sort of Switzerland in the foothills of the Himalayas. Now, in the autumn of 1948, it was a place of great strategic importance to both India and Pakistan. In late October, Pathan tribesmen, aided by Pakistan, made incursions into Kashmir which triggered a hasty accession of the Maharajah to India and to a remarkably rapid airlift of Indian troops to repel the invaders. When British Paramount News first dealt with the Kashmir crisis it is interesting that they included it with coverage of the Dussehra festival in the states of Gwalior and Jaipur. The film showed the two rulers seated on their thrones and receiving the homage of their subjects, apparently oblivious to the threat posed by the Indian Government to their traditional authority and powers.[42] British Movietone News focused on the evacuation of British civilians by the RAF from Kashmir, whilst Universal News emphasised the attack on St Joseph's convent in Baramula by tribesmen.[43] Turner remarked that he had received no assistance from the Indian Government in taking his Kashmir film and that correspondents were not made welcome.[44] This is interesting as the newsreels covered the story very much from an Indian point of view. The tribesmen were shown on screen almost as wild men with long, dishevelled grey beards. In contrast, the Prime Minister of Kashmir, Sheikh Abdullah, who made himself available to journalists, was presented as tall, upright and heroic. His training of a Kashmir national militia was viewed sympathetically, as was the airlift of Sikh soldiers to repel the invaders. When Nehru returned to his native Kashmir to celebrate the country's independence in May 1948, the viewpoint was very sympathetic, and generally speaking, there was no recognition of Pakistan's claims.[45] This may well have been due to the lack of newsreel film from the Pakistan side, as stated earlier. However, a notable exception came from the American-owned news magazine *March of Time* and its cameraman-director, Peter Hopkinson.[46]

Hopkinson was filming separate *March of Time* films on India and Pakistan. He was able to reach Srinagar with the Indian troops in October, but more importantly he was able to take the last plane to Rawalpindi before the winter set in. From there he was able to join the Azad (Free) Kashmir troops who were under attack from Indian forces, and to film their leader, Sardar Ibrahim.[47] Hopkinson saw incontrovertible evidence that Pakistan had sent its soldiers clandestinely into Kashmir, but he felt that its case was a strong one and had not been put to the world. He believed that India was determined to destroy Pakistan and that the Kashmir crisis was about to lead to what he called 'the bloodiest civil war in history'.[48] Hopkinson, who came to be suspected of working for the Indian Government, was expelled from Kashmir and was lucky to be allowed to keep his film intact. He was distinctly left-wing in his politics and felt increasingly out of sympathy with his American employers, who were largely concerned with the Cold War allegiances of India and Pakistan.[49]

On 21 June 1948 Turner filmed his last assignment on his Indian mission, the tumultuous departure of Lord and Lady Mountbatten from India. This marked the end of a period of unusually prolonged interest in Indian political life shown by the British newsreels. As we have seen, the newsreels have their drawbacks as an historical source. Even when photographed by Indian cameramen, such as the Parkash brothers, the newsreels as finally presented saw India principally through western eyes. Until June 1948, the casual British cinema-goer might almost have assumed from watching the newsreels that the Raj was still in place. True, the last British troops were shown leaving India at the end of February 1948, but the ceremonial of British rule still remained in use and the Mountbattens were always in pride of place. For this sense of continuity, Mountbatten was responsible, as we have seen. The newsreels were fascinated with the unusual and exotic aspects of India: princely India took up a good deal of attention. Despite attempts to contrast the old and the new India, there was still a tendency to fall back on the former. Because of the restricted function of the newsreels within the cinema industry and the limited time available for these international stories, it was perhaps inevitable that they should resort to the shorthand of stereotype. However, newsreels remain a valuable record of empire and of the way in which decolonisation was made understandable and perhaps palatable to British audiences. The raw material provided by the cameramen/journalists in the form of film and supporting documentation is too valuable a source for historians to ignore.

Acknowledgements

My particular thanks are to John Turner, who kindly answered my queries by correspondence and agreed to be interviewed by me on videotape at the BUFVC. Others who helped by correspondence are T. Mathra, Homai Vyarawalla, Narain Thapa and Leo Enticknap. I am very grateful to the excellent archivists who help film researchers, notably Luke McKernan and Linda Kaye at the BUFVC, Paul Sargent and Kay Gladstone at the Imperial War Museum, staff at the BFI, ITN Archives, BBC Written Archives, Caversham, the Hartley Library at the University of Southampton and the British Library, Oriental and India Office Collections.

Notes

1. There is now far less reason for historians to fight shy of newsreel as a source because much of the footage and its accompanying documentation is available on the internet. The main place to search for material is the excellent newsreel database maintained by the British Universities Film and Video Council (BUFVC), www.bufvc.ac.uk, which leads the researcher into documentary and film sources, the latter via the Pathé website, www.britishpathe.com
2. British Movietone News showed film of Nehru in front of a microphone in the Constituent Assembly, Issue no. 50A, 'The New Dominions', 21 August 1947, but the speech comes from another source as the newsreels filmed mute and added soundtrack later. This soundtrack was usually commentary or music; it was difficult to synchronise speech afterwards.
3. An informed, though necessarily speculative, contemporary estimate of the worldwide audience for newsreels was that every week 215 million people watched them, one in ten of the population: P. Baechlin and M. Muller-Strauss, *Newsreels Across the World* (Paris: UNESCO, 1952), p. 9.
4. Arts Enquiry, *The Factual Film* (London: Oxford University Press, 1947), p. 140.
5. G. Clement Cave (managing editor of Pathé News), 'Newsreels Must Find a New Policy', *Penguin Film Review*, 7, 1948; L. Enticknap, 'The Non-Fiction Film in Britain, 1945–51', unpublished PhD diss., University of Exeter, 1999, pp. 77–9, 82–3, 95.
6. P. Addison, *Now the War is Over: A Social History of Britain 1945–51* (London: BBC/Jonathan Cape, 1985), pp. 129–30.
7. N. Reeves, *The Power of Film Propaganda: Myth or Reality?* (London and New York: Cassell, 1999), pp. 162–4. Sydney Bernstein's cinema questionnaire (1946) found that 41 per cent of respondents found newsreels 'good', 49 per cent 'fair', 8 per cent 'poor', while 2 per cent were 'don't know'; cited in Enticknap, The Non-Fiction Film in Britain, 1945–51', pp. 88–9.

8. Paramount in particular disliked it: *Arts Enquiry*, p. 138.

9. Minutes of Newsreel Association of Great Britain and Ireland [NRA], British Film Institute [BFI], 14 July 1947, minute 2386; J. Turner, *Filming History: the Memoirs of John Turner, Newsreel Cameraman* (London: BUFVC, 2001). It appears that the influence of Commander Sir Arthur Jarratt, a friend of Mountbatten's, was important in reaching this agreement, see Campbell-Johnson to Mountbatten, 11 July 1947, MB1/E30, Mountbatten MSS, Hartley Library, University of Southampton.

10. Telegram, Brockman to Campbell-Johnson, 16 July 1947, no. 2003-S, Mountbatten, MSS EUR F200/114, British Library Oriental and India Office Collection [BLOIOC].

11. NRA, minute 2395, 31 July 1947.

12. Turner, *Filming History*, pp. 116–17.

13. See P. Woods, ' "Chappatis by Parachute": The Use of Newsreels in British Propaganda in India in the Second World War', *South Asia*, 23, 2 (December 2000), pp. 106–8.

14. J. Mohan, *Dr P. V. Pathy: Documentary Film-maker (1906–61)* (Pune: National Film Archive of India, 1972), p. 45.

15. See Baechlin and Muller-Strauss, *Newsreels across the World*, p.38 for the dominant role of royalty in stories about Britain in the American newsreels.

16. See J. Morgan, *Edwina Mountbatten: A Life of Her Own* (London: HarperCollins, 1991).

17. See A. Campbell-Johnson, *Mission with Mountbatten* (London: Robert Hale, 1951), p. 106; Ved Parkash's dope-sheet for British Paramount News, 12 June 1947, 'India Accepts the Plan', Reel 7, British Universities Newsreel Database [BUND], http://joseph.bufvc.ac.uk/BPN/040576/040576_d.pdf, in which it is shown that Mountbatten repeated parts of his speech for the newsreels so that it would synchronise with an All India Radio recording which would accompany the film back to London. In the end this part of the film was not used.

18. This is very well brought out in J. Masselos, 'The Magic Touch of Being Free: The Rituals of Independence on August 15', in *India: Creating a Modern Nation* (New Delhi: Sterling, 1990), pp. 37–53.

19. Ibid., p. 40.

20. Photo of shot list, British Paramount News, issue 1719, 21 August 1947, http://joseph.bufvc.ac.uk/BPN/040680/040680_s.pdf.

21. *Constitutional Relations Between Britain and India: The Transfer of Power, 1942–47*, vol. XII, 8 July–15 August 1947 (London: HMSO, 1983) [hereafter TOP] document 489, Viceroy's Personal Report no. 17, L/PO/6/123:ff. 245–63, para. 67.

22. See British Movietone News, issue 931A, 10 April 1947, 'Asiatics Peg Their Claim', showing meeting of 1 April 1947.

23. See, for instance, the typed commentary for British Paramount News, issue 1733, 9 October 1947, 'Gandhi, 78 Acclaimed by All' – though an apparently unconvinced editor has pencilled 'Ridiculous' in the margin of the commentary script, http://joseph.bufvc.ac.uk/BPN/040751/040751_c.pdf.

24. See despatch no. 5, Sir L. Grafftey-Smith, U.K. High Commissioner, Karachi, to Arthur Henderson, Minister of State, Commonwealth Relations Dept., 25 August 1947, L/PJ/10/136, BLOIOC.

25. Note the concern expressed by the BBC at the lateness of a published programme of events from Karachi and the impact this might have on the balance of their coverage, Mosley to Stephenson, 5 August 1947, India: Transfer of Power file, 1 March 1947 to February 1948, BBC Written Archives, Caversham Park.

26. These were British Movietone News and Universal News, NRA Minutes, BFI, Box 3, meeting 4 December 1947, item 2443.

27. Turner, *Filming History*, p. 118; the nationalistic film journal *Filmindia* complained that this material was patronising, presenting Indians as 'still a very primitive people'. *Filmindia*, 13, 10, October 1947, pp. 8–9. This seems over-sensitive and was clearly not Turner's intention. This scene-setting was typical shorthand used by newsreels and it is paralleled by Ved Parkash's pictures of Lahore with camel-carts, street vendors and such-like, which prefaced the Pakistan celebrations.

28. TOP, vol. XII, document 489, Viceroy's Personal Report no. 17, L/PO/6/123:ff 245-63, dated 16 August 1947, para. 66; Campbell-Johnson, *Mission with Mounbatten*, p. 160.

29. Remarkably, there is colour film showing this rainbow. It is in the Col. Frank Hodgkinson collection at the Imperial War Museum, London. It was used in the Carlton TV series *The British Empire in Colour (2002)*, episode 1. 'Tryst With Destiny'. Hodgkinson was ex-Indian Army and a keen amateur photographer. He was attached to Mountbatten's staff, L/MIL/14/1519, BLOIOC.

30. Turner, *Filming History*, p. 120.

31. *Filmindia*, 13, 10, October 1947, p. 7.

32. Commentary to issue 47/68, 25 August 1947, http://joseph.bufvc.ac.uk/Pathe/101936/101936_c.pdf.

33. Pathé, commentary to issue 47/66, 'India Takes Over', 18 August 1947, http://joseph.bufvc.ac.uk/Pathe/101926/101926_c.pdf.

34. Pathé commentary to issue 47/76, 'Peace – the Eleventh Hour', 22 September 1947, http://joseph.bufvc.ac.uk/Pathe/101983/101983_c.pdf.

35. For example, British Movietone News issue no. 953A of 11 September 1947. Modern audiences cannot help but notice the parallels with Diana, Princess of Wales.

36. See the dope-sheets for British Paramount News issue 1728, 22 September 1947, 'Delhi Riots Kill Thousands', http://joseph.bufvc.ac.uk/BPN/040727/040727_d.pdf; for details of the situation in Delhi, see G. Pandey, *Remembering Partition: Violence, Nationalism and History in India* (Cambridge: Cambridge University Press, 2001), chapter 6. Despite calls in *Filmindia* for stricter censorship of film of riots, the Government of India held firm to a policy of not placing restrictions on the access of photographers and journalists, *Filmindia*, 13, 12, December 1947, 7–9; Mountbatten Mss, Hartley Library, MB1/D20/7.

37. Ibid., http://joseph.bufvc.ac.uk/BPN/040727/040727_c.pdf.

38. Turner, *Filming History*, pp. 129–30.

39. Campbell-Johnson, *Mission with Mountbatten*, pp. 279–80. Remarkably two of the world's greatest photographers, Margaret Bourke-White and Henri Cartier-Bresson, were in Delhi at the time, both taking photos of the Mahatma for news magazines. See C. Cookman, 'Margaret Bourke-White

and Henri Cartier-Bresson: Gandhi's Funeral', *The History of Photography*, 22, 2 (Summer 1998), 199–209.

40. Turner *Filming History*, p. 130.
41. Ibid., pp. 131–2.
42. Issue 1740, 3 November 1947, 'India Despatch Shows Land of Ironic Contrast'. For the situation of the princely states, see I. Copland, *The Princes of India in the Endgame of Empire, 1917–1947* (Cambridge: Cambridge University Press, 1997).
43. Issue 962, 10 November 1947, 'British Civilians Evacuated from Kashmir'.
44. G-B. News cameraman's report dated 2 November 1947 with British Para- mount Newsreel no. 1744, 17 November 1947, http://joseph.bufvc.ac.uk/ BPN/040807/040807_d.pdf.
45. Although a reader in *Filmindia* complained of anti-Indian bias in a Gaumont-British commentary on Kashmir, *Filmindia* xiv, 5, May 1948, p. 67, col. 3.
46. News magazines such as *March of Time* or *This Modern Age* differed from newsreels in that they were made at less frequent intervals and often went into great depth on one issue. *March of Time* (MOT) was also well known for its outspoken commentaries and creative use of film material. See R. Fielding, *The March of Time, 1935–1951* (New York: Oxford University Press, 1978).
47. See P. Hopkinson, *Split Focus: An Involvement in Two Decades* (London: Rupert Hart-Davis, 1969), pp. 118–23.
48. Hopkinson to H. Maurice Lancaster, European Director MOT, 31 January 1948, Hopkinson Collection, BFI, Box 1, Notebook 3. MOT: India (2) 1947–49 correspondence.
49. *Split Focus*, p. 153; The *March of Time* Indian edition was heavily edited and released as 14th year no. 4, 'Asia's New Voice', 18 February 1949, whilst 'The Promise of Pakistan' appeared in the UK only, as 15th year no. 5.

10
Purity, Obscenity and the Making of an Imperial Censorship System

Deana Heath

> The tone of the Empire comes from you the authors of our land. If the tone is pure, the blood will go on pulsating through the whole world carrying with it purity and safety. If the stream of the blood is impure, nobody can tell the effect it will have right through our Empire.[1]

While the British Home Secretary William Joynson-Hicks was undoubtedly the most avid exponent of the purported effect of 'impure' literature on Britain's linguistic – and by extension racial and national – purity, he was by no means the first. By the late nineteenth century, community organisations and the state, as well as the newly emergent medical profession, had come to form a 'medico-moral alliance' in Britain which attempted to shift the focus away from viewing 'purity' (a term that nominally referred to the campaigns against prostitution, but was in fact applied to a wide range of moral and social crusades) as a moral question to regarding it as a medical and racial concern.[2] Whatever the immediate targets of the members of such an alliance, their larger goals were intimately connected with the preservation of the British 'race', nation and Empire. Attempts to regulate 'obscene' literature – that is, to 'juridif[y] those channels – differentiated by age, gender, class and culture – through which the literature of erotic formation circulates'[3] – thus became an aspect of the racial purity movement. 'Obscene' literature in the shape of new forms of print culture, such as sexology texts and naturalistic fiction (which not only deployed many of the techniques and literary tropes found in pornography but were readily available to a rapidly expanding mass readership), became regarded as 'a pathological agent invading bourgeois homes and schools', while the new, cheap and decidedly popular publications that had begun to mushroom in the 1880s, such as 'pornographic' postcards, mutoscopes, stereoscopes and advertisements for birth control products and aphrodisiacs, were deemed 'a threat to the procreative behaviour, well-being and public decency of the popular classes'.[4] The growth of such publications coincided with what Joss Marsh refers to as a 'mania for "Saxon" English' in Britain following the publication of the first volume of the *Oxford English Dictionary* which, in addition to spurring scholarly and popular interest in the English language, 'produced the rude and hardy Saxons as Englishhood's direct linguistic ancestors, fit progenitors of the master race' and thus 'held out the promise not only of a return to origins...but of racial purity'.[5] Since racial identity in Britain throughout the 1880s and up to the First World War continued to be regarded largely in cultural and historical terms rather than in terms of biology,[6] in threatening Britain's culture and civilisation, such 'obscenity' undermined the very basis of Britain's racial superiority.

'Degeneracy' in British culture not only translated into the degeneracy of the British 'race' and nation, but also undermined Britain's very justification – and, some critics feared, its very ability – to govern vast portions of the globe. As the MP and National Vigilance Association (NVA) member Samuel Smith declared in 1888, 'man becomes corrupted to the very core of his being' through exposure to obscene literature, which meant that 'Nations that abandon themselves to such practices slowly decline, and by an inevitable law of Providence are swept away by manlier and purer races'.[7] The only way to prevent such a calamity, according to Smith, was to purge the nation and Empire of obscene literature. This was, however, easier said than done. Although by the 1870s London had managed to rid itself of its dubious reputation as the 'smut capital of Europe', this had been achieved through driving the more professional pornographers to France, where they promptly drummed up a lively trade in obscene and erotic books, magazines and indecent postcards throughout both Britain and its Empire via the post.[8] The difficulty for moral reformers such as Smith in combating the trade was that the state was reluctant to serve as moral regulator of what Ian Hunter, David Saunders and Dugald Williamson refer to as the 'pornographic field'.[9] This was in part a product of the notion of the ideal state in Britain, which was conceived of until the Edwardian era largely as a limited one.[10] But it was also a product of the setback the Government had received in 1886 in its efforts to regulate the moral realm with the repeal, achieved by a massive campaign by feminists and social purity activists, of the Contagious Diseases Acts, following which legislation pertaining to immorality 'was seen to lie outside formal politics'.[11] But while the state may have desired to remain aloof from the task of moral censorship, by the 1880s such detachment was already, in fact, no longer possible. Not only had the governmentalisation of the social realm in Victorian Britain contained a heavy moral component, but the pressure exerted by moral reform organisations had secured the passage of a number of legislative enactments pertaining to obscenity.[12] The sweeping to power of purity activists in municipalities throughout Britain following the passage of the Local Governments Act in 1888 resulted in the further co-option of the state to the moral reform agenda,[13] the repercussions of which were felt not just in Britain, but throughout the whole Empire.

Creating an imperial censorship system

That the drive to regulate 'obscene' literature should become an imperial project was almost inevitable in light of the long-standing connections, ranging from popular fiction to children's books, between British literature and the Empire. The connection between imperialism and sexuality had also long been apparent, particularly the difficulties of policing the sexual behaviour of Britain's subjects throughout the Empire. By the 1880s there was a growing awareness, as Ronald Hyam reveals, that Britain 'did not merely sell cotton clothes to all the world: it also exported nude photographs'.[14] Purity activists such as Alfred Dyer and Josephine Butler, therefore, began turning their attention to the Empire, particularly to India (the former out of fear, apparently, that 'obscene photos would set off another mutiny in which all the white women would be ravaged'; and the latter with the aim of overturning the Contagious Diseases Acts in India).[15] The NVA, fearful that realistic novels such as translations of the works of Emile Zola were in India 'bought in tens of thousands, and were regarded as samples of European civilization',[16] likewise established a branch there and forged links with purity organisations throughout the Empire.[17]

Such activities reveal the extent to which the cultural interconnectedness of the Empire, facilitated through technological advancements such as the telegraph and the steamship, was growing in the late nineteenth century. But such interconnectedness was also aided through the activities of British publishers and booksellers, who in the 1870s began to make a concerted effort to expand their trade throughout the Empire, with Australia and India as their primary targets.[18] The imperial trade was cultivated through a number of means, such as colonial libraries, news agencies and fiction bureaux, and the establishment of publishers' branches and representatives in the colonies. Such an expansion needs to be considered partly in terms of what Luke Trainor refers to as a late nineteenth-century 'reorganization of the production of knowledge'.[19] But it also needs to be understood in the context of cultural imperialism, for beginning with the 'advance guard' John Murray (who established a colonial library in 1843 due to his fear that American publishers were infiltrating the Empire and damaging the loyalty of imperial subjects to the Queen), British publishers and booksellers undertook a concerted campaign to culturally re-colonise the Empire.[20] The impact of such a campaign was profound. In Australia, by the 1880s the largest imperial market for British books and periodicals, British imports (coupled with the establishment of British publishers' branches in Australia) destroyed the nascent publishing and independent bookselling industry which had begun to emerge there during the mid-nineteenth century, and by the end of the Second World War only a fraction of the books sold in Australia had originated there.[21] While the situation was not as dire in India, by the late nineteenth century Britain's second largest imperial literary market, by 1894 India was importing five million packages of books and newspapers a year from Britain, a figure that had reached an incredible twelve million packages by 1911.[22]

Although somewhat daunted by the scale of the imperial book and periodical trades, by the end of the nineteenth century the British Government had developed a *modus operandi* for regulating obscene publications throughout the Empire. Since publications emanating from Britain posed the danger of 'corrupting' Britain's colonial subjects, colonial and later dominion governments were to be 'assisted' in regulating the circulation of obscene publications within their own borders, particularly those that originated in Britain. But since the expanding cultural interconnectedness of the Empire meant that 'obscene' works from colonies such as India and Australia were making their way to Britain, the British Government also found itself having to undertake the task of protecting Britain from being rendered 'uncivil' through contamination by the obscene effluvium of its Empire.

For Britain's Australian and Indian colonies, the latter form of regulation was generally greeted with greater equanimity than the former, at least in the case of Australia. Thus when in 1913 the British Government requested the Australian Government to take action against William Chidley's *The Answer* (which aimed to rectify the incorrect manner in which, according to its author, mankind was having sex), the Australian Postmaster-General accordingly declared the book 'indecent, obscene and grossly offensive' and advocated that criminal proceedings be taken against its sender to prevent further copies reaching the United Kingdom.[23] The response of the Indian Government to such requests was rarely so agreeable. As the Director of the Indian Intelligence Branch noted in 1936, 'If H. M.'s Government would help us to keep out of India Communist literature printed in London then I think we should as a quid pro quo help them to keep out of England literature which they regard as offensive.' But 'Since they don't help us I see no reason why the Government of India should incur odium in this country by issuing what would be regarded as a puritanical notification.'[24]

'Assisting' colonies to regulate the trade in 'obscene' publications within their own borders was fraught with even greater tensions, particularly, again, in the case of India. By the early twentieth century the British Government had begun to attempt to overcome the appearance of excessive intervention in the governance of its colonies, at least in the moral realm, through couching such requests in the guise of an international moral crusade. It did so primarily through the aegis of the 1910 International Agreement for the Suppression of Obscene Publications. The Agreement sought to tackle the international traffic in 'obscenities' through sharing information among signatory powers on the traffic in obscene publications within and between their borders, but since it was only administrative in nature and did not require signatories to institute legislative changes in order to enable them to comply with its provisions, it was largely ineffective.[25] This led the British Government to advocate the passage of the International Convention for the Suppression of the Circulation of and Traffic in Obscene Publications, sponsored by the League of Nations, in 1923. Of the 28 nations that had signed the Obscene Publications Convention by the end of the decade, Britain was not only one of the few countries actually to implement it, it also dutifully submitted its annual report on obscene publications to the League in painstaking detail.[26] It furthermore exerted continued pressure on the governments of 37 colonies, dominions, protectorates and mandated territories to comply with and enforce the Convention in their territories, and to notify the British Government of all possible infractions against it. While the British Government was assiduous in informing fellow signatories of infractions against the Convention committed by their citizens, it provided Britain's colonies and dominions with far more numerous and detailed warnings of such infractions – warnings that were not always listed in annual reports to the League.[27] Colonial governments were informed as to what publications they should refuse entry to, were notified of discoveries made through the post about the trade in obscene publications within their borders, and were advised on what course of action should be taken in regard to the recipients of such wares.

No one was more assiduous in alerting the Empire as to the nature of the licentious books circulating within it than a Scotland Yard detective with the unfortunate name of A. Crapper. In 1925, for example, Crapper informed the Australian Government that a letter had recently been stopped in the post addressed to the Librairie du Palais Royal in Paris requesting 'that certain objectionable books, including "The Perfumed Garden", an obscene work, be sent to the bookseller Robertson & Mullens in Melbourne', while other obscene books, such as *Forbidden Fruit*, had been requested to be sent to a Mr J. Mendes of 386 Flinders Lane, Melbourne. While Crapper noted with some generosity that 'Robertson and Mullens are a firm of repute and it seems probable that the books to be sent to them were ordered on behalf of clients without any knowledge as to their true nature', Mendes was another matter. Since he might, according to Crapper, 'be a dealer in questionable books', it was advisable 'to have some inquiry made as to his identity and occupation'.[28] Crapper even went out of his way to save the Australian Government from having to carry out its own examination of questionable publications by suggesting that it prohibit whatever publications the British Government issued warrants against, advice that the Australian Government invariably followed.[29] Thanks to Crapper and his cohorts, the Convention thus afforded the British Government with the ability to document, regulate and restrict the consumption of obscene publications throughout the whole Empire.[30]

While the Australian Government was an enthusiastic supporter of Britain's efforts to help it regulate its trade in obscene publications, it none the less evinced considerable reluctance to ratify the Obscene Publications Convention. Even after Australia eventually ratified the Convention in 1935, its annual reports to the League of Nations were generally inaccurate because the Government reported only those cases of obscene publications that had gone to trial (usually none), and not the thousands of publications stopped at the docks or seized by the police.[31] It was not that the Australian Government was opposed to the Convention; it was simply so assured as to the infallibility of its own censorship system that it did not deem an international treaty necessary to improve upon it. As the Director of the Attorney-General's Department noted in 1930, the Australian Government had already managed to implement 'a very strict examination of literature', particularly in relation to the rest of the Empire, for 'books prohibited in Australia are sold openly, not only in foreign countries, but in other parts of the British Empire' – including Britain.[32] It was, in fact, from Britain itself that 'some of the worst examples of obscene and indecent writing' were imported into Australia.[33] Australia's system of censorship, it was convinced, thus rendered Australia more moral, pure and virtuous than the imperial metropole.

The Indian Government was also unenthusiastic about acceding to the Obscene Publications Agreement and Convention, although for different reasons. Not only was there a sense among British officials in India that, when it came to the international trade in obscene publications, 'India was more sinned against than sinning'[34] and hence had little to gain by participating in an international system to regulate the trade, but rather than priding itself, like Australia, on the efficacy of its censorship apparatus, such an apparatus, at least in the case of 'obscene' publications, was virtually non-existent. As the Director of Criminal Intelligence C. R. Cleveland remonstrated in 1912, he was extremely loathe to 'undertake anything of the nature of a regular bureau of obscenity' since his department was 'dropping far more important work in order to keep our staff small and we ought to avoid new work of doubtful effectiveness and character'.[35] Although the Indian Government was eventually pressured into acceding to the Agreement, since it was 'unwilling to appear not to be in sympathy with an object which is itself excellent', compliance on paper did not, however, translate into compliance in reality, and little was done to implement it.[36] Most British members of the Government were equally opposed to signing the 1923 Obscene Publications Convention, but many of their Indian counterparts in the newly expanded imperial legislature favoured it – not because they saw it (as did some British members) as a means to see India ranked among the 'civilized' nations of the world, but because they viewed it as a means of defending India's civilisation from 'corruption' by the West. That much of India's moral corruption came from Britain not even many British Indian officials could deny, for although India's annual reports to the League reveal that many of the 'obscene' publications imported into India came from Europe, they also reveal that, as in the case of Australia, they came from other parts of the Empire, including Britain itself.[37]

As the Governments of both India and Australia were well aware, not only did 'obscene' books, magazines and photographs circulate wherever the Union Flag flew, but in terms of the circulation of such material the Empire had become like a giant web with Britain at its centre. 'Obscene' South African photographs were to be found in India, 'obscene' Indian periodicals in Burma, and the typescripts of 'markedly obscene' books from Fiji in Australia.[38] London itself was the nexus through which much of this traffic was conveyed, the thread along which 'obscene' publications travelled from France to Jamaica, the United States to Nigeria, or Germany to South Africa. London was also a master spinner, churning out volumes of books that were seized by customs officials in Australia, periodicals that were prohibited in Canada, and even obscene gramophone records in a local language that were destroyed in Uganda.[39] But the proliferation of 'obscene' publications circulating between and within Britain and her colonies was not the only reason that Britain's attempt to create a viable imperial censorship system was doomed to failure. An additional reason was that, while the British were beset by worries that their 'race' was declining and was in danger of falling from its exalted position at the head of the Great Chain of Being, Australians and Indians were beset by similar fears (thanks, in part, to the dissemination of British print culture throughout the Empire) – fears that, as in Britain, were reflected in a drive to regulate the 'obscene', but that worked in ways that were detrimental to Britain's interests.

Although motivated by similar fears, racial discourse in both colonies (as well as their conceptions of, and attitudes towards, the obscene) was more complex than in Britain. While in Australia one strand of the discourse deemed Australians to be 'purer', 'whiter', offshoots of the British 'race,' a competing strand regarded the Australian 'race' as more degenerate than its British counterpart thanks to the debilitating effects of Antipodean life wrought by the hot climate and racial miscegenation. Both racial optimists and pessimists in Australia were united in the belief that the greatest danger to the strength and purity of the Australian race came not from within but from without, and from the 'white' races as well as the 'yellow'. As *The Australian Star* declared in 1897, 'We have evolved here a healthy, clean-living race, and the Australian type must be kept intact, and its physique protected from the foul strains that the age, the social conditions, and the sins of older races have bred in the bone until it has become a hereditary curse.'[40] The Australian colonies and later Commonwealth sought to protect Australia from such 'sins' by erecting a system to censor imported publications which, according to a deputation to the Australian Minister for Trade and Customs in 1935, should function in the nature of a 'sanitary system' or as a 'quarantine to prevent plagues'.[41]

Indian conceptions of and attitudes towards racial degeneracy were even more heterogeneous than Australian ones, in large measure because so many different conceptions of race coexisted in Indian society. Some of these pre-dated colonialism (as in the case of Indian conceptions of terms such as *jati, khun* and *samaj*),[42] while others were clearly derived from colonial discourse (such as the identification of the term *race* with *nation*). Although the multivalency of racial discourse in Indian society produced an array of overlapping and often competing conceptions of who exactly belonged to the Indian 'race' (Hindus or Muslims, Aryans or non-Aryans, caste Hindus or Untouchables) and what the basis of that inclusion was (biological, cultural or religious), what united the various strands of racial discourse in India was the belief that the Indian 'race', however constituted, had become degenerate and was in need of 'purification'. As in both Australia and Britain, this entailed the purification of language and literature, for as one Indian official declared in 1924:

> the modern tendency of freer expression of thought in unrestrained language has resulted in the throwing off of the many helpful restraints which preserved the cleanliness and dignity of social intercourse and if obscene literature is allowed to add its baneful influence to unfettered expression of thought, the standard set up by centuries of civilization will be greatly lowered . . .[43]

Indian print culture was deemed, however, to be twice as much in need of purification as its Western counterpart, for in addition to containing indigenous forms of obscenity such as *shrinagar ras* poetry, it now contained new types of obscenities derived from 'the great countries beyond the seas'.[44] Thus while Britain may have incited the regulation of the obscene in India and Australia, and while it continued to police the morality of its Empire beyond the Second World War, the creation of an imperial censorship system served to promote the production of alternative political rationalities in its colonies which, rather than enhancing the cultural interconnectedness of the Empire and of ensuring Britain's place as the centre of virtue and civility within it, constructed the imperial metropole as a source of impurity, corruption and degeneracy.

Notes

1. Speech by Home Secretary William Joynson-Hicks to the Author's Club, *Daily Telegraph*, 12 December 1928. Cited in Alan Travis, *Bound and Gagged: A Secret History of Obscenity in Britain* (London: Profile Books, 2000), pp. 67–8.

2. See Frank Mort, *Dangerous Sexualities: Medico-Moral Politics in England Since 1830*, second edition (London: Routledge, 2000); Alan Hunt, *Governing Morals: A Social History of Moral Regulation* (Cambridge: Cambridge University Press, 1999); Lucy Bland, *Banishing the Beast: Sexuality and the Early Feminists* (New York: The New Press, 1995); and Sheila Jeffreys, *The Spinster and Her Enemies: Feminism and Sexuality, 1880–1930* (London: Pandora Press, 1985).
3. Ian Hunter, David Saunders and Dugald Williamson, *On Pornography: Literature, Sexuality and Obscenity Law* (New York: St. Martin's Press, 1993), p. 52. *Obscenity*, like the terms *morality*, *virtue* and *civility*, was a socially determined concept that changed according to who was reading or viewing the work in question, and when and where they were doing so. Such a belief was enshrined in the ruling passed by Lord Chief Justice Sir Francis Cockburn in 1868, which became Britain's test of obscenity for almost a century, that the obscenity of a given work was determined by 'whether the tendency of the matter charged with as obscenity is to deprave and corrupt those whose minds are open to such immoral influences': *R* v. *Hicklin*, 3 QB 360.
4. Hunter, Saunders, and Williamson, *On Pornography*, pp. 52–3.
5. Joss Marsh, *Word Crimes: Blasphemy, Culture, and Literature in Nineteenth-Century England* (Chicago and London: The University of Chicago Press, 1998), p. 205. The publication of the first volume of the OED in 1884 coincided, significantly, with the publication of the new Revised Version of the King James Bible (1881–84), which led to a growing loss of faith in the literalness of the Bible and a new ' "faith" in "Englishry" ' (p. 209).
6. Jose Harris, *Private Lives, Public Spirit: A Social History of Britain 1870–1914* (Oxford: Oxford University Press, 1993), p. 235.
7. Letter to the *Standard*, reproduced in the NVA journal the *Vigilance Record*, 15 August 1888, p. 80.
8. Edward Bristow, *Vice and Vigilance: Purity Movements in Britain Since 1700* (Dublin: Gill and Macmillan, 1977), p. 50.
9. The 'pornographic field' is 'the field of disparate institutions historically responsible for the channels through which erotica have been disseminated and the cultural interests and abilities through which erotica have been consumed': Hunter, Saunders and Williamson, *On Pornography*, p. 10.
10. Brian Harrison, 'State Intervention and Moral Reform in Nineteenth-Century England', in Patricia Hollis (ed.), *Pressure from Without in Early Victorian England* (London: Edward Arnold, 1974), p. 305.
11. Mort, *Dangerous Sexualities*, p. 104.
12. The governmentalisation of the moral realm culminated in legislation such as the Married Women's Property Acts of 1870 and 1882, the Education Acts of 1870 and 1902, the Acts designed to combat cruelty against children beginning in 1889, and the Incest Act of 1908. Statutes pertaining to obscenity included the Obscene Publications Act 1857; the Post Office Protection Act 1884, which prohibited the sending of indecent or obscene items through the post; the Indecent Advertisements Act 1889; by-laws under the London Council (General Powers) Acts 1890 and 1896; and the Customs Laws Consolidation Act 1876, which provided for the seizure of obscene or indecent articles.

13. Hunt, *Governing Morals*, p. 154; Harris, *Private Lives*, p. 254; and Jeffrey Weeks, *Sex, Politics and Society: The Regulation of Sexuality Since 1800*, 2nd edn. (London and New York: Longman, 1989), p. 23

14. Ronald Hyam, *Empire and Sexuality: The British Experience* (Manchester: Manchester University Press, 1990), p. 3.

15. Bristow, *Vice and Vigilance*, p. 87.

16. *Hansard's Parliamentary Debates*, 8 May 1888, pp. 1708, 1713. The problem with translations of French novels such as Zola's, according to the NVA, was that 'The literary merits of foreign works are apt to be blurred by translation; and, what is even of more importance, modern literature bears a relation to the national life, manners, and habits of thought which is not appreciable to the foreigner. In a realistic French novel the literature is far more, and probably the vice is less, to a Frenchman than to an Englishman, who will lose little – whatever he may gain – by total ignorance of the whole realistic schools': *Vigilance Record*, June 15, 1889, p. 5.

17. The NVA took a great interest in both social purity and moral censorship in the Empire from its inception, and maintained contact with moral reform organisations throughout the empire. See, for example, 4/NVA/S.88/Box 108, Women's Library, London.

18. Since both Australia and India contained large numbers of English speakers, their importance as markets for British publishers and booksellers was evident as early as mid-century. In 1853, for example, while exports to Canada totaled £35,863, those to the Australian colonies already amounted to an impressive £138,695. Although British book exports to Canada continued to increase throughout the nineteenth century, they did not increase at the same rate as British exports to Australia due to the increasing dominance of the US in the Canadian book trade. By 1869 India was vying with Canada for second place in the Empire, with British book imports in the three presidencies of Bengal, Bombay and Madras totaling £44,130: Simon Nowell-Smith, *International Copyright Law and the Publisher in the Reign of Queen Victoria* (Oxford: Clarendon Press, 1968), p. 92; CUST 7/22 and 8/110, The National Archives, Kew; and George L. Parker, *The Beginnings of the Book Trade in Canada* (Toronto: University of Toronto Press, 1985).

19. Luke Trainor, 'British Publishers and Cultural Imperialism: History and Ethnography in Australia, 1870–1930', *Bibliographical Society of Australia and New Zealand Bulletin*, 20, 2 (1996), p. 100. Such a reorganisation included new modes of literary production, a transition from free enterprise to monopoly capital and increased international competition, as well as the growth of democracy and concurrent class and gender shifts. For a more detailed examination of some of these shifts, see Norman Feltes, *Literary Capital and the Late Victorian Novel* (Madison: University of Wisconsin Press, 1993).

20. Letter from John Murray III to Sir Francis Head, 20 November 1843, cited in James Barnes, *Free Trade in Books: A Study of the London Book Trade Since 1800* (Oxford: Clarendon Press, 1964). Colonial libraries were editions that were designed for sale only in the colonies. Murray was ahead of his time in that no other publisher established a colonial library until the 1880s. For more information on the colonial edition in Australia and India, see Graeme Johanson, *A Study of the Colonial Edition in Australia, 1843–1972*

(Wellington, NZ: Elibank Press, 2000); and Priya Joshi, *In Another Country: British Popular Fiction and the Development of the English Novel in India* (New York: Columbia University Press, 2002).

21. See Wallace Kirsop, 'The Four Phases of Australian Book-Trade History', *Books for Colonial Readers – The Nineteenth Century Australian Experience* (Melbourne: Bibliographical Society of Australia and New Zealand in Association with The Centre for Bibliographical and Textual Studies, Monash University, 1995) and 'Bookselling and Publishing in the Nineteenth Century', in D. H. Borchardt and Wallace Kirsop (eds.), *The Book in Australia* (Melbourne: Australian Reference Publications, 1988); and Martyn Lyons, 'Introduction', in Martyn Lyons and John Arnold (eds.), *The History of the Book in Australia, 1891–1945: Towards a National Culture in a Colonized Market, 1890–1945* (St. Lucia: University of Queensland Press, 2001).

22. 81–83/January 1895, Separate Revenue (Post Office, General), A, Finance and Commerce Dept., National Archives of India, New Delhi; and 6–10 October 1911, Post Office, A, Dept. of Commerce and Industry, National Archives of India, New Delhi. The nature of the market in India (such as its size and linguistic diversity, the differences in the types of publications that were popular in India versus in Britain, and the fact that reprints – largely pirated – of British books could be sold much more cheaply there than works imported from London) meant that British publishers faced much stiffer competition in India than in Australia. Additional problems were posed by the linguistic diversity of India and the differences in the types of publications that were popular there.

23. MP341/1/0, 1913/9411, Box 157, Australian Archives, Melbourne. William Chidley was fined £3 plus costs for publishing an obscene book, and London was duly informed that the required action had been taken.

24. Note by Bamford, 10 May 1936, 712/32, Judicial, A, Home Dept., National Archives of India, New Delhi. In light of the difficulty of determining how to constitute the obscene in colonial India, colonial officials generally refrained, as one official put it in 1890, from 'attempt[ing] to raise the native standard by punishing offences against our own': D. Ibbetson, Esq. to S. S. Thorburn, Esq., 21 February 1890, 547–83/October 1890, Public, A, Home Dept., National Archives of India, New Delhi.

25. While purity organisations such as the NVA and the Swiss Association Against Immoral Literature had begun holding international conferences on the trade in obscene publications since the 1880s, it was not until the meeting of the first International Congress against obscene publications in Paris in 1908 that sufficient pressure was exerted on European governments to initiate an international regulation of the trade. The holding of an International Convention for the Suppression of the White Slave Traffic by a number of European governments in 1904 doubtless provided an additional incentive to undertake a similar convention on obscene publications, particularly since, as the League of Nations reported in 1927, there had long been 'direct evidence of the association between the Traffic in Women and the Traffic in Obscenities': International Conference', *Vigilance Record*, 15 November 1888; NVA Executive Minutes, June 1886 to April 1890, 4/NVA/104, Women's Library, London; and clippings in file GB/106/4/NVA/S.88/B, Box 107, Women's Library, London.

26. Many countries were reluctant to even sign – France, for example, did not ratify the Convention until 1940. See Memorandum from League, 4 June 1932, A425/126, 1943/2649, Australian Archives, Canberra.

27. See, for example, CO 323/1656/6, The National Archives, Kew; HO 45/20913, The National Archives, Kew.

28. Crapper to Secretary, Prime Minister's Department, 7 October 1925, A981/4, LEAGUE OBS 6, Australian Archives, Canberra.

29. Crapper to Secretary, Prime Minister's Department, 28 May 1924, A981/4, LEAGUE OBS 6, Australian Archives, Canberra.

30. Although the 'trade' on the whole seems to have been not entirely worthy of Britain's robust efforts to stamp it out, by 1931 the Home Office was convinced that, in both Britain and the Empire, 'grossly obscene wares are rarer now than they were a few years ago': 'Reply to Questionnaire on Obscene Publications', 9 March 1931, A981/4, LEAGUE OBS 2, Australian Archives, Canberra.

31. For an overview of the regulation of the trade in obscene publications in Australia, see Deana Heath, 'Creating the Moral Colonial Subject: Censorship in India and Australia, 1880s to 1939', PhD diss. (University of California at Berkeley, 2003), Ch. 5.

32. Memo, Director, Attorney-General's Department to Department of External Affairs, 20 January 1930, A981/4, LEAGUE OBS 4, Australian Archives, Canberra.

33. This was in part thanks to 'the contraction of distance due to quickened communications' between metropole and colony: T. W. White, speech, Wesley Church, Melbourne. Printed in 'Report of "The Star" Public Debate held in the Melbourne Town Hall February 26 1935', in folder 'Book Censorship No. 2. Lists-Cabinet approval etc.,' T. W. White Papers, MS 9148, National Library of Australia, Canberra.

34. *Extract from Council of State Debates*, 11 March 1924, 570/1923, Judicial, Home Dept., National Archives of India, New Delhi.

35. C. R. Cleveland to Home Department, 5 July 1912; 1 December 1912, 193–204/April 1913, Judicial, A, Home Dept., National Archives of India, New Delhi.

36. 193–204/April 1913; 246–47/August 1913; and 388–93/April 1914, Judicial, A, Home Dept., National Archives of India, New Delhi.

37. See, for example, 838/29, Judicial, Home Dept., National Archives of India, New Delhi. As in the case of the Agreement, India also signed the 1923 Convention.

38. A989/1, 1944/1300/20/1; and Doc. no C.73.M.70.1941.IV., A981/4, LEAGUE OBS 7, Australian Archives, Canberra.

39. A981/4, LEAGUE OBS 7, Australian Archives, Canberra. See also 989/1, 1944/1300/20/1, Australian Archives, Canberra.

40. 'The Restriction of Aliens', *The Australian Star*, 18 November 1897, p. 3.

41. 'Report of proceedings of deputation to the Hon. T. W. White, DFC, VD, Minister of State for Trade and Customs, RE Censorship of Books held at Commonwealth Public Offices, Treasury Gardens, Melbourne. Tuesday, 10th September, 1935, at 4:30 PM', folder marked 'Book Censorship', Papers of T. W. White, MSS Mss. 9148, National Library of Australia, Canberra.

42. These terms are generally translated as *caste, blood* and *society*, although such terms can have a multitude of meanings.

43. 'Opinion of Rao Bahadur R. S. Thakur, Deputy Commissioner, Hoshangabad', contained in a letter from W. N. May, Esq., Commissioner, Nerbuddar Division, to Secretary to the Governor, Central Provinces, Legal Department, 27 June 1924, 570/1923, Judicial, Home Department, National Archives of India, New Delhi.
44. Speech by the Hon. Dr Sir Deva Prasad Sarvadhikary, *Extract from Council of State Debates*, IV, 19 (11 March 1924), 570/1923, Judicial, Home Dept., National Archives of India, New Delhi.

11
Peripheral Politics? Antipodean Interventions in Imperial News and Cable Communication (1870–1912)

Denis Cryle

Media dependency, news monopoly and the role of the state

A study of the historical evolution of trans-Tasman press and cable connections within the British imperial context, such as is proposed here, requires from the outset a broad conceptual framework, including an understanding of recent communication historiography and of the ways in which it addresses contemporary concerns with globalisation, information flows and media convergence. The insights of the Canadian economic historian and communication pioneer Harold Innis[1] remain a valuable point of departure for this purpose. In the wake of Geoffrey Blainey's[2] similar preoccupation with the tyranny of distance, recent work by Australian and New Zealand communication scholars[3] has been informed by similar geographical concerns. Osborne and Cryle observe in the preface to their special Australasian *Media History* issue of 2002 that:

> [Perhaps] more important than quantity is the need to reconceptualise Australian media history to acknowledge more clearly its dependent interconnections with broader Australian historical experience and to relocate it more substantially within the larger framework of Australian reconnections with larger worlds.[4]

The contemporary Canadian scholar Dwayne Winseck, revisiting Innis's earlier insights concerning the potential for new monopolies of knowledge[5] associated with information technology, has aptly credited the late nineteenth-century telegraph with effecting 'a kind of media convergence' involving the press, newsagencies, cable companies, governments, railways and stock markets. He argues that the period 1840–1910 saw 'the economics of news gathering tilted from competition towards monopoly and to efforts to secure the commodity value of information'.[6] At the same time the countervailing tendency of colonial press interests to coalesce in response to perceived London-based monopolies of both content and carriage, when combined with the proximity and dependency of trans-Tasman news connections, creates specific regional scenarios which are worthy of renewed investigation.

In the introduction to her recent study of India and the British press, Chandrika Kaul acknowledges the seminal influence of Innis's work for understanding empire, but qualifies his analysis of power and communication as 'insufficiently dynamic', since:

> It is not a one-off effect but the beginning of a process of negotiation and struggle. While it is true that the immediate impact of a new technology is to consolidate an established elite, other groups will also seek access to that technology and the information and influence it yields.[7]

The extension of the international cable via Suez and India to Australia in 1872, and to New Zealand by 1876, brought about a much awaited but protracted integration of periphery with metropole.[8] If the Eastern Telegraph Company underpinned an emerging communication monopoly, the pre-eminence of Reuters in India, described by Kaul as 'the only agency in a position to provide a news imperial service',[9] was equally significant for the press of the 'Far East', perpetuating, in a British imperial context, the emerging monopolies of knowledge envisaged by Innis. In spite of its significant market advantage, however, Reuters' ascendancy was, as previously intimated, never automatic. Recent case studies of its influence across different colonies confirm a range of outcomes in its negotiations with the colonial press.[10] Reuters' share of the international news market remained surprisingly tenuous, not only in Canada and South Africa, but also in Australia and New Zealand, as the comparative study to be undertaken here will confirm.

In the context of colonial communications, the rhetoric of monopoly evolved and intensified through the period under examination, precipitating a series of lively and sustained campaigns against the inadequacies of imperial news supply such as Potter and Rantanen[11] have outlined it. If the prospect of Reuters as a monopoly supplier galvanised newspaper proprietors into collective opposition by the mid-1880s, attacks on the Eastern Telegraph Company as the sole information carrier became more protracted and public over time. Its monopoly as the first trans-Atlantic carrier had been eroded by American cable companies, but its continued domination of the Eastern international route and its high carriage charges aroused the resentment of colonial newspapers and governments alike. In 1872, cable rates for all parties were an exorbitant 10/4 a word. By the turn of the century, the press rate was half that for government messages and one third of the ordinary rate.[12] In part, this decrease was due to pressure mounted from the 1880s by British-based campaigners like Henniker Heaton, a British MP and former Australian journalist,[13] as well as by colonial governments who administered the domestic telegraph and by sections of the press, not least the emerging provincial press associations.

Despite real technological improvements by British-based business interests, colonial dissatisfaction with the imperial news system intensified most notably during and after periods of war and imperial crisis, when the cheaper or deferred press rates were impracticable and press business had to be despatched at more exorbitant rates. The role of the state as arbiter and intermediary, at various levels, can easily be lost sight of in these seemingly interminable discussions over imperial communication. In this respect, Simon Potter's recent observations that:

> State intervention, while acceptable in some forms, was seldom allowed to interfere with the commercial interests of private sector press enterprises. As the volume of news travelling around the empire increased before, during and after the First World War, it became clear that the imperial press system would remain dependent on private enterprise[14]

appear too undifferentiated when applied to the pre-war situation, since they do not take sufficient account of the mediating and subsidising roles played by colonial governments, their roles in overseeing the local transmission of overseas cable news, in convening inter-colonial communication policy and participating in the regular imperial conferences which culminated in the establishment of the jointly government-owned Pacific Cable by the turn of the century. Thus it will be argued that a countervailing tendency to public monopoly and public utility vied at this period with the exigencies of private enterprise,[15] and created precedents for state intervention on security and strategic grounds.

One result of these complex communication debates is that colonial government inquiries and records remain a significant source of information, as well as newspapers, private and colonial business records. News and cable services, while deemed essential, were too often viewed as cryptic, erratic and expensive. Kevin Livingston, in his *Wired National Continent*,[16] has shown that, in the case of Australia and New Zealand, the colonial press was an active participant in communication debates concerning postal charges and the efficacy of the telegraph, while senior public servants canvassed and debated such issues openly as newspaper correspondents. Consequently, Van Cuilenburg's and McQuail's policy assumptions, that 'communications [were] effectively kept out of the sphere of public debate' and that 'the policy terrain was effectively depoliticised',[17] appear too categorical in view of the rapidity with which cabled information had become integral to colonial administration and business.

Trans-Tasman connections: the United Press Association and cable news negotiations (1870–1895)

In the case of Reuters, the established British and imperial news agency expanding along the Eastern network, however, Antipodean resistance proved to be both more immediate and more concerted. In view of Reuters' success in India and the exorbitant charges resulting from its market dominance,[18] it was not surprising that sections of the press in Australia and New Zealand viewed Reuters intentions with considerable suspicion, especially the established daily newspapers which were most reliant on regular and timely overseas news cables. In 1872, the Melbourne *Argus* and the *Otago Daily Times*, two leading trans-Tasman newspapers which were to play leading roles in their respective press associations, agreed under controversial circumstances to an annual agreement whereby the *Argus* would act as Reuters' agent in New Zealand for a fee of £500.[19] The initiator, Julius Vogel, thereby opened up the possibility of a trans-Tasman newspaper coalition and compounded the difficulties which Reuters would encounter in the Antipodes.

In Victoria, the intentions of the Melbourne *Argus* co-proprietor Lachlan Mackinnon towards Reuters were already clear in correspondence of March 1870 to his editor. Writing to J. S. Johnston, Mackinnon confided:

> We must work however so as eventually to be independent of Reutter. Depending on him would be humiliating as well as dangerous. If he had a monopoly he could at pleasure shut up any

paper in the Colony by refusing to give it telegraphic news. Mind that in two years we shall have to publish daily telegraphs and from all parts of the world. My idea on this point is that an organization embracing every paper now in the Colonies should be formed so as to ignore Reutterism altogether.[20]

His letters reveal a personal rebuff at the hands of Reuter and an aware-ness of the Indian situation, where newspapers paid Reuters a £4,000 annual news subsidy as well as covering domestic telegraphic charges. The newly formed APA would follow suit but with the important concessions secured by the Australian press and noted by Putnis that:

> The *Sydney Morning Herald* and the Melbourne *Argus* agreed to take the Reuter service, but in London rather than Melbourne, thus allowing Australian editors to make their own selections for trans-mission. Reuter's press operation in Australia was much smaller than would have been the case had Melbourne been the point of sale.[21]

Mackinnon worked tirelessly to include the *Sydney Morning Herald* as the leading newspaper in the rival colony of New South Wales within his organisation, but his influential association did not become the universal or representative association he initially espoused. Instead, it began by excluding local competitors, as well as newspapers in the other Australian colonies and in the regions.

The eclipse of Greville and Bird as Reuters' New Zealand agent and its ability to make consistent headway in the Australian market[22] gave Australian–New Zealand press cooperation, in the form of the Vogel–*Argus* agreement, an initial fillip, threatening Reuters' ambition to become the regional supplier of international news. The arrival of Henry Collins[23] in Australia, corresponded with the initial formation of the New Zealand Press Association in 1878 and of its stable successor, the United Press Association (UPA) in 1880.[24] The UPA's predecessor, the New Zealand Press Association, had taken both Reuters and APA messages,[25] offering these at a 25 per cent reduction to its own members. Once the UPA emerged as the sole local association, two years later, Collins, on behalf of Reuters, moved to close the New Zealand market and shut out the Australian service entirely by offering a 20 per cent reduction on its current agreement. Collins' further promise, to 'furnish UPA subscribers with a service of Australians news per cable of such an improved and extended [quality] as will render any supplemen-tary service unnecessary',[26] proved sufficiently attractive for the UPA to conclude an initial two-year agreement with Reuters and agree to the closure of the supplementary Australian service.

By 1882, however, when this agreement was due to expire, complaints were voiced by UPA members about the Reuters service, to the point where a prospective decline in subscribers prematurely threatened the existence of the Association itself.[27] Despite its 20 per cent concession, Reuters was criticised for charging all recipient newspapers the same fee irrespective of their size, or the quantity of the cable news which they took.[28] But the most regular complaints were directed at the content of the service. In her Indian study, Kaul[29] estimates that at least half of the news sent by Reuters to its Far Eastern customers, including Australia and New Zealand, was general to all, rather than country-specific. Antipodean subscribers complained that its news was not sufficiently local. With Mackinnon and the Melbourne *Argus* pressing it to take an independent Australian service, the UPA persisted under the terms of its agreement, but proceeded in September 1880 to 'write to Reuters asking for greater expediency in Australian messages and also greater accuracy in translation of the Melbourne *Argus* and *Age* specials to be forwarded by agents through the evening papers'.[30] Press dissatisfaction with Reuters simmered in New Zealand throughout the 1880s, peaking at an historic confrontation in 1887 when Collins' further offer was dramatically declined in favour of an Australian-based service. Reuters' international coverage faced increasing criticism in 1882 over inadequate Middle East reporting to the point where UPA subscribers exerted pressure on the directors to switch to the *Argus* or *Age* for an international service. Henry Brett, a UPA director and influential proprietor of the *Auckland Star*, after studying the rival Australian services, strongly recommended for the *Argus*.[31]

In 1887, the Australian press, represented by the *Sydney Daily Telegraph*, began negotiations with the UPA by demanding an even larger figure for the full service than Reuters but, unlike Collins, was still prepared to negotiate separate prices for international and Australian cable news. Unexpectedly for the UPA and for Reuters, the Sydney delegation had, at a late hour, conspired with the *Age* and the *Argus* associations to cut out Reuters, by offering to replace it with a fully Australian-based service.[32] Fenwick, a long-serving director and head of the UPA, recalled with triumph the 'veritable bombshell for Reuters representatives' which its late switch of allegiance produced on an over-confident Collins. Although available accounts of the episode differ in details concerning the individual Australian actors, they concur on the historical significance of the 1887 agreement, which was renewed regularly over the next 25 years.[33]

By playing off prospective suppliers against each other, the UPA had achieved a highly advantageous agreement, reducing its European and international cable news costs from £4,000 to £1,000. Under the terms of the same triennial agreement, the UPA established an office in Sydney to organise its own Australian news service, which expanded to as much as one third of its total incoming cable news by the early 1890s.[34] The most costly and newsworthy items of the UPA's Australian service were its steady stream of special cables from major Australian newspapers covering popular sporting events and the turf in particular. The 'specials', which were supplied to its subscribers at additional cost, appealed to both its morning and evening newspapers on the grounds of their brevity and timeliness. Sports coverage, along with local market prices, remained central to the UPA's ongoing cable news agreements throughout the late nineteenth and early twentieth centuries, although it continued to exercise relative independence in its choice of individual Australian suppliers.[35] Indeed, a common predilection for sport and gambling by Australian suppliers and New Zealand receivers alike helped to sustain their anti-Reuters posture. For the same reasons, Reuters official First World War service, with its wordy parliamentary news, official documents and Dominion politics, was subsequently deemed to be unattractive to readers and 'cut pretty severely'[36] by the New Zealand Association.

Fenwick's subsequent claim, on behalf of the Association, that 'the New Zealand press had the benefit of the cheapest cable service ever known anywhere'[37] applied more to content than to carriage however, since continuing high cable charges pressured both the Australian and New Zealand Associations to increase their subscription rates to the detriment of smaller members.[38] In 1886, with the international press rate still at 2/8 a word, the UPA observed that cable charges between Australia and New Zealand 'threaten to seriously affect the supply of foreign intelligence'.[39] Following the example of the Australians, the UPA successfully lobbied the Post Office for a reduction in the domestic press rate from of 2d to 1d per word, but was unable to secure comparable reductions from the Eastern Telegraph Company.

Consequently, over the period 1880–95, subscriptions for the larger New Zealand morning and evening dailies, as the main recipients of the *Argus* and sporting specials, doubled from £500 to £1,000 per year, while fees for the smaller dailies also rose, albeit more slowly.[40] The prospect of ongoing increases disturbed smaller proprietors who took their grievances to parliament, demanding an inquiry into the Association's system for fixing fees and recommending legislation for their abolition.[41] While such counter-measures did not materialise in the short term, the issue would resurface in the New Zealand legislature, maintaining internal political pressure on the Association, in concert with the external financial pressures to which it remained vulnerable. Like the APA, its Australian counterpart and supplier, the United Press Association began by championing the local interest and inhibiting Reuters' access to Far East news markets. Once its local ascendancy became established, however, it appeared less willing to explore cheaper cable options and alternatives on behalf of its membership. To this end, a wider campaign, including public and government players, as well as sectional and commercial interests, would be required.

Cable diplomacy: the Pacific news experiment (1886–1912)

Although Reuters' loss of Australasian press traffic did little to alter the monopoly of cable carriage, the Eastern Telegraph's service to the Far East, rarely without its critics, was itself coming under significant challenge, not least from local politicians and entrepreneurial competitors. In the case of Australia and New Zealand, rivalry with John Pender's Eastern Telegraph Company began within five years of the cable reaching Darwin and constituted a challenge 'more formidable than any he had previously encountered'.[42] In the late 1870s, Audley Coote, an Australian capitalist, proposed laying a cable to Singapore on behalf of the rival Siemen Brothers.[43] Coote's preoccupation with Asia–Pacific communication and his willingness to pursue unconventional means, including non-British capital, were reminiscent of Julius Vogel's vision for New Zealand of an alternative cable via the Pacific. By 1886, amid public opposition from Sir John Pender, Coote, along with F. C. Rowan and Randolph Want, was promoting a cable to San Francisco on behalf of the newly formed Pacific Telegraph Company. In a bid for colonial support, Rowan lobbied press and officialdom in Australia and New Zealand on the company's behalf. Along with arguments about the strategic need for a Pacific route in the event of imperial hostilities, Rowan and Coote also identified reduced cable prices as a potential benefit to newspapers in their memorandum for the Federal Council session of January 1886.[44]

In Charles Todd (South Australia) and E. C. Cracknell (New South Wales), Rowan publicly engaged two Postmasters-General who had invested their influential careers in the Eastern line and its overland extension from Darwin to Adelaide.[45] Rowan on Coote's behalf, contested Cracknell's objection to the Pacific cable on the grounds that

Pacific traffic would amount to no more than 300,000 words per annum in the event of a 100 per cent price reduction to 5 shillings per word.[46] Rowan's counter-assessment, based on reduced rates of 3 shillings per word (ordinary) and 1s 6d per word (press), estimated that traffic would treble with further cost reductions, although he conceded that this might be less attractive to the press than to the public in the short term, 'because the cover rates accorded to them have probably brought them already [more] than ordinary messages to their normal limit'.[47] Undeterred, Rowan extended his campaign to New Zealand where he debated with Julius Vogel the timing and extent of colonial government subsidies.[48] Both these men were present and poised to play active roles at the decisive London cable deliberations of the following year.

In view of Pender's promise of price reductions and their own existing arrangements, established press interests were loath to commit to an alternative cable scheme.[49] Rowan lobbied metropolitan Australian and New Zealand newspapers with mixed results. In Melbourne, the *Age* expressed its support for the Pacific Telegraph memorandum,[50] but the *Argus*, which continued to play a dominant role in the APA, opposed any colonial commitment to a Pacific proposal.[51] Stressing its 'possible international importance in case of war', Rowan responded by pointing out that the *Argus* was effectively discounting 'any scheme which might commercially compete with that of the existing Company'.[52] Both the APA and the *Argus*, were loath to explore alternative cable arrangements, in part because their press business to the Far East was insufficiently influential to sway Pender, but equally from a concern that reduced press rates arising from a Pacific route could encourage new local competitors.

At the London Jubilee Conference in 1887, with Sir John Pender at the height of his influence, delegates exerted renewed pressure on his Eastern company by advocating the construction of a Pacific cable on imperial grounds.[53] Once the Canadians, led by Sir Sandford Fleming, swung their considerable weight behind the proposal, Vancouver rather than San Francisco became the favoured North American destination on the grounds of empire loyalty, with a transcontinental land link to the Atlantic via the Canadian Pacific railway. Successful motions at the Conference for a thorough Pacific feasibility survey, a difficult feat of engineering in view of the depth and unbroken stretches of ocean involved, challenged the Eastern Extension monopoly primarily on security grounds by pointing out the vulnerability of the existing Suez Canal and African routes.[54] The other significant aspect of this intervention was the conception of the Pacific cable, as a joint state enterprise rather than as a private one as had been generally the case. The adherence of the established Australian colonies, New South Wales, Victoria and South Australia, aided by Eastern's new policy of collective negotiation, however, postponed any concerted challenge until the turn of the century. Of the Australian colonies, only Queensland defied Eastern by commissioning a French telegraph company to construct an under-water cable to New Caledonia in 1893[55] and threatening to renege on the payment of its Eastern subsidy, while New Zealand signalled its intention in 1889 to duplicate the trans-Tasman line in defiance of Eastern's own proposal.[56] In 1896 when an Imperial Committee deliberated the trans-Pacific cable in London, New Zealand was unrepresented,[57] but by 1901, when the Pacific Cable Board was eventually finalised, New Zealand took its place along with the Australian, Canadian and British Governments.[58]

The years 1886–87 marked a high point in Antipodean dissatisfaction with both imperial news supply and cable communication. But, if discontent with Reuters was largely a private matter on the part of the Australian and New Zealand press associations, the criticisms of the Eastern Telegraph Company, which drove advocates of the Pacific cable, assumed increasing public prominence in parliament and the press as well as at conferences.[59] Sections of the colonial press were by now more inclined to seize upon Heaton's outspoken denunciations of the Eastern 'octopus'. Along with the *Brisbane Courier* in Queensland, the *Age*'s London correspondent reproduced Heaton's anti-Eastern rhet-oric and his persistent denunciations of it as a 'colossal monopoly'.[60] By 1890, the Eastern company responded to colonial complaints about cable breakages and protracted delays by laying a series of duplicate cables to Australia and New Zealand. Pender remained confident that appeals to imperial sentiment by his opponents, in the case of a trans-Pacific route, would be overshadowed by business considerations.[61] Emboldened by the protracted debate with Pender and his Eastern Tele-graph Company, colonial advocates of the Pacific route were by 1894 calling for the nationalisation of Eastern's established network on the grounds of public and imperial interest.[62]

While individual colonial spokesmen and newspapers took an anti-Eastern line, the Australian Press Association did not support calls for a Pacific cable. Victoria, the home colony of both the *Argus* and *Age* remained wedded to the existing service via Adelaide, while Lachlan Charles Mackinnon, the influential *Argus* manager and cousin of the former proprietor of the same name, recognised that the advent of a cheaper alternative would lessen the dependence of Australian and New Zealand papers upon his established service. Although the UPA continued its agreements with the Australian Press Association rather than with Reuters at this time, it continued to press for more favourable terms including a new clause in 1895 granting it the option of 'obtaining directly from Europe any cable of special interest to New Zealand' as long as it was not obtained through 'a rival agency'.[63] In Victoria, the cable monopoly now shared between the *Argus* and *Age*, inhibited new daily competitors like the *Herald* and *Telegraph* while regional Victorian newspapers resorted to a meagre Reuters service.[64] Many Australian regional newspapers, in particular, simply could not afford to subscribe to the service. Consequently, their cable news was mostly confined to inter-colonial items in the case of Australia or to domestic news in the case of smaller New Zealand subscribers. It was only by their persistent agitation and lobbying that both the APA and UPA came under greater government scrutiny from the mid-1890s, with the reintroduction of a Bill to suppress Association fees into the New Zealand legislature.[65] Australian legislators were slower to act until a Senate Select Committee, established at the federal level in 1909, took the unprecedented step of subsidising an Independent Cable Service to offset the APA monopoly.[66]

In 1902, on the eve of the opening of the Pacific cable, it was clear that the imperial crisis and war in South Africa had worked in favour of the existing imperial news system, by expanding the flow of cable news east to Australia and New Zealand, and strengthening the commercial power of the locally-based press associations.[67] Hugh Denison, proprietor of the Sydney *Sun*, subsequently recalled that the Australian press paid as much as £100,000 for overseas cables at the time of the Boer War,[68] while the regional NSW proprietor, Thomas Temperley, remembered that detailed reporting of the Boer War was 'a luxury for the very rich'.[69] In 1903, for example, a mere 300 press messages were sent via the Pacific route from a total traffic of 18,000 words, rising to only 890 of the 37,000 sent in the following year.[70] The APA continued to boycott the Pacific cable, preferring the Eastern service 'for solely commercial reasons'.[71] In March 1909, prior to the Senate inquiry, it made a significant concession by allocating a portion of its incoming traffic (11,000 words) to the Pacific route, but private messages via this service continued to outnumber press traffic by as much as 10 to 1.[72] When Mackinnon called, as a witness to the Senate inquiry, was pressed on this point, he insisted that the Pacific cable was unreliable, depending as it did the Atlantic leg on American companies which are 'very casual with Pacific business'.[73]

New Zealand Association reports suggest that Mackinnon may have been prepared to give ground over Pacific traffic as early as 1904[74] but that the *Sydney Morning Herald* remained intransigent. Competition for the *Herald* and the APA was growing more strongly in New South Wales than in Victoria. The New South Wales Provincial Press Association, driven by the frustrations of the cable situation and the prospect of press amalgamations in country centres,[75] was becoming increasingly active on behalf of its constituents. Two of its members, Thomas Mitchell Shakespeare (*Grafton Argus*) and Thomas Temperley (*Richmond River Times*), were prime movers in establishing the Australian Provincial Press Association,[76] with offices in Sydney at the terminus of the Pacific line. In the wake of the Senate Committee of 1909, it was Temperley, on behalf of the Independent Cable Service, who visited Canada and negotiated significant concessions from the Canadian Pacific Railway Company for a 5,000-word weekly cable service via Vancouver and the Pacific at a considerably reduced rate.[77]

A further incentive in 1909 for press traffic on the 'All Red Route' was an agreement at the first Imperial Press Conference in London to reduce cable costs from 1 shilling to 9d a word.[78] Governments represented on the Pacific Cable Board, including Australia and New Zealand, took the initiative in lowering their cable costs and subsequently enjoyed a three-fold increase which continued exponentially during the First World War. The main beneficiaries of these developments were the evening papers, which began to take their afternoon messages via the Pacific route. The New Zealand Association extracted concessions from Mackinnon on the grounds that its 'evening papers were badly served'.[79] In the wake of government intervention, the regional grip of the *Argus-Sydney Morning Herald* combine became more tenuous. In New Zealand, the UPA, as it had with Reuters in the late nineteenth century, entered into negotiations with new Australian rivals of the *Argus*, including the recently formed Independent Cable Association and the emerging *Sun-Herald* group, spearheaded by Hugh Denison and Theodore Fink.[80] By 1912, the UPA was organising its own supplementary coverage of New Zealand Premier Cook's UK visit, in addition to arranging with the Independent Cable Service for a supply of Canadian government cables.[81]

To conclude, a series of developments in 1909 brought to a climax colonial attempts to intervene in the imperial press system, most notably on the issue of cable rates and information monopolies. Heaton's anti-monopolistic rhetoric, imported from Britain, appealed to both colonial Liberal and Labour politicians, as did the Fleming's Pacific cable scheme on the grounds of imperial defence. More particularly, the Antipodean press, having negotiated an arm's length relationship with Reuters during 1886–87, the first significant moment for this study, was less easily weaned from the Eastern monopoly, preferring to lobby it collectively for subsidies and concessions, until the combination of internal and external pressures from competitors and governments proved too great. By 1909 however, the Empire was again in crisis. With the outbreak of the First World War, the imperial news system reasserted itself as it had previously done during the Boer War. The greatly expanded flow of cable news from London would not only consolidate the Pacific cable project, the great cause of the interventionists, but also strengthen Reuters' relationship with the British Government and result in greatly enhanced profits for the Eastern Telegraph group. For the Antipodean press, the first round in these complex and ongoing negotiations was over; but the second contest, between established cable interests and Marconi's broadcasting alternative, was only beginning to be felt throughout the Dominions. The relative enthusiasm with which Antipodean newspapers and the dominion press in general, embraced the new international possibilities offered by broadcasting can only be fully understood in the context of its enduring dissatisfaction with pre-war cable and news arrangements.

Notes

1. Harold Innis, *Empire and Communications* (Victoria, Toronto: Press Porcepic, 1986).
2. Geoffrey Blainey, *The Tyranny of Distance* (Melbourne: Sun Books, 1966).
3. Patrick Day, *The Making of the New Zealand Press: A Study of the Organisational and Political Concerns of New Zealand Newspaper Controllers* (Wellington: Victoria University Press, 1990).
4. Graeme Osborne and Denis Cryle, 'Special Issue: Australasian Media History in 2002', *Media History*, 8, 1 (June 2002): 7.
5. Paul Heyer and David Crowley, 'Introduction' to Harold A. Innis, *The Bias of Communication* (Toronto: University of Toronto Press, 1995), p. xix.
6. Dwayne Winseck, 'Back to the Future: Telecommunications Online Service and Convergence from 1840 to 1910', *Media History*, 5, 2 (1999): 138, 140.
7. Chandrika Kaul, *Reporting the Raj: The British Press and India c. 1880–1922* (Manchester and New York: Manchester University Press, 2003), p. 5.
8. Peter Putnis, 'The Business of Empire: Henry M. Collins and the Early Role of Reuters in Australia', *Australia Journal of Communication*, 24, 3 (1997): 11–26.
9. Chandrika Kaul, 'Imperial Communication Fleet Street and the Indian Empire 1850–1920's', in Michael Bromley and Tom O'Malley (eds.), *A Journalism Reader* (London and New York, 1997), p. 63.

10. Peter Putnis, 'The Business of Empire' and 'Reuters in Australia: The Supply and Exchange of News, 1859–1877', *Media History*, 10, 2 (2004): 67–88; Simon J. Potter, *News and the British World, The Emergence of an Imperial Press System 1876–1922* (Oxford, Clarendon Press, 2003).
11. Terhi Rantanen, 'The Struggle for Control of Domestic News Markets', in Oliver Boyd-Barrett and Terhi Rantanen, *The Globalization of News* (London: Sage, 1998), p. 38.
12. Kevin Livingston, *The Wired Nation Continent: The Communication Revolution and Federating Australia*, (Melbourne: Oxford University Press, 1996), p. 187.
13. John Henniker Heaton, 'Penny a Word Telegrams through the Empire', in Royal Colonial Institute, *Report of Proceedings* (London: The Institute, 1909), pp. 3–36.
14. Potter, *News and the British World*, p. 9.
15. Jan Van Cuilenburg and Denis McQuail, 'Media Policy Paradigm Shifts Towards a New Communications Policy Paradigm', *European Journal of Communication* 18, 2 (2003): 181.
16. Livingston, *The Wired Nation Continent*, pp. 40ff.
17. Van Cuilenburg and McQuail, 'Media Policy Paradigm Shifts', p. 189.
18. Kaul, 'Imperial Communication', p. 62.
19. Day, *The Making of the New Zealand Press*, p. 212.
20. Lachlan MacKinnon to T. S. Johnston 24 March 1870 (Johnston Letters, University of Melbourne Archives).
21. Putnis, 'The Business of Empire', pp. 20–1.
22. Putnis, 'Reuters in Australia', pp. 71–2.
23. Putnis, 'The Business of Empire', p. 19.
24. George Fenwick, *The United Press Association Formation and Early History* (Dunedin: Otago Times, 1929), p. 7; New Zealand Press Association Minutes, 1879 (Alexander Turnbull Library, Wellington Acc 75–213).
25. Ross Harvey, 'Bringing the News to New Zealand: The Supply and Control of Overseas News in the Nineteenth Century', *Media History*, 8, 1 (2002): 27.
26. New Zealand (United) Press Association, Minutes, 1880, pp. 11–12.
27. Ibid., 1882, p. 57.
28. Fenwick, *The United Press Association*, p. 13.
29. Kaul, 'Imperial Communication', p. 63.
30. NZPA (UPA), Minutes, 1880, p. 20.
31. NZPA (UPA) Minutes, 1882, p. 57.
32. James Sanders, *Dateline-NZPA The New Zealand Press Association 1880–1980* (Auckland: Wilson and Horton, 1979), pp. 22–3.
33. Fenwick, The *United Press Association*, p. 14. Fenwick's account (pp. 13–14), for example, refers to Watkin Wynne of the *Sydney Daily Telegraph* as the Australian negotiator, while Sanders' NZPA history (pp. 23–4) mentions F. W. Ward of the same paper. On the issue of co-operation between Australian papers, Putnis (1997, p. 23) states that the *Age* and *Argus* did not operate a joint service until 1891, while Inglis (1980, p. 31) gives the merger as occurring in 1895.
34. Fenwick, *The United Press Association*, p. 15.
35. NZPA (UPA), Minutes 1885, p. 130; 1886, p. 179.
36. Ibid., 1920, p. 11.
37. Fenwick, *The United Press Association*, p. 15.

38. Sanders, *Dateline-NZPA*, p. 28.
39. NZPA (UPA), Minutes, 1886, p. 148.
40. Sanders, *Dateline-NZPA*, p. 29; Harvey, 'Bringing the News to New Zealand' (2002), pp. 30–1.
41. Sanders, *Dateline-NZPA*, pp. 28–9.
42. Hugh Barty-King, *Girdle Round the Earth: The Story of Cable and Wireless and its Predecessors to Mark the Group's Jubilee 1929–1979* (London: Heinemann, 1979), p. 63.
43. Coote entry, *Australian Dictionary of Biography* (Melbourne: Melbourne University Press, 1969), 3, p. 455.
44. Memorandum for Federal Council sitting at Hobart, January 1886, in F. C. Rowan, *Letterbooks, 1883–88* (National Library of Australia), pp. 28, 34.
45. Livingston, *The Wired Nation Continent*, pp. 100–1.
46. Rowan to the *Age*, 18 May 1886 in *Letterbook*, p. 170.
47. Rowan to the *Age*, 3 May 1886 in *Letterbook*, pp. 139ff.
48. Rowan to Coote, 23 February 1886; Rowan to R. Want, 21 May 1886 in *Letterbook*, pp. 77ff.
49. Rowan to R. C. Want, 16 December 1885 in *Letterbook*.
50. Rowan to the editor of the *Age*, 30 March 1886 in *Letterbook*, p. 114.
51. Rowan to the editor of the *Argus*, 29 March 1886 in *Letterbook*, p. 110.
52. Ibid.
53. Barty-King, *Girdle Round the Earth*, p. 77.
54. W. D. Le Sueur, 'The Jubilee Conference of 1887', in George Johnson (ed.), *The All Red Line. The Annals and Aims of the Pacific Cable Project* (Ottawa: James Hope and Sons, 1903), pp. 51–4.
55. Livingston, *The Wired Nation Continent*, p. 145.
56. Barty-King, *Girdle Round the Earth*, p. 91.
57. F. Hamilton, 'The Imperial Conference of 1896', in Johnson, *The All Red Line*, p. 190.
58. R. Bruce Scott, *Gentlemen on Imperial Service: A Study of the trans-Pacific Telecommunications Cable* (Victoria: Sono Nis Press, 1934), p. 6.
59. Gerald Newton Savory, 'Colonial Business Initiatives and the Pacific Cable. A Study in the Role of Private Enterprise in the Development of Imperial Communications' (MA diss., University of Washington 1972), p. 111.
60. Livingston, *The Wired Nation Continent*, p. 123.
61. Hamilton, 'The Imperial Conference of 1896', p. 226.
62. George Johnston, 'The Ottawa Conference of 1894', in Johnson, *The All Red Route*, p. 185.
63. NZPA (UPA) Minutes 1895, p. 58.
64. Select Committee on Press Cable Service in Australian Senate, *Journals* (1909), 1, 309.
65. Sanders, *Dateline-NZPA*, pp. 28–9.
66. Select Committee on Press Cable Service, *Report*, p. 288.
67. Potter, *News and the British World*, pp. 45ff.
68. Robert Donald, *The Imperial Press Conference in Canada* (London and New York: Hodder & Stoughton, 1992), p. 171.
69. T. H. Hardman, *A Parliament of the Press: The First Imperial Press Conference* (London: Horace Marshall, 1909), p. 50.
70. Hardman, *A Parliament of the Press*, p. 137.

71. Lachlan McKinnon, Evidence to Select Committee on Press Cable Service, p. 317.
72. Ibid., p. 316.
73. Ibid., p. 317.
74. NZPA (UPA) Minutes, 1904, p. 295.
75. R. B. Walker, The *Newspaper Press in New South Wales, 1803–1920* (Sydney: Sydney University Press, 1976), p. 185.
76. Rod Kirkpatrick, *Country Conscience: A History of the New South Wales Provincial Press, 1841–1995* (Canberra: Infinite Harvest Publishing, 2000), p. 175.
77. Independent Cable Association of Australasia, Company File 1910 (New South Wales Archives Office 3/5801 3455).
78. Hardman, *A Parliament of the Press*, pp. 112, 123.
79. NZPA (UPA), Minutes 1910.
80. Theodor Fink, 'History of the Herald', in Fink Papers, Box 5, File 2 (University of Melbourne Archives MSS 97/127).
81. NZPA (UPA), Minutes 1910, p. 1.

12

A 'Sense of Common Citizenship'? Mrs Potts of Reefton, New Zealand, Communicates with the Empire

Ross Harvey

Introduction

A 'sense of common citizenship', claimed Sir Sandford Fleming in 1906, would be an outcome of publishing 'even small portions of...Empire news' in newspapers throughout the Empire.[1] In 1876 the final piece in the essential infrastructure of an imperial press system, the cable connecting New Zealand to the rest of the Empire, was in place. But what did this mean for newspaper readers in the more remote corners of the Empire? Were they too preoccupied with local commercial interests and with earning a living to pay much heed to news about parts of the world that they had left and were unlikely to return to? Certainly, one newspaper proprietor in Reefton, New Zealand, in the mid-1890s thought that it was worth persevering to preserve her membership of the United Press Association (UPA) and, through this, access to news from the Empire. Why? Was a sense of common citizenship sought, or can the decision be explained on other grounds?

Reefton, a remote mining town in the north-west of the South Island of New Zealand, is almost as far away from London as one can get. It might be considered that this isolation from the rest of the British Empire resulted in newspapers that were almost completely preoccupied with local, provincial and, occasionally, national events. Yet in the mid-1890s Mrs M. A. T. Potts, proprietor of one of Reefton's three newspapers, the *Inangahua Times*, fought energetically to maintain her newspaper's membership of the UPA. This chapter examines the case of Mrs Potts and the *Inangahua Times* in an attempt to establish what motivated the proprietors of small country newspapers to join and participate in press associations, and what readers of these newspapers gained from such memberships. This attempt may lead to a better understanding of the value of press association membership and participation in an imperial press system to these proprietors.

Although the role and significance of press associations in the development of an imperial press network have been demonstrated by Potter, Kaul, Boyd-Barrett, Rantanen and others,[2] the literature is silent on the question of what motivated newspaper proprietors to join and participate in press associations. Discussions of an imperial press network, such as those by Potter and Kaul,[3] suggest that it developed for commercial and ideological reasons, promoting the development of trade for the benefit of Britain and promoting British ideals to the rest of the world. But these 'big picture' discussions are principally concerned with the large and powerful metropolitan newspapers of the Empire, *The Times, The Times of India, The Argus* and their counterparts, and typically do not address small newspapers and their interests.[4]

This chapter seeks answers to three questions in the context of New Zealand country newspapers in the late nineteenth century: What did the proprietors of these newspapers gain from participating in press associations? What did readers gain from reading these newspapers? Did proprietors and readers have any sense of participating in an imperial press system? It is based on the archives of the New Zealand Press Association and on extant issues of the *Inangahua Times* published in the 1890s. It is a case study in the ingest and distribution of imperial news in New Zealand, a country that provides a near-ideal case study for examining the 'wider saga' of the formation of neo-Britains.[5] New Zealand in the 1890s had only one effective source for news from overseas; consequently, the imperial press system's New Zealand branch was uniform.

New Zealand, 'the most distant of Britain's possessions'

Some key factors about New Zealand and its relationship to the Empire affected its newspapers. One was the timing of access to the telegraph and with it the ability to participate fully in the Empire. New Zealand was connected by telegraph with the rest of the world only in 1876. After that year the development of the New Zealand Press Association shaped the way in which news was sourced, its nature, distribution and control by government. Another factor was the nature of settlement in nineteenth-century New Zealand, with many small farming and mining settlements and small cities. Consequently 'geographical conditions in New Zealand were particularly conducive to the establishment of small-town newspapers'.[6] A third factor is New Zealand's small physical area and population. This resulted in being able to support only one press association, leading to a monopolistic situation that significantly altered the nature of the news, how much of it was available and the very operation of the newspapers.

Perhaps most significant was the distance of New Zealand from the hub of the Empire and most of the other colonies and dominions. Shipping routes, postage costs and government subsidies determined the frequency and freshness of contact with the rest of the Empire. Communication, as Chandrika Kaul notes, plays 'a vital role in shaping political, institutional and cultural structures...especially so in the case of empires, with the extensive spatial dimensions inherent in this form of political organisation'.[7] New Zealand governments certainly recognised the importance to their developing nation of encouraging efficient communication channels using all possible means. The penny charge by the British Post Office on newspapers sent to and from New Zealand was in 1847 considered to 'operate prejudicially upon the diffusion of information which it is enlightened policy to encourage by all available means';[8] twenty years later the New Zealand Parliament was still debating the need to abolish postage on newspapers because 'in a public point of view it was highly desirable to encourage to the utmost the free circulation of newspapers in the Colony'.[9]

Although New Zealand was only 'a subplot in the diaspora of Europeans that sent as many as 50 million from the Old World to the New',[10] it became a keen and committed part of the Empire. But was the colonial experience weaker and less effective because communications were difficult? We should keep in mind that New Zealand was considered 'More English than England!', resulting perhaps from its isolation, so that it clung to 'the ideas traditionally associated with the Victorian Age which nurtured her in infancy and early youth', and was 'untouched by the revolutionary solvents of the twentieth century'.[11]

Mrs Potts and the *Inangahua Times*, Reefton

The New Zealand Press Association archives in the Alexander Turnbull Library, Wellington, include correspondence in 1894 and 1895 between Mrs M. A. T. Potts and the United Press Association. This correspondence, almost entirely concerned with maintaining a cable news service to Mrs Potts' newspaper, the *Inangahua Times*, Reefton, is clear evidence of the significant value placed on receiving a cable service. Why did the impecunious Mrs Potts feel it necessary to go to extraordinary lengths to ensure that her newspaper was supplied with the cables, especially when if she had waited one day she could have copied, legally, the same news from other papers? Why did she consider the cabled news as so essential? Her persistence is all the more extraordinary in light of the frequently expressed contemporary opinion that much of what was sent by the wires was padding and was 'not news'.[12] The conventional answer is the business advantage that publishing cabled news provided, so that Mrs Potts' newspaper could sell more copies, attract advertising and turn a profit – or at least provide her with a living. But this does not fully explain the lengths to which Mrs Potts was prepared to go. Did the inhabitants of Reefton, an isolated town in 'the most distant of British possessions',[13] consider that they needed to be in touch with the rest of the Empire? Would they have purchased the *Inangahua Times* if it did not contain current news from the rest of the Empire and the world? To what extent was Mrs Potts aware of being part of a wider imperial press system? Or can her concerns be explained simply on economic grounds?

In November 1875, William Joseph Potts became the proprietor of the *Inangahua Times*, a morning newspaper published three times per week in Reefton. This newspaper had been established by the Inangahua Times Company (Limited) earlier that year and Potts had initially operated it on their behalf.[14] In 1888 Mr Potts enquired about joining the United Press Association and was advised that he could subscribe to one of three classes:

> The first class contains everything...The second class contains all but 'specials'; the third contains the ordinary foreign cables & a summary only of Australian news.[15]

For third-class service Potts was entitled to 'a main service of foreign news (without sporting or commercial, except the result of one or two races) & a summary of Australian news (also excluding sporting except the results of such races as the Melbourne Cup)'. He could also choose between two ways of receiving inter-provincial news (news from within New Zealand), either taking a supply of news 'condensed in Wellington' or 'from the agents direct'.[16]

Potts subscribed and the first issue with 'UPA Telegraphic News' was on 10 August 1888. Issues prior to this had used headings such as 'Latest Cablegrams. By Electric Telegraph (Copyright)' for overseas news, or 'Telegrams. (From Our Own Correspondent)' for news originating in New Zealand; the headings for 10 August 1888 read 'Latest Cablegrams.

(By Electric Telegraph-Copyright.) Per United Press Association', 'Australian (Per Press Association.)', 'Telegrams' for New Zealand news, and 'Parliamentary. United Press Association'. In later issues New Zealand news was prefaced by 'Colonial Telegrams. By Electric Telegraph Per United Press Association' and, although there were small variations, the one constant was attribution to the Press Association. The 10 August 1888 issue also indicated that the previous day an evening edition had been published for the first time. It would contain, courtesy of 'a thoroughly efficient telegraphic service, all the latest British and foreign, as well as inter-colonial, inter-provincial, and Parliamentary intelligence' up to press time each evening. As a result, readers would 'enjoy the same advantages as are offered in all the metropolitan towns'.[17] The Association explained elsewhere that 'newspapers which pay for importing' cable news from overseas currently are protected by law for preferential use for 18 hours, after which 'the cablegrams may be copied by any non-subscribing newspaper gratis'.[18]

We next read about the *Inangahua Times* in the Press Association archives through correspondence with Mrs M. A. T. Potts, widow of William Potts, who died on 23 January 1891. Mrs Potts leased the newspaper to Messrs Noble and Calvert, but the lessees did not pay the fees required to maintain its Press Association membership. Mrs Potts issued the *Inangahau Times* as a morning daily from 1 May 1891, apparently to compete with the two other newspapers in Reefton, which were also being issued daily. (That three daily newspapers could appear in Reefton, which had a population of just 2,000,[19] is remarkable.) She indicated that 'no effort will be spared in making the paper a reliable record of daily news, and its columns will be found to contain the latest cablegrams [British and foreign, including Australian news], telegrams [New Zealand news], mining and general news'; its intended audience was 'tradespeople and others [who] will find in the *Inangahua Times* a journal commanding an extensive circulation...The mining industry, being the principal mainstay of the district, will always be faithfully supported and its claims consistently advocated.'[20]

Only a few 1893 issues of the *Inanagahua Times* survive so it is difficult to be precise about what happened next. Edward H. Canavan, apparently hired as manager, enquired of the Press Association in November 1893 about the currency of the newspaper's membership. He had 'observed from the last annual report of the Assn that the membership has ceased', and 'its owner would not like to be deprived of a valuable asset through the carelessness of her lessees', Noble and Calvert.[21] By early January 1894 Canavan could see little likelihood of the paper continuing, with three daily papers serving this small community 'too much...there is little use keeping on the subscription unless the payments can be made smoothly and regularly, and for this I can see no certainty at present'.[22] Mrs Potts, however, thought differently, taking more direct control near the start of 1894.[23] In late January 1894 she wrote to W. H. Atack, the Association's manager, to request more time to pay the outstanding debts. She noted that 'of course being connected with the Press Association adds considerably to the value' of the property and 'for this reason I ask you to grant me another month'.[24] Meanwhile, the Press Association discussed recovering its debts from Mrs Potts.[25] Canavan, apparently still with the *Times*, was more sanguine about the business recovering and urged the Association to continue its service until at least one of the three Reefton papers ceased, suggesting that a nominal service 'in the way of mining reports, etc.'[26] be provided. The Association found this acceptable and suggested that the *Times* act as the Association's correspondent to settle the outstanding account.[27] Mrs Potts cabled her agreement, but noted that Canavan had left her employ and was editing one of the opposition papers, the *Reefton Guardian*, and she requested authorisation for the editor of the *Inangahua Times* to act as the Press Association's special correspondent.[28]

Mrs Potts finally made up her mind to rejoin the Association. In a letter to Atack dated 8 April 1894, she requested the exact terms and a statement of her debt to the Association. She had been left in an embarrassing financial situation on the death of her husband but was now free of this debt, although she requested that the Association 'make all the allowances you possibly can'. Canavan, she considered, had 'acted in a most shabby manner' by publicly indicating that the *Times* has been struck off the Association's list of subscribing papers and that the Association was intending to take 'immediate proceedings for piracy',[29] and she requested in a telegram to the Association that it 'instruct Mr Canavan to discontinue sending Association telegrams'.[30] Meanwhile, counter to their earlier decision, the Association had apparently given Mrs Potts notice that she must settle her debt with them, suggesting that if she settled within a fortnight then she should be allowed to resume the cable service, otherwise 'we must cut her off completely'.[31]

These threats appear to have spurred Mrs Potts into action, and she advised Atack in a letter dated 24 April 1894 that she had instituted proceedings to recover the £20 owing the Association.[32] Three weeks later she suggested that she pay the current subscription and 'an additional sum of £3 per quarter in liquidation of my former tenants' liability (£30)'. She was 'endeavouring – whilst struggling against tremendous odds – to act fairly, & honestly & you must admit that it is hard that I should be held responsible for the debts of others' and lamented that 'had I known, during the time that Messrs. Noble & Calvert were leasing the paper, that the Press Association fees were unpaid I could have insisted on their fulfilling the terms of agreement but I was completely in the dark'.[33] One day later she again wrote to Atack with a third proposal, her ability to pay based on the likelihood that one of the two rival newspapers would shortly be moving its plant from Reefton to Nelson.[34] Meanwhile she continued her battle against her rival's alleged piracy, at the end of June forwarding a copy of the *Inangahua Herald* extra for 25 June 1894 with the comment: 'The enclosed speaks for itself. The *Herald* is not an Association paper but continues to be ahead of all of us in important items of news.'[35]

Agreement was reached at the end of June 1894. Mrs Potts had purchased the goodwill of the *Reefton Guardian*, and will 'henceforth have a better chance of success', although for the next few months she must limit the number of telegrams she received and requested 'only the most <u>important</u> news until such time as I can recover lost ground'.[36] She also cancelled the inter-provincial service[37] but changed her mind only two days later:

> I am willing to subscribe to both the inter-provincial service & Cable, as there is no other alternative. It will be a struggle for the first 6 months, & if it is at all possible to make some reduction in Cable fee – just for the time being – I would be very thankful . . . I have limited Cable messages to 500 words, but think the limit had better be <u>700</u> for Cablegrams & telegrams during the Session. Please do not send commercial Cablegrams, they are of no interest here.[38]

Correspondence between the Association and Mrs Potts after this date is largely concerned with payments. Mrs Potts fought doggedly to ensure that she secured the most favourable arrangement. Some comments suggest the value of the arrangement to her newspaper. In August 1894 she noted that clipping from other newspapers was not possible for her evening daily because 'the train does not arrive here with the morning (Greymouth) papers until ½ 7 p.m. so you see it is impossible for us to copy. (Our contemporary the "Herald" however does so in a most flagrant manner, & with impunity.)'[39] She explained further: 'Monday is the only day on which the train reaches Reefton early (11.30 a.m.) On that day we have two trains & the Grey River Argus comes by the morning train therefore that is the only opportunity we have of clipping from our contemporaries.' She again complained about the 'the piracy of Cable News' by the rival *Herald* 'without contributing a penny for the privilege'.[40] A further complaint followed, the *Times* editor noting that 'Mrs Potts has to pay sometimes as much as £4 per week to the Telegraph Office for wires, and it is annoying to find that which she has to pay for appearing in the opposition paper'.[41]

All was not yet running smoothly. In a private letter to Atack in November 1894, Canavan, now editor of the *Reefton Guardian*, painted a gloomy picture of the likelihood of the *Inangahua Times* surviving. It was 'financially defunct – the plant mortgaged and the business shattered by severe competition' and Mrs Potts is unable to pay her staff.[42] Canavan's comments should not be taken at face value, for the *Reefton Guardian* closed some time in 1894. In fact, by March 1895 Mrs Potts was reporting to Atack that an agreement between the two Reefton papers had resulted in increased advertising revenue because, 'instead of separately competing with each other for cheap work as has hitherto been the custom', a fair price was received.[43]

Canavan's prognosis of the financial health of the *Times* may have had some factual basis, for at some stage in 1895 Mrs Potts had reduced her supply of cabled news (although 1895 and 1896 issues examined do not show any evidence of this). In July she reinstated her subscription to the cablegrams 'in order to meet the requirements of the public & to compete with other papers circulating in the district',[44] but to her 'astonishment & indignation' when she received the first supply of cables she discovered that it had already been 'circulated all over the town' by the *Herald* two hours earlier. Cash flow was still clearly a problem, as she set a limit for cables of '400 words daily, & inter provincial telegrams 200 words... or an average equal to about £1 per week which is all I can afford just now', and noted that on Mondays she could copy from the Grey River *Argus* and on Wednesdays no wires were required after 11 am, as 'we publish early (half holiday)'.[45] In a later letter to Atack she further explained the situation:

I wired to you not to send messages after 10 a.m. on Wednesdays because the *Times* is published at midday every Wednesday & of course any messages received after publication on Wednesday afternoon are useless for publication in Thursday's paper as they all appear in the Greymouth 'Star' which arrives here every night

(Wednesdays included) by the 7 p.m. train. Last Wednesday week the days messages amounted to 10/. That was so much money thrown away, as if we want to copy stale messages we can copy from the 'Star' but of course the advantage of being connected with the Association is that we receive the same messages every day as the Greymouth papers, & have them published here before the arrival of the evening train. If there were a morning or midday train we could then copy from the 'Argus', & you would only have to send a few in the afternoon. The messages last week amounted to £2.16 which I would not like to pay *every* week.[46]

But by the start of 1896 'the present dullness' was again causing Mrs Potts to consider discontinuing her cable messages. She suggested that the Association should permit the *Times* some leeway because it was possibly unique in New Zealand in that it was 'unable to copy its morning contemporary's cables & telegrams'.[47] This letter is the last of any significance between Mrs Potts and Atack, with an exception in October 1899, where the ongoing complaint against the *Herald*'s piracy was reiterated:

> our morning contemporary 'Inangahua Herald' is publishing cables in a more barefaced manner... We received a wire on Friday morning for publication in the evening but in the afternoon the Herald published all the news as an extra... The editor's son is in Wellington & probably clips cables from Wellington papers & forwards them to Reefton. In order to prevent Press Ass messages being published second hand we have now to issue an extra. Can nothing be done to prevent this.[48]

What the *Inangahua Times* contains

Why is it worth recounting in some detail this story? It perhaps tells us a little more than has previously been understood about the role of the Press Association and the way it operated, and it strongly reiterates the value placed on getting the cabled and telegraphed news, despite frequent setbacks such as piracy of news. The story also reveals the curiously ambivalent role of the Press Association in providing country newspapers with cable service. It was surprisingly patient (more accurately its manager, Atack, was patient) in its attempts to accommodate Mrs Potts' vacillations, apparently acknowledging the attempts she was making to meet her obligations. However, it was unwilling to act against the *Inangahua Herald* for its alleged piracy of telegrams. Its attitudes and actions in relation to the Reefton newspapers may be explained in part by its monopolistic nature. No other supply of overseas news was available to newspaper proprietors in New Zealand at the time. There was no significant competition after 1878 and some considered that the Press Association enjoyed 'a vicious monopoly which is being worked to the detriment of small and struggling newspapers'. An opposition association based on a cabled supply of Australian and European news from Sydney and charging members 'nothing beyond wire charges'[49] was proposed in 1894 by Joseph Ivess, but was unsuccessful. In such a dominant position the Press Association had little need to respond to the complaints of small and struggling country newspapers.

Another point illuminated by this story is the value placed by the *Inangahua Times* on getting cabled and telegraphed news, despite frequent piracy. We can assume that the principle of exclusivity, as noted by Rantanen in relation to news agencies, was operating at the level of the individual newspaper for Mrs Potts; that is, 'in news provision the news quickly becomes common property, so in order to survive economically the news agency must be able to exclude from using the news those newspapers which do not pay for it'.[50] Those newspapers that can provide the news exclusively, at least initially, have an edge over those who cannot. But for New Zealand country newspapers the Press Association's cable service was not satisfactory. The Wanganui Herald Newspaper Co. in 1895 complained to the Association about the 'excess of quantity' of both overseas and New Zealand news it was provided with (it must be realised that the newspapers paid the cable charges) and also about the quality, 'which is frequently not of a standard justifying its despatch to us'. The Wanganui Herald Newspaper Co. had discussed this matter with a 'large number of journals' who, with one exception, all agreed that improvements were required. The matter was urgent because:

A daily supply of well selected telegraphic items is an absolute necessity and a considerable quantity of that wired us & other up-country journals does not come under that category & puts us to great unnecessary expense.... it is the opinion of a large number of our up-county contemporaries that there is great cause for complaint in this connection ... We regret having to speak so plainly but the matter is one of vital importance to the proprietors of up country papers & needs immediate amendment.[51]

But the Potts story does not illuminate our understanding about two of the questions posed at the start of this chapter: What did readers gain from reading the newspapers that did participate in the press association? And, did proprietors and readers have any sense of participating in an imperial press system? In relation to news from overseas the journalistic world expressed some scepticism about its value to readers, Alan Mulgan in 1934 advising that 'it is a rule in journalism that, generally speaking, local news is more important than news from a distance' and that 'large numbers of people are not interested in overseas news, or a large part of such news. They are either not sufficiently intelligent or well-informed, or they are too busy to care.'[52] But apparently Mrs Potts did not subscribe to this view. To seek a better understanding of these matters we turn to a reading of the extant issues of the *Inangahua Times* for 1894 to 1896, the period covered by the correspondence between Mrs Potts and the Press Association.

Unfortunately, the newspapers themselves provide few clues about the importance of cabled news to its readers. The limitations of this chapter preclude reporting on the exact nature of the news reported in the *Inangahua Times*, but a general description of the numbers from 1894 to the start of 1896 indicate its flavour. Each number was 28 columns in total (four pages, each of seven columns). A typical number (and there was remarkably little variation over this period) comprised 23–4 columns of advertising and 4–5 columns of news (liberally interpreted to include a wide variety of literary matter), on rare occasions rising to seven columns. For instance, the number for 1 February 1894 consisted of about 23½ columns of advertising and about 4½ of news, made up of editorial comment (¾ column), 'Local and General' (1¾), Australian news (attributed to the UPA, ½), cablegrams ('British and Foreign', attributed to the UPA, ½), telegrams (New Zealand content, UPA attribution, ½) and sporting (¼) (the measures are all approximate). This was little different from the 10 July 1894 number where one might expect an increase in cabled news because it was the second day of the newspaper's change from a morning to an evening issue. Here the 4½ columns of news consisted of editorial comment (½ column), 'Local and General' (¾), cablegrams ('British and Foreign', attributed to the UPA, ¼), telegrams (New Zealand content, UPA attribution, ½), mining intelligence (½) and other (attributed to 'Own Correspondent', ¾).

This balance varies little in the numbers available to us now from this period (1894 March to April and mid-October to December are missing), although sometimes there was no editorial, infrequently correspondence was included, and more often 'mining intelligence' or sports results were provided. This was definitely a mining town newspaper: a standing advertisement in the 1894 numbers indicates 'special attention given to mining matters, local & foreign'. (Numbers exist of a *Mining Sheet* issued weekly by the newspaper in 1894 and 1895 to provide readers with 'the latest mining news at the earliest possible hour'.[53]) It was also definitely a local Reefton newspaper, with a very strong emphasis on Reefton news, and a New Zealand newspaper, with reporting of significant events elsewhere in New Zealand, and with only occasional editorial comment about matters outside New Zealand, these being usually but not solely British events. An examination of the newspapers reveals little evidence that it was being produced for readers who eagerly sought news from outside its shores. The editorials, when they are included, are usually not related to wider world issues or views, focusing instead on mining and national (that is, New Zealand) matters, especially sittings of Parliament. Even where one could expect a change in the quantity and nature of overseas news, such as where the Potts–UPA correspondence suggests that changes in the newspapers were made, the newspapers provide little obvious evidence that these changes were made.

Statements made in some numbers of the *Inangahua Times* promise more. On 25 June 1894 it incorporated one of its rivals, appearing for the first time as the *Inangahua Times and Reefton Guardian*. Its editorial advised readers that 'new arrangements have been made for the supply of the latest intelligence, so that the stirring events taking place in Parliament will, together with the general and local news have extended space in our columns'. However, if any changes were made they are not evident. On 2 July 1894 the change from morning to evening issue was foreshadowed for the following week. The editorial in this number noted that 'in progressive times' change is desirable, making it 'necessary to keep abreast of current developments'; this could be best accommodated by publishing in the evening to allow 'all reports of public meetings to be done justice to'. This was desirable, it was explained, because 'a paper should be a faithful reflex of local events ... a proper epitome of local history, and can be used to send abroad in lieu of personal correspondence'. It noted, too, that changing to being issued at 4 pm would enable the newspaper to make the most of its subscription to the Press Association (it being 'the only paper in the district subscribing' to its services) and so 'we have decided to take the whole of the original cablegrams and telegrams' rather than the more limited supply that morning issue necessitated because of the closure of the telegraph stations at midnight. Again, however, no obvious change to the nature and quantity of news is discernable from a scrutiny of the newspapers around this date.

Conclusion

Potter suggests the emergence of a 'mutual interdependence' between Britain and the Dominions as a consequence of the embryonic imperial press system that was developing in the late nineteenth century.[54] This limited case study has examined the one-way traffic of news from the rest of the world to the Dominion of New Zealand. (We must, of course, acknowledge that traffic in news was not all one-way. A more comprehensive study would need to investigate the supply of news from New Zealand to the rest of the Empire, initially as monthly supplements to the well-established newspapers or as separate titles – for example, the *Illustrated New Zealand Herald*.) This limited case study has not revealed any inkling of 'mutual interdependence'. The investigations in it have not enabled the questions posed at the start of this chapter to be answered with any degree of certainty. This reading of the *Inangahua Times* suggests that it remained determinedly a local newspaper, despite the inclusion of news from elsewhere in New Zealand and beyond. What we can say is that for Mrs Potts in Reefton in the mid-1890s, the provision of the most recent news from overseas, as well as from within New Zealand, was very important, and she went to considerable lengths to ensure that this supply was unbroken. What we cannot determine precisely from this study is the value of this supply of news to the newspaper's readers and to its commercial viability. Further studies are needed for more precise conclusions to be drawn. Whatever Mrs Potts' motives, the *Inangahua Times* outlasted its competitors and survived until 1942.

Notes

1. Sandford Fleming, 1906, quoted in S. J. Potter, *News and the British World: The Emergence of an Imperial Press System* (Oxford: Clarendon, 2003), p. 66.
2. Potter, *News and the British World*; C. Kaul, *Reporting the Raj: The British Press and India, c. 1880–1922* (Manchester: Manchester University Press, 2003); O. Boyd-Barrett and T. Rantanen (eds.), *The Globalization of News* (London: Sage, 1998).
3. Potter, *News and the British World*, Kaul, *Reporting the Raj*.
4. An exception is Potter, *News and the British World*, who pays some attention to the situation of country newspapers in New Zealand; for example, p. 33.

5. J. Belich, *Making Peoples: A History of the New Zealanders* (Auckland: Penguin, 1996), p. 277.
6. P. Griffth, R. Harvey and K. Maslen (eds.), *Book & Print in New Zealand: A Guide to Print Culture in Aotearoa* (Wellington: Victoria University Press, 1997), p. 130.
7. Kaul, *Reporting the Raj*, p. 3.
8. *New-Zealander* (13 October 1847): 2.
9. 'Postage on Newspapers', *New Zealand Parliamentary Debates*. House (19 August 1868), p. 513.
10. M. King, *The Penguin History of New Zealand* (Auckland: Penguin, 2003), pp. 169–70.
11. *The Cambridge History of the British Empire: Volume VII Part II: New Zealand* (Cambridge: Cambridge University Press, 1933), p. 7.
12. *Report of the Press Telegrams Committee*, N.Z. House of Representatives. *Appendices to the Journals* (1880), I.-5, p. 22, no. 433.
13. H. Brett, *The New Zealand Press Association: What Is It?* (Wellington: NZPA, 1898).
14. The *Inangahua Times* is available in microfilm and also at http://paperspast.natlib.govt.nz.
15. NZPA Archives, Atack to W. J. Potts, 25 May 1888.
16. NZPA Archives, Atack to W. J. Potts, 8 August 1888. {PRIVATE}
17. *Inangahua Times* (10 August 1888), p. 2.
18. Brett, *The New Zealand Press Association*, p. 3.
19. G. H. Scholefield, *Newspapers in New Zealand* (Wellington: Reed, 1958), p. 255.
20. *Inangahau Times* (1 May 1891).
21. NZPA Archives, Canavan to Atack, 4 November 1893.
22. NZPA Archives, Canavan to Atack, 19 January 1894.
23. *Inangahua Times* (2 January 1894) 2: 'owing to the sudden change of management of this paper, a doubt exists as to whether our list of subscribers is complete'.
24. NZPA Archives, M.A.T. Potts to Atack, 31 January 1894.
25. NZPA Archives, Brett to Atack, 1 February 1894.
26. NZPA Archives, Canavan to Atack, 1894.
27. NZPA Archives, Brett to Atack, 30 March 1894.
28. NZPA Archives, M. Potts to Atack, 7 April 1894.
29. NZPA Archives, M. A. T. Potts, to Atack, 8 April 1894.
30. NZPA Archives, M. Potts to Atack, 12 April 1894.
31. NZPA Archives, Brett to Atack, 24 April 1894.
32. NZPA Archives, M. A. T. Potts to Atack, 24 April 1894.
33. NZPA Archives, M. A. T. Potts to Atack, 14 May 1894.
34. NZPA Archives, M. A. T. Potts to Atack, 15 May 1894.
35. NZPA Archives, Thomson? and Innes? to Atack, undated.
36. NZPA Archives, M. A. T. Potts to Atack, 25 June 1894.
37. NZPA Archives, Potts to Atack, 4 July 1894.
38. NZPA Archives, M. A. T. Potts to Atack, 6 July 1894.
39. NZPA Archives, M. A. T. Potts to Atack, 2 August 1894.
40. NZPA Archives, M. A. T. Potts to Atack, 9 August 1894.
41. NZPA Archives, Gillon to Atack, undated (late September or early October 1894).

42. NZPA Archives, Canavan to Atack, 29 November 1894.
43. NZPA Archives, M. A. T. Potts to Atack, 27 March 1895.
44. NZPA Archives, M. A. T. Potts to Atack, 23 July 1895.
45. NZPA Archives, M. A. T. Potts to Atack, 25 July 1895.
46. NZPA Archives, M. A. T. Potts to Atack, 18 August 1895.
47. NZPA Archives, M. A.T. Potts to Atack, 8 January 1896.
48. NZPA Archives, M.A. T. Potts to Atack, 16 October 1899.
49. Printed circular 'The Anglo-Colonial Press Association', signed 'Joseph Ivess, Promoter', To the Proprietor of [blank], Stratford, 25 October 1894: in NZPA Archives, {PRIVATE} Letterbook 30 November 1891 to 7 February 1895.
50. T. Rantanen, 'The Struggle for Control of Domestic News Markets (1)', in O. Boyd-Barrett and T. Rantanen (eds.), *The Globalization of News* (London: Sage, 1998), p. 36.
51. NZPA Archives, Wanganui Herald Newspaper Co. to Atack, 21 June 1895.
52. A. Mulgan, 'World Affairs in the Press', *Lectures in Journalism: Digest of Extension Course June–September 1934, Auckland University College* (Auckland: Auckland University College, 1934), p. 7.
53. Held by the Alexander Turnbull Library, Wellington.
54. Potter 2003, pp. 15–16.

13

'That some must suffer for the greater good': The *Post Courier* and the 1969 Bougainville Crisis

Philip Cass

This chapter examines the way in which the *Post Courier*, then Papua New Guinea's only daily newspaper, covered the emerging crisis on Bougainville in the second half of 1969 as landowners resisted attempts to begin work on the Panguna copper mine. It argues that although the *Post Courier*'s reporting could be interpreted as favourable towards the mine's owner, Conzinc Rio Australia; it could also, paradoxically, be interpreted as broadly developmental. The *Post Courier*'s reporting of the dispute in 1969 hints at the more violent conflicts to come in 1975 and 1990 and reflects the conflict between the need for national unity and national consciousness in a developing nation and micro-nationalist movements.

The Island of New Guinea was initially divided among Australia, the Netherlands and Wilhelmine Germany. Queensland annexed Papua, the south-east segment of the island, in 1883 when Queensland was still a separate colony.[1] This move outraged London, which was not keen on its colonies having colonies of their own. In 1906, the recently federated dominion of Australia accepted sovereignty over what had by then become British New Guinea.[2] The western half of the island had already been annexed by the Dutch as an outgrowth of its control of the Netherlands East Indies, and in 1885 Kaiser Wilhelm authorised the Deutsche New Guinea Kompagnie to administer German New Guinea on its behalf. Berlin assumed direct control a decade later.

Australia seized New Guinea from the Germans in 1914 as its first contribution to the British Empire's struggle with Germany. After the war Australia was granted control of New Guinea under a mandate from the League of Nations. In the period up to the Japanese invasion of 1942, the people of Bougainville had only limited contact with

Europeans. The harbour at Kieta, which was in Nasioi territory, made a natural entry point to Bougainville for missionaries, planters and colonial administrators.[3] The Nasioi, on whose land the Panguna mine would later be established, were thus exposed to Europeans from an early stage.

During the Second World War Bougainville was heavily fought over. Most local people hid in the bush, while a minority collaborated with the Japanese and a larger number assisted the Australian coast watchers. It was only after the war that the Australian administration had either the necessary resources or the incentive to begin to extend a range of services to the island. After the war the mandate over New Guinea was resumed under the auspices of the United Nations. In practice, Australia ran Papua and New Guinea as one territory and the United Nations acted as if both territories were under its mandate. Under the terms of the mandate, Australia was obliged to prepare the indigenous people for self-government and eventual independence.

While Hudson makes a cogent argument about the colonial nature of the Australian administration in Papua New Guinea, it is very difficult to see the Territory of Papua New Guinea itself as a colony in the same way as New Caledonia, for instance.[4] It was never intended as the site of large-scale European settlement and for decades offered no real financial incentives. It can probably be argued that even a firm like Burns Philp derived a steadier income from its trade stores than from copra plantations subject to fluctuations in the world market.

In fact, we must look to Fiji, a British colony, to find an Australian firm making money from a colonial enterprise. This was Colonial Sugar Refineries, which ruthlessly exploited the indentured workers brought from India to work on the sugar plantations, a crop imported to provide the British colonial administration with a source of revenue to offset the costs of running the islands.[5] This is not to say that many Australians did not share expansionist ideas about the Pacific. Thompson demonstrates quite clearly that there were certainly elements in Australian politics, the commercial community and the public who longed for Australia to fulfil a sub-imperial role in the Pacific and who advocated, at various times, the annexation of Fiji and New Caledonia.[6] However, the British Government consistently made it clear that it would not condone such moves, and Papua New Guinea remained the only Pacific territory of any size administered by Australia.

Australia had a very ambivalent attitude towards PNG after 1945. It recoiled from the idea that it was administering a colony, but at the same time it refused to set a firm date for independence or self-government and resented what it regarded as ill-informed advice from UN inspectors. It also managed the country in a very inefficient manner. The Territory's administrator was poorly paid, unable to directly control the recruitment of staff and subject to constant interference by the Department of Foreign Affairs in Canberra.[7] The motivations of Australian officers in the field and the administration in PNG's capital, Port Moresby, were often far removed from those of cabinet ministers and senior public servants in Canberra. The willingness of Canberra to intervene, to bypass the PNG administration completely, ignore the advice of its officers in the field and its inability to deal sensitively with the Nasioi, were all to blame for the crisis on Bougainville in 1969.

However, the events that unfolded on Bougainville in 1969 had their origins in New Guinea's tangled colonial past as much as in Canberra's desire to curry favour with the mining company Conzinc Rio Australia. The real origins of the Bougainville tragedy lay in a conference in Washington in 1898 when representatives of Germany, the United States and Great Britain met to discuss under what rules each country could have access to each others' colonial markets in the Pacific and West Africa. As an inducement to the Germans, the British, who claimed the Solomon Islands, redrew their colonial boundaries so that Bougainville, which ethnically and geographically was part of the Solomons, became part of German New Guinea. It was a classic case of two imperial powers 'swapping natives' without any thought for the consequences.[8] For Papua New Guinea the consequences of the carelessly drawn imperial boundaries have been tragic. When Australia was granted a League of Nations mandate over New Guinea, no attempt was made to redraw the imperial boundary and Bougainville remained part of New Guinea.

After the First World War, the Administrator, Sir Hubert Murray, set up 'native' plantations and imposed a head tax to defray expenses, while the Australian Government pursued what was then the orthodox policy among metropolitan powers that overseas territories should not be a financial burden.[9] The pursuit of a source of revenue that would make Papua and New Guinea at least partly self-reliant financially continued after the Second World War and, in 1964, it appeared that a solution had been found when surveys showed that there were commercially viable deposits of low grade ore – and probably gold – in the coastal mountain range on the east of the island. The ore body was estimated to have a yield of 900 million tones. Conzinc Rio Australia, a subsidiary of the British mining company Conzinc Rio Tinto, spent Aus$21 million exploring the site.

CRA negotiated a development agreement with the Australian Government which contained provision for a payment of a small part of the mining royalties to local landowners, along with compensation payments. Eventually, about 60 square miles – less than one per cent of the total island area of Bougainville – was acquired for the open cut mine, with 80 per cent of this being set aside for a tailings dump. CRA was given generous tax concessions by the Australian Government in Canberra.[10]

Neither the Australian Government nor the administration in Port Moresby had ever found the equivalent of Fiji's sugar crop to offset the costs of running the Territory, but a copper mine offered just such a prospect. By the time the mine was opened, it may have seemed that it could make PNG nearly economically self-sufficient.

There was opposition to CRA from the very beginning by the Nasioi people who were the traditional landowners. The American anthropologist Ogan, who lived among the Nasioi in the early 1960s when CRA was conducting its preliminary explorations, portrayed the local people as verging on the xenophobic and opposed to all external influences.[11] The Nasioi's dislike of foreigners encompassed not just white expatriates, but people from other parts of PNG.[12]

The proposed copper mine at Panguna provided a focus for resistance to the administration, renewed calls for independence and helped clarify Bougainvilleans' political aspirations. In 1968 elected politicians joined with undergraduates at the University of Papua New Guinea in Port Moresby and students at the Catholic seminary in Lae to call for a referendum on the future of Bougainville in 1970.[13]

Leo Hannett, then a university student and later a prominent leader of his people, said:

> Our historical, ethnic, racial, geographical and political ties are with the Solomons Group, the ties are stronger than any that exist between Bougainville and any other parts of the Territory. Many of the people of Bougainville have parts of their families and relatives living in the Solomons. Much as we cherish the friendship of our Papuan and New Guinean brothers, our customs and beliefs differ and no real ethnical bonds exist.[14]

May cites the opposition to the mine as a manifestation of micronationalism and places it within the context of similar movements across PNG in the post-war period. He observes that, in general, 'micronationalist movements reflect the circumstances of their origins' and characterises their objectives as 'broad, ambitious and ill-defined'.[15] The opposition movement on Bougainville had very clearly defined aims, at least in its early phase, but these (the abandonment of the mine or exclusive access to its wealth) do not sit entirely easily with the micro-nationalist sentiments expressed by Hannett, which were based on an idealised sense of ethnic identity. Hannett and the other students demanded a referendum to determine whether the island would remain part of PNG, become independent or join the British Solomon Islands Protectorate.

Opposition to the proposed mine and the land resumptions came from many sources, including Catholic priests on Bougainville and plantation owners whose land was wanted for the mine. Fathers Mahoney, Moore and Wiley were inspired in their opposition by their own experiences of strip mining in the United States. As Downs puts it, they

> shared an uncommon concern [at that time] for the preservation of Bougainville's natural environment [and] expressed distrust of anything that reminded them of the gutted Appalachian valleys pouring their slag into the green land of Ohio.[16]

The New Guinea Planters' Association also became involved when it was decided to acquire Arawa plantation forcibly as the basis for the township which would house the mineworkers and their families. Another important figure was Paul Lapun, a Bougainvillean nationalist elected to Papua New Guinea's first House of Assembly in 1964. He used the House as a forum for Bougainvilleans' concerns about the mine and acted as a respected figurehead for younger politicians and protesters. He introduced a bill which ensured that 5 per cent of government royalty receipts would be paid to all landowners in all future mining operations in PNG.

The final complication of an already complicated situation was the question of who owned the copper and who should benefit from it. The administration and the Australian Government operated on the principle that the minerals were owned by the Government. The Nasioi thought the minerals belonged to them and that they should receive all or the majority of the financial benefits of the mine's profits. Some Bougainvilleans felt that if profits from the mine were exclusively theirs, the revenue could be used to fund an independent Bougainville. Australia's Minister for External Territories, Charles Barnes, visited the island in 1965 and told the Nasioi they could expect no compensation for their land, only for houses and trees.[17]

The Australian attitude was made quite clear in a statement by the Director of Lands and Mines, Don Grove, in 1966:

> It is the practice in most newly developing countries throughout the world for the minerals to be owned by the Government, which then controls all the prospecting and mining activities [and] from the ownership of the minerals flows a payment of royalty ... If the law were to be changed ... a very few people could become rich and the whole of the rest of the Territory would be deprived of its proper share of benefits of the mining.[18]

This was the position to which the Territory's administration, the Australian Government and later independent Papua New Guinea governments would stick: that the Bougainville copper mine was a resource for the whole of PNG and not just one part of it. Profits from the mine would be used to benefit the whole of the Territory and, later, the whole country. As trustees of the Territory of Papua New Guinea, Australians were, as Nelson puts it, 'asked to create a nation'.[19] Benedict Anderson's concept of the imagined community has been cited so often that one hesitates to use it again, but if every a new country was fashioned out of the imagination, it was Papua New Guinea. With 1,000 languages and as many tribes, a geography that allowed the Highlanders to live in total isolation until the 1930s and levels of cultural development that ranged from hunter-gathering to sophisticated trading and exchange cycles, there was probably no more fragmented and diverse a population on earth.[20]

Within the boundaries of the colonial map inherited from the 1898 conference, therefore, Australia had to create a sense of national, as opposed to clan or district identity, negotiate the future of the Territory with the newly created indigenous educated elite, and find a way to ensure that PNG would enjoy a stable future.

Barnes saw the Bougainville copper mine as vital to the future of the Territory. 'If the CRA project is allowed to falter, the Government's policy for the economic, social and political development ... will be placed in jeopardy,' he said.[21] Barnes seems to have been prepared to do anything to keep the project going, including sending in the Pacific Islands Regiment and importing Asian labourers who would be 'more amenable to control and discipline'.[22]

By 1969 CRA was in a position to begin work on the mine in earnest, with an expectation that production would begin in 1972. By the end of that year it was clear that Australia would have to make concrete plans for the future. An Australian Federal election was due in the second half of 1969, and Gough Whitlam, leader of the opposition Australian Labor Party, had several times called for self-government or independence for PNG at the earliest opportunity.

1969 was a watershed for the Territory of Papua New Guinea. It was the year the South Pacific Games were held in Port Moresby and the year that the young Michael Somare and the Pangu Pati began to flex their muscles in the House of Assembly. It was the year that expatriates were told to substitute the word 'national' for 'native', and the year that the Tolai of the Gazelle Peninsula marched through the streets of Rabaul to protest at a visit by Australian Prime Minister John Gorton.

It was also the year that PNG gained its first daily newspaper. An amalgamation of the *South Pacific Post* and the *New Guinea Times-Courier*, the Australian-owned *Post Courier* was aimed at expatriates and the small group of English-literate indigenes. It was, to all intents and purposes, the only newspaper in the country for most people. There were several church or mission-backed publications with tiny circulations, but the majority of the indigenous population relied for news and information on either the Australian Broadcasting Commission station 9PA in Port Moresby, or regional stations broadcasting in Tok Pisin and Tok Ples and run by district administrations.

The *Post Courier* gave little space to Bougainville until police were called in to clear villagers trying to block the forced resumption of land designated for the establishment of a mining town. The *Post Courier*'s reporting of the progress of the mine needs to be read within the framework of the political changes occurring in PNG and against the larger issue of the future of the Territory. The idea of creating a united and unified nation was central in all the media. Thus, in a complete reversal of the usual situation in newly developed countries, the Australian-owned newspapers and the Australian Government radio service displayed many of the characteristics of the developmental journalism found in newly independent media.

Definitions of development media broadly include such functions as the promotion of nationalism, national unity and a sense of national identity as a means of uniting disparate tribal groupings and language groups. National identity is often centred on a particular symbol, such as a flag, and it can be argued that the Bougainville mine fulfilled such a role in the *Post Courier*.[23]

The mine could be presented as a symbol of progress and a guarantor of a bright future for PNG as a whole. In an age of optimism and rapid change, it seemed only reasonable and sensible that a gigantic and profitable copper mine was a good thing. The *Post Courier* devoted several front pages to the dispute between landowners and CRA and gave extensive coverage on inside pages. There was always a hope that disputes with landowners could be settled in the traditional manner with appropriate compensation payments. The compensation package offered to Nasioi landowners and the provision of local infrastructure, jobs and income-producing activities was generous in comparison with similar projects in other parts of the world.[24]

While the *Post Courier* generally supported the notion of the mine as vital to the Territory's future, it did not do so uncritically. It covered the opposition in detail, reported the critical comments of leaders such as Lapun and Hannett, and devoted space to the views of the villagers affected by the forcible resumption of land at Rorovana. The paper acknowledged in its editorial column that the issue for the landowners was not the amount of compensation being offered, but a desire to retain their heritage.[25]

In mid-1969, exasperated by the refusal of villagers to sell their land, the administration threatened that unless a sale was negotiated, land near the Arawa plantation and the Loloho plantation at Anewa Bay would be forcibly resumed. Anewa Bay was marked as the site of a port, while Arawa was to be the site of a township for mineworkers. Police had been flown into Bougainville earlier that year and now another 60 police, including a riot squad under the command of Deputy Police Commissioner Barry Holloway, were flown into Kieta. Taking a Benthamite position, the Acting Assistant Administrator, Tony Newman, declared that the copper mine would benefit the entire Territory and that it was inevitable that some people must suffer for the greater good.[26]

The clash with the Rorovana people came on 1 August when CRA employees, protected by police, moved onto their land near Kieta. The *Post Courier* reported that 25 village women wrestled with riot squad police. Some of the women, who were trying to remove a concrete marker, were bare-breasted, a fact widely reported in the Australian press. After 30 minutes one peg was uprooted. About 600 local people watched the struggle, but did not take part. Once the peg was removed, the local people left.

The *Post Courier* did not ask why it was the women who took part in the removal of the peg and not the men. If they had, they might have uncovered a major blunder on the part of CRA, the Canberra Government and the Port Moresby administration. The women were leading the protest for the simple reason that on Bougainville, customary land ownership is matrilineal, not patrilineal. The administration, the Government and the mining company were dealing with the wrong people – the men. As Ursula Rakova told Radio Australia many years later:

In Bougainville land is passed on from mother to daughter...the customary boundaries are well managed by women...rather than men...My brothers will not know the boundaries of the land. I will know that because my mother will tell me, my brothers will marry and go help their wives. I...will look after the land.[27]

By dealing only with the men, the administration was weakening the traditional social structure and creating great problems for the future.[28] It is worth asking why the administration dealt with the men and not the women. There was anthropological evidence dating back to the 1930s that the Bougainvilleans were matrilineal, information which must surely have been available to the administration from experts at UPNG or the Australian School of Pacific Administration.[29]

Paul Lapun and fellow MHA Donatus Mola presented the administrator, Donald Hay, with a petition on 31 July. It contained some prescient words:

The trouble itself, and the means by which a solution is attempted, have obvious political implications for the future not only of Bougainville District, but...for the whole of...Papua New Guinea. We feel that this trouble will not be solved merely by the completion of some satisfactory sale arrangements of individual pieces of land with individual landowners...The trouble can only be solved and the success of the mine...assured, when the majority of the people in the Bougainville District can recognise that the project is good for Bougainville because it provides for the District genuine economic and social benefits which are adequate, fair and just.[30]

CRA chief Sir Maurice Mawby dismissed claims that that Bougainvilleans might rebel over the mine as 'ludicrous', but his comments, under the headline 'Hannett claim ludicrous says CRA chief', ran on the same page as a story reporting that police had used tear gas and batons to remove 65 Rorovana people who tried to stop bulldozers working.

The coverage of the incident in the Australian press was hostile, with the Sydney *Sun* running its coverage under the heading 'Australia's Shame'. The *Australian*, the country's only national daily, wrote:

> The use of tear gas and clubs this week to enforce alien land laws on the uncomprehending people was a damning indictment of the administration of Papua New Guinea, which is to say of Canberra.[31]

The story gained international coverage, with newspapers running pictures of Rorovana women confronting police and CRA workers.[32] On Bougainville the CRA bulldozers worked without interruption as soon as the clash was over. Opposition to the mine intensified and took on new guises which forced work to stop completely. Villagers from 72 settlements in the Kieta sub-district formed the Napidakoe Navitu Association to co-ordinate opposition to the mine, with 1,500 people reportedly attending the association's first meeting.[33] They began daily sit-ins, forcing CRA to suspend work. While more police were flown to Bougainville and a two-day truce was negotiated, Australia's Minister for External Territories, C. E. Barnes said: 'a handful of Bougainville people could not be allowed to delay a project on which the future of two million people... depended'.[34]

The Rorovana people were allowed to speak for themselves in a full-page interview with the journalist James Hall, who interviewed Willie Bele. The interview is eloquent in its depiction of a frustrated, fearful and suspicious people; but just like the administration and CRA, the *Post Courier* was talking to the wrong people. When Bele was asked who owned the land, he said he didn't know and he was being quite truthful. As a man, he had no right to know women's business.[35]

The manager of the Arawa plantation, Kip McKillop, who was in Sydney to launch legal proceedings over the land resumptions, said he was having difficulty obtaining labour to run the plantation. Workers whose contracts expired had left, while workers from Rabaul would not come because of the dispute and when some did come, most left to work for CRA.[36]

Barnes made a major speech to the House of Representatives defending the mine, saying it would provide jobs, training, development and indirect taxes. 'The Territory gets more out of the copper project than the company does,' he claimed. On Bougainville the Napidakoe Navitu Association declared that it would handle all land negotiations and that the administration would no longer be able to deal with individual owners.[37]

The seriousness with which the Australian Government viewed the situation was revealed when Prime Minister Gorton agreed to meet Lapun and Bele and said the Government was prepared to renegotiate the sale of disputed Rorovana land.[38]

The Government and CRA sought to solve the problem by massively increasing the amount of compensation being offered for the Rorovana land. This now entailed rent of Aus$7,000 a year for the land, Aus$30,000 compensation for damage to the lands and Aus$7,000 worth of shares in Bougainville Mining Ltd. The *Post Courier* estimated that the package worked out at Aus$1,000 an acre, far more than the Aus$600 an acre being touted as a price for the Arawa plantation land.[39]

Even then, not everybody was satisfied. Pangu Pati secretary Albert Maori Kiki, touring Australia as a guest of several unions, said the PNG administration was 'creating a big mess which the Territory's citizens will have to clean up'.[40] Barnes reacted furiously, claiming one of the sponsoring unions was 'communist dominated'.[41] Negotiations with the Rorovana people continued, even as CRA resumed work. Napidakoe Navitu sent representatives to Port Moresby to deal with the Director of Agriculture. Paul Lapun said the high price put on the Rorovana land had not been what decided the people to lease it to CRA. He said it had been the administration's promise not to try to resume any more land without talking to the people first.[42]

As 1969 began to wind down, the Bougainville story became less immediately important. The Australian elections were underway and the Government's handling of the various crises in PNG was being used as a political issue by Labor. However, after narrowly losing the 1969 federal election, Whitlam cynically and brilliantly exploited the situation in PNG, using it as a stick with which to beat the reinstalled Coalition Government. The Coalition Government would still not say when self-government or independence would come. Barnes claimed that PNG would be ready for self-government within a decade when it had developed a sound economic basis, part of which would come from the Aus$300 million it was estimated would be invested in Bougainville.[43] In contrast, Whitlam ended the year with a declaration that as soon as Labor was elected, PNG would have home rule, possibly as soon as 1972.[44]

True to his word, Whitlam granted PNG independence when he became Prime Minister. In September 1975, only two months before Whitlam was sacked by the Governor General, the Australian flag was lowered at Murray stadium in Port Moresby. PNG had been granted independence, but while it had a flag, a national anthem and an enthusiastic population, it had no manufacturing industries, no real jobs to absorb its university graduates and the Government had only one guaranteed source of income – revenue from the Bougainville mine.

Trouble continued to flare on the island until attacks on mine property in 1989 by the self-styled Bougainville Revolutionary Army led to a full-scale civil war. By the time that war was over, Bougainville's civil structure lay in ruins, thousands of people had died, the PNG economy had collapsed, the army had led a coup to prevent the civilian government using mercenaries and the bright hopes of 1969 had been crushed.

In the post-1975 era, relations between Australia and Papua New Guinea collapsed. Australia seemed to turn its back on its nearest neighbour and PNG, buoyed up by the illusory wealth of a rentier economy, overspent, overvalued its currency and became prey to all the sharks that circle the shores of newly independent nations.

Perhaps the greatest example of the change in relations between the two countries came with the newspaper coverage of the war. A comparison of the coverage of the early stages of the conflict by the *Australian* and the *Times of PNG* showed a curious reversal.[45] The *Australian* consistently supported the PNG Government and the return to production of the mine for the financial good of the country, while the *Times* was extremely critical of the PNG Government's handling of the war and sensitive to the human suffering caused.

It was curious that the only national daily circulating in the former metropolitan power supported the PNG Government's call for national unity and economic stability, while the only locally owned newspapers in PNG (the *Times'* sister paper, *Wantok*, was equally sympathetic) should be so sensitive to micro-nationalist sentiment that threatened to tear the country apart.

The chief lesson to be drawn from the *Post Courier*'s coverage of the 1969 clash is that when the media is owned by expatriates it will, however well intentioned and however sympathetic towards the aspirations of the indigenous peoples, it will still see things through the eye of the metropolitan power. This is not to say that the *Post Courier* was blind to the mistakes made by the administration in Port Moresby or the Government in Canberra, but it did not question the need for the Panguna mine or the need for some Nasioi to be sacrificed for the greater good.

Notes

1. R. Thompson, *Australian Imperialism in the Pacific* (Melbourne: Melbourne University Press, 1980), p. 51.
2. W. J. Hudson, *New Guinea Empire* (Sydney: Cassell, 1974), p. v.

3. E. Ogan, 'The Bougainville Conflict: Perspectives from the Nasioi', *State, Society and Governance in Melanesia*, Discussion Paper 99/3, 1999.

4. Hudson, *New Guinea Empire*, pp. vii–viii.

5. A. J. Strathern and P. J. Stewart, *Fiji in the Pacific* (Brisbane: The Jacaranda Press, 1994), pp. 49–51.

6. Thompson, *Australian Imperialism in the Pacific, passim*.

7. I. Downs, *The Australian Trusteeship Papua New Guinea 1945–1975* (Canberra: Australian Government Publishing Service, 1980).

8. D. Stephen, *A History of Political Parties in Papua New Guinea* (Melbourne: Lansdowne Press, 1972), p. 152.

9. Hudson, *New Guinea Empire*, pp. 14–15.

10. M. Somare, *Sana: An Autobiography* (Nuigini Press: Port Moresby, 1975), p. 121.

11. E. Ogan, 'Business and Cargo: Socio-economic Change among the Nasioi of Bougainville', *New Guinea Research Bulletin*, No. 44 (1972): 183.

12. R. F. Mikesell, *Foreign Investment in Copper Mining: Case Studies of Mines in Peru and Papua New Guinea* (Baltimore, MD: Johns Hopkins University Press, 1975), p. 81.

13. Stephen, *A History of Political Parties in Papua New Guinea*, p. 150.

14. Papua New Guinea House of Assembly, *Hansard*, I:2 (1968), p. 433.

15. R. J. May, *State and Society in Papua New Guinea: The first 25 Years* (Canberra: Australian National University Press: 2000) at http://epress.anu.edu.au/sspng/mobile_devices/index.html.

16. Downs, *The Australian Trusteeship Papua New Guinea 1945–1975*, p. 343.

17. M. O'Callaghan, in A. Carl and L. Garasu (eds.), *Weaving Consensus: The Papua New Guinea-Bougainville Peace Process* (London: Conciliation Resources, 2002) at http://www.c-r.org/accord/boug/accord12/index.shtml.

18. Downs, *The Australian Trusteeship Papua New Guinea 1945–1975*, pp. 344–5.

19. P. Cotton, 'PNG Celebrates 25 Years of Independence', *Focus* (September 2000): 1.

20. B. Anderson, *Imagined Communities*, (London: Verso, 1991).

21. B. Burton, 'Documents Highlight Australian Role in PNG Conflict', *Asia Times*, 6 January 2000.

22. Ibid.; See also Downs, *The Australian Trusteeship Papua New Guinea 1945–1975*, p. 477.

23. A. J. Strathern and P. J. Stewart, 'Mi les long yupela usim flag bilong mi': Symbols and Identity in Papua New Guinea', *Pacific Studies*, XXIII: 1/2 (2000).

24. Mikesell, *Foreign Investment in Copper Mining, passim*.

25. *Post Courier*, 30 July 1969.

26. *Post Courier*, 28 July 1969.

27. Radio Australia, *Time to Talk*, programme two, 'Women and Land in Bougainville', at http://abc.net.au/timetotalk/english/issues_two.htm.

28. Australian Parliament, Joint Standing Committee on Foreign Affairs, Defence and Trade, 'Bougainville: The Peace Process and Beyond'. Completed inquiry presented to Parliament, 27 September 1999.

29. T. Havini, 'Bougainville's totems autonomous: Naboin, Nakas, Nakaripa, natasi', at http://www.avicam.com/muse/havini.php.

30. *Post Courier*, 4 August 1969.

31. M. Havini and R. Havini, 'Bougainville – The Long Struggle for Freedom', Paper presented to the UN International Conference on Indigenous Peoples, Environment and Development, (Zurich, 1995).
32. A. McIntosh, 'The Bougainville Crisis: A South Pacific Crofters' War', *Radical Scotland* No. 44 (May 1990).
33. Australian Parliament, Joint Standing Committee on Foreign Affairs, Defence and Trade, 'Bougainville: The Peace Process and Beyond'. Completed inquiry presented to Parliament, 27 September 1999.
34. *Post Courier*, 14 August 1969.
35. *Post Courier*, 13 August 1969
36. *Post Courier*, 14 August 1969.
37. *Post Courier*, 15 August 1969.
38. *Post Courier*, 22 August 1969.
39. *Post Courier*, 11 September 1969.
40. *Post Courier*, 15 September 1969
41. *Post Courier*, 24 September 1969.
42. *Post Courier*, 30 September 1969.
43. *Post Courier*, 10 October 1969.
44. *Post Courier*, 30 December 1969.
45. P. Cass, 'A Comparison of the Coverage of the Bougainville Crisis in the *Australian* and the *Times* of PNG', *Australian Journalism Review*, XIV: 2 (1992).

14

The Influence of the British Empire through the Development of Communications in Canada: French Radio Broadcasting during the Second World War

Alain Canuel

The second half of the nineteenth century was the crucible in which international communications was forged. In 1866, a young American engineer, Cyrus Field, established a communications link between the Old and New Worlds by means of a submarine cable. The Great Powers henceforth had a new instrument of communications which strengthened the links between them, and even more importantly brought them closer to their colonies and possessions. For nearly half a century, submarine cable would dominate the world of communications and bring the continents closer together. This technology helped shape an era when the links between Canada and Great Britain were very strong.

Great Britain, which was the first power to possess this technology, was soon followed by France. From 1870 on, Great Britain pursued its interests in India by laying a submarine cable from Malta to Alexandria and from Suez to Karachi.[1] Communications with India and America stimulated the development of new cable industries, which gave the Great Powers powerful and complex networks: as evidence, India and England exchanged at least 100 telegrams in 1870; in 1895, they exchanged more than two million. It is clear that at the dawn of the Second Industrial Revolution, colonial expansion could have hardly been conceived without telegraph links between the home country and its distant possessions: 'Cable had become an essential part of the new imperialism.'[2]

Among the member countries of the British Empire, Canada was certainly the country which most benefited from the process of development of imperial communications, particularly since the installation of the first transatlantic submarine cable. The present study proposes to retrace the principal steps in the evolution of the submarine cable, telegraph and radio in Canada from a perspective which takes into account both imperial projects and national initiatives.[3] Our analysis will look as well at the creation of a short-wave radio station which was established with the intent to converge the means of communication with wartime goals as well as at the role that the French public radio played in Canada as a means of propaganda in the Second World War.

Submarine cable (1866–1901)

In 1866, Cyrus Field established the first permanent link between Canada and Great Britain.[4] This technological feat opened the door to a new mode of communication and imperceptibly transformed the role of the Dominion, which henceforth served concurrently as a relay for the British Empire network and the industrial countries.[5] Even more than the telegraph, the submarine cable created an interdependence between the two countries. Yet, the motives were not the same: England, conscious of the decline of its naval and military force, first tried to remedy the deficiency through these new technological capabilities while at the same time affirming its supreme authority within the Empire, an authority which constituted the very framework of its existence. For Canada, 'the existence of a telegraphic route [between Europe and America] represented a positive factor in the development of the colonies'.[6] With the submarine cable, especially the one linking Vancouver to Australia (finished in 1902), Canada became an essential link in the British imperial communications network, which had began its development in 1866.[7] There is no doubt that this technology brought a certain unity to the British Empire and that the cable monopolies often anticipated or favoured imperial needs. At the beginning of the twentieth century, the British submarine cable network was divided into two categories: strategic and non-strategic. Just before the First World War, a study report indicated that you would have to cut 15 (strategic and non-strategic) cables to isolate Canada from England.[8]

Imperial wireless chain (1911–26)

At the beginning of the twentieth century, wireless telegraphy arrived. Once again, Canada and Great Britain were noted as being the major beneficiaries of the first transatlantic electronic communication without submarine cable. On Friday, 12 December, Guglielmo Marconi established the first wireless communication between Poldhu (Wales) and St. John's (Newfoundland). Although the international submarine cable network had not yet been completed, the industrialised countries spread wireless telegraphy around the world, thus superimposing a new international communications network on the old one. This technological breakthrough constituted an important step in the annals of Canadian communications. It reinforced Canada's position with regard to the two great powers of Great Britain and the United States. The axis of communication between the two continents rested once more on the triangular basis of Great Britain/Canada/United States, and the importance of Canada as a player in this respect should not be underestimated. Before the First World War, the British Government was interested in constructing an imperial chain of radio stations capable of linking Great Britain with her overseas dependencies and Dominions, a chain that the enemy could not cut in the event of war as easily as the submarine cables. This was a project of national importance; it was also a project that no organisation in Britain was able to carry out, except for the Marconi Company, which had the technical knowledge and trained personnel for this kind of project. The technical superiority and the lead of the Marconi Company before the First World War gave the British Government access, in the event of war, to relatively secure communication links within the British Empire and to maintaining communications with allied countries, especially the United States.

The Marconi Company submitted a plan to the British Government in 1910 for a wireless chain throughout the British Empire. Needless to say, the question of imperial communications became more urgent during the years preceding the war. Most of the British telegraph lines passed through a number of different countries and the possibility that the service might be interrupted for political reasons (because war was imminent) forced the Government to sign a contract with Marconi in 1912 for the establishment of an imperial wireless network. In the end, the completion of the project was deferred until 1926, in large part due to the war, but also because of pressure from some members of the British Parliament and from cable company owners. It seems from the events that occurred before the war that Canada was not really consulted about the cable project, except during the Imperial Conferences of 1911 and 1918. If the First World War was pivotal in transforming the world of wireless into the world of radio by passing from the electric to the electronic era, it was also key in transforming the political status of Canada. In 1916, the British Prime Minister, David Lloyd George, recognised that the position of the Dominions with regard to external affairs had been completely revolutionised in the course of the previous few years and that the Dominions since the war had been given equal rights with Great Britain in the control of foreign policy of the Empire. This revolution manifested itself in the course of the Second World War both by an accentuation of a Canadian nationalist sentiment and by a manifest desire for greater collaboration with England to defeat the enemy.

There is no doubt that in the Canadian Government of William Lyon MacKenzie King, politicians like Bruce C. Claxton, who played a key role in Canada's participation in the war, had integrated the imperial message and saw themselves not only as Canadians but more as members of a larger Imperial ensemble.[9] From then on their role was to ensure that all public agitation against the war effort was stifled and that a sustained campaign for greater participation in the war by the Quebec population become imperative.

Radio (1919–36)

The development of radiotelephony during the first quarter of the century was closely linked to Canada's political situation. Before the First World War, radiotelephony was used by Great Britain as an instrument, a tool for maintaining the Empire. After the war, it can be said that this technology mainly evolved towards radio broadcasting, and that a new form of cultural imperialism had appeared in Canada. Radio, which developed in the wake of these two technologies, had never fully rid itself of the imperialist stamp because it was founded by the same capitalist regime which sustained the feasibility of two international communications networks. Hence, radio did not rid itself fully of the stigmata of the imperialism which encouraged and profited from the birth of the submarine cable and the wireless telegraphy. Nevertheless, we should not conclude that countries situated on the peripheries could not control this postwar technology and assure themselves a certain measure of autonomy. From this point of view, the dichotomy of centre versus periphery constitutes the substratum of communications. This conformity to the standardised models of the Great Powers necessitated different modalities of application linked to the particularities of each country, to their expectations, their aspirations and their capacity for absorbing systems. Thus, for example, Canada opted for a hybrid formula which embraced both privatisation (the American model) and state ownership (the British model) of radio.[10] The influence of the British model was seen primarily at the level of organisation and network management. The politicians in charge as well as the commissioners charged to rule Canadian radio often made reference to Great Britain, while remaining conscious that marked differences between the two countries did not allow them to apply the model in its entirety. Nevertheless, the British model did serve more than once as a guide for Canada in finding answers to thorny questions. One can think, for example, of the British Broadcasting Company, which was created in 1922 as a private company with commercial interests and which would become, thanks to the intervention of the state, the British Broadcasting Corporation (BBC) in 1926. There is no doubt that Canada always seriously considered the British approach before acting; it did this, for example, in 1936 before lodging its Bill on radio broadcasting, which aimed at regulating and controlling radio broadcasting in Canada.

The influence of the British model was also felt at times when certain problems seemed insoluble. In the spring of 1933, at the express demand of the Canadian Prime Minister, Richard B. Bennett, the Director of Public Relations of the BBC, Gladstone Murray, came to Ottawa to carry out a study of problems the Canadian Broadcasting Commission had encountered. Of the three reports submitted to the Government, the first called on the Prime Minister to lodge, as quickly as possible, Bill 99 modifying the Broadcasting Law of 1932; while the third report, based on the example of the BBC, insisted on the fact that 'the public organization responsible for broadcasting in Canada must be a corporation independent of the government of the day and protected from political interference'.[11]

The participation of Canada in the First World War and its admission to the League of Nations in 1921 greatly modified inter-imperial relations; the results obtained at the Conference of 1926 clearly demonstrated this. To a certain extent, the Statute of Westminster (1931) sanctioned this sovereignty. Before the Second World War, the unity of the Empire relied on the common allegiance of the nation-members to one sovereign. With the Westminster Accord, and in the following years, the reins of colonial dependence disappeared one after another, thus permitting Canada to acquire a more marked international personality.

We can affirm that the development of radiotelephony during the first four decades of the century in Canada was closely linked to its political situation. On the one hand, the creation of a shortwave station helped Canadians to understand better the profound discontent which existed between the will of the directors of public radio broadcasting to develop activities in concert with England and the hesitation and even objections of the Minister of Transportation, C. D. Howe (whose principal task was to manage the war effort in Canada), with regard to such an initiative where Canada would not have absolute control. On the other hand, the use of French-language public radio during the Second World War went back obligatorily to the political goals of William Lyon MacKenzie King with the emergence of the combination of a war propaganda paired with a nationalist propaganda.

The shortwave station

The federal government's intention to furnish Canada with an international shortwave transmission station during the war was not realised until 1942, and the official opening of the Canadian Broadcasting Corporation's International Shortwave Service did not occur until 25 February 1945. From the beginning of the hostilities, the president of the board of governors of the Corporation, Leonard W. Brockington, intervened directly with Prime Minister King to garner his support for a shortwave station. This intervention failed even though Canada's participation in the war showed its unwavering support of Great Britain. Why didn't the federal government pursue the project when they had declared the radio service essential to the war on 5 September 1939? The incapacity of the Corporation to free itself totally from the political powers and to obtain the necessary credits for the establishment of an international shortwave station gives us a partial answer. There are other factors: the obstinacy of C. D. Howe held the project back considerably and diminished its impact when faced with an imperialistic strategy between Canada and England which was supposed to be reinforced during the war. Without the unconditional support of Howe for this project, all the measures put in place by the King Government with regard to creating a more effective radio network would have had an effect only if Canada possessed its own shortwave station.

The general discontent of the population as reported in the leading Canadian newspapers, as well as repeated criticism from the opposition, put pressure on the King Government. In the House of Commons, some members saw the necessity of countering enemy propaganda, whereas others judged that a powerful shortwave transmission station 'is particularly recommendable in order to supplement the existing British station and to encourage cooperation within the Empire as well as for general spreading of the truth throughout the world'.[12] When radio came to be considered an essential service, the Corporation informed Howe of the availability of a shortwave transmitter, which the RCA Victor Company of the United States said was ready to be sold to Canada. The major reason cited by Gladstone Murray, Director-General of the CBC, was based on the tradition of cooperation between Canada and Great Britain in times of war: 'I know that the BBC has serious fears about its Daventry installation, which is very exposed to aerial attack. If this installation was destroyed and if we had in Canada a shortwave transmitter of 50 kilowatts, we could maintain the British service in times of War.'[13]

Murray's argument was a good one, but Howe did not take any action on the recommendation. Because of the Government's inaction in this case, the opposition attacked Prime Minister King, 'recommending the use of a shortwave radio station "to counterbalance unfavourable propaganda"' and to 'refute Hitler's false propaganda concerning the War effort in Canada'.[14] When war was declared, Canada, which supported England financially, could not hide behind budgetary restrictions to justify its inaction, especially when a shortwave station constituted a necessity for the British Government in times of war. The *Financial Post* considered 'that after the expenses incurred by Canada for the fabrication of armaments, the cost of a shortwave transmission station would be insignificant – hardly more than that of a bomber'.[15]

In October 1940, the proposition, which England presented to Canada to build a shared shortwave transmission station, was also rejected by Howe, now Minister of Munitions and Services.[16] Anxious to allay fears, the British Government specified that Canada was mistaken if it thought that England intended directing the station's programming towards the United States.[17] One month later, Howe informed the War Committee of the British Government's revised position in which they would be willing to assume part of the capital, operations and maintenance costs of the shortwave station, if Canada agreed to build it and guarantee its financing until the end of the war. Furthermore, England proposed sending an engineer specialised in shortwave as well as a small group of persons with expertise in propaganda. All these concessions were fruitless for Howe rejected the British proposition for a second time, with the full support of the Cabinet War Committee. In January 1941, the British Government made a final attempt to convince Canada of the necessity of constructing a shortwave transmission station. This time they went directly to the Minister of National War Services, J. T. Thorson. Favourable to the idea, Thorson decided that Canada's involvement in the shortwave transmission project would not cause serious problems with the United States.[18] This divergence of opinion between Thorson and Howe would, however, not put in question the facts which had already been brought to the attention of the Government. Despite this, in 1942 the CBC prepared detailed reports on technical costs, costs of services and production; evaluated all the initiatives that had been undertaken so far by the various players; and underlined the impact that any delay would have. Certain reports went so far as to include commentaries that supported the project, notably that of the Office of Governors and those of certain deputies of the House of Commons, and presented press clippings from Canadian newspaper editorials and articles which supported the shortwave transmission project.[19]

However, it was not until 18 September 1942 that the Canadian Government by Order in Council (C.P. 8168) approved the construction of a shortwave station. Even though the CBC got the go-ahead, there was a delay of several months before they got the American-made transmission equipment. Howe, considered the architect of Canadian industrialisation during the war, did not think much of shortwave's potential as a psychological weapon. Let us not misunderstand this; when war was declared, the Corporation had been in existence for only three years. Even if the state radio had demonstrated on several occasions that it had the experience necessary to operate internationally, that would not be enough to convince the Canadian Government, and especially Howe, of the usefulness of a shortwave station *a fortiori* if it cost 'as much as a bomber'. In the absence of shortwave propaganda, the Canadian Government put more emphasis on censorship, because it let them control public opinion by keeping points of view and arguments that displeased it from public consideration.[20] In the Government's mind, propaganda promoted national unity with the goal of convincing the population of Quebec of the necessity of participating in the war.[21]

Propaganda on state radio

Because it was seen as a rapid and effective means of disseminating information, radio became a favoured tool of manipulation, a vector for the diffusion of the Government's ideas. Because it was the only information source which could bring hour-by-hour coverage of the war's progress to the public as well establishing direct contact with Canadian troops and the Allies, radio became a very powerful means of applying pressure and of indoctrination. In Canada, and more particularly in Quebec, the use of radio for both wartime and ideological propaganda stemmed directly from the aims of the King Government. Furthermore, government interference in the Corporation was largely focused on the French language network. Unable to cover the full spectrum of propaganda, we will limit our study to two headings: the first will consider the nationalist propaganda of the King Government; the second will consider the attempts to deal with the subversive propaganda of the enemy. It is essential to consider the propaganda with regard to Quebec since 'The primary challenge of the King Government, during the world conflict, was not so much the application of censorship rules and the denunciation of subversive propaganda as the conscription crisis which threatened to compromise national unity.'[22]

When Europe entered the war, Canada saw its subliminal identity crisis resurface. Memories of the First World War experience left no doubt as to the opposition of Quebec to conscription. From here on, state radio propaganda took the form of a nationalist propaganda which served the interests of the MacKenzie King Government in having 'essentially as [its] objective to conciliate the two nationalisms of Quebec and of English Canada, which oppose each other and harm national . . . unity and the War effort'.[23] The other propaganda aimed at countering that of the enemy which emphasised the precariousness of the political situation in Canada, notably during the plebiscite of 1942. When the task was responding to enemy propaganda, it was naturally towards Quebec that the Federal Government turned its major efforts, as it believed that the situation in the province had created an unhoped-for opportunity for the enemy to destabilise Canada.

On 10 November 1941, Claude Melançon, Associate Director of Public Information, wrote to the Minister of Justice, Ernest Lapointe, to voice his concerns about the effect of Vichy propaganda on Quebec. This propaganda, he affirmed, 'successfully exploits the anti-British sentiment of a certain press and of a good number of our pseudo-intellectuals'.[24] Some days later, the Canadian Minister of Foreign Affairs attempted to sum up the methods and effects of the propaganda directed at French Canadians. To counter the shortwave broadcasts and the activities of the French consuls in Canada, it was proposed to keep monitor transmissions from Paris and Vichy. In return, Canada would produce recorded broadcasts – since shortwave was not available in 1941 – which would be sent to the BBC so that they could be retransmitted to France. It was also judged important to provide French Canadians with alternative radio broadcasts. Melançon wrote that it would be possible to use certain broadcasts transmitted by the BBC and destined for Canada such as Radio News Reel to 'diffuse information which would show the real face of the Pétain collaborators'.[25] Towards the end of January 1942, Radio Vichy announced an increase in the number of transmission hours broadcast to North America.[26] A few weeks later, Melançon wrote to Lester B. Pearson to express his fears concerning the Vichy transmissions. In a letter addressed to a colleague, Pearson wrote:

> Another way of meeting this situation would be by counter radio propaganda through French programmes in Quebec. Practically nothing seems to be done in this direction. Melançon tells me that the C.B.C. French-speaking officials concerned are averse to propaganda even for our own cause. I have made an examination of the French C.B.C. broadcasts for the forthcoming week. There are only talks that have nothing to do with the War and practically no effort is being made through this medium to enlighten opinion and strengthen morale. That is, I think, an astonishing situation. We allow Vichy and Paris to broadcast every day their views of the War and we refrain almost entirely from telling our own people about the issues involved.[27]

This last remark was symptomatic of the political climate which prevailed in Canada, and particularly in Quebec, at the beginning of 1942. Rather than present an argument based on taking action directed at Europe in order to counter the propaganda coming from Vichy and Paris, Pearson opted for an internal propaganda programme which would permit the Government 'to inform our people on the questions which the War raises'. We can easily understand this attitude, which favoured a national approach over an international one, when we know that, by this time, Prime Minister King had already decided to seek a plebiscite to ask the Canadian population if it agreed to 'liberate the Government of all obligations resulting from previous engagements which restrain the methods of recruitment for military service'.[28]

The precarious situation which prevailed at Radio Canada in 1942 could not help but diminish the concerted efforts to support a propaganda programme directed at Germany and France. Thus, the Subcommittee on French Broadcasts (composed of representatives of the Canadian ministries) compiled a list of subjects which the Commission of Information in Times of War had to deal with. These were then transmitted to the BBC for diffusion.[29] To help create these broadcasts, personnel in Ottawa used reports from the intelligence services of the Political Warfare Executive and those of the Canadian and American censorship boards.[30] At the time Canada did not have the expertise necessary to produce quality texts of its own. The BBC went so far as to refuse to broadcast material from Canada which did not meet its own criteria, such as material which did not sufficiently reflect their representations of Canada for a European audience.

In December 1943, Canadian bureaucrats were divided as to the preference to accord to organisations which used Canadian propaganda. Was it necessary to work more closely with the British Political Warfare Executive or with the American War Information Office? For both technical (experience, organisation and cooperation) and political reasons, the Ministry of External Affairs favoured closer collaboration with the British Political Warfare Executive, without completely abandoning the American War Information Office in New York. Another important consideration concerned those in the political office in Canada. The country had to present itself not as a colony, but as a world power which could demonstrate leadership in international affairs.[31] In Ottawa, decision-makers were beginning to understand the importance of making Canada known as a discrete member of the United Nations; and to this end, they decided to exploit the tools made available for the activities of psychological warfare.[32] From an historical point of view, we can easily understand that the choice between the British Political Warfare Executive and the American War Information Office for diffusing Canadian propaganda was difficult. Canada had always developed a collaborative approach with Great Britain for the development of imperial communications. For example, in July 1924, the British Government launched the construction of imperial wireless beam stations between Great Britain, Canada, India and South Africa. Canada was the first among the countries involved to have an operational beam link with Great Britain.

During world conflict, we have observed that the Canadian Broadcasting Corporation-Radio-Canada became an instrument of propaganda; an instrument which had, at such times, to influence and convince. Furthermore, we have seen that the state radio had also to monitor national interests in the field of radio broadcasting. This balance between its activities linked to the war and those linked to its national development was not always easy to achieve, taking into account limited budgets and above all the many institutional and ministerial relationships on which the Corporation depended during the war. At the national level, the King Government discovered that communications were an important element of national sovereignty; at the international level, the psychological war as practised by the allies

230 *Alain Canuel*

(more particularly the United States and Great Britain) showed that Canada could not compete at a time when a real revolution in the world of international communications was taking place.

Conclusion

Relations between Canada and Great Britain in the course of the second half of the nineteenth and the first half of the twentieth centuries were complex. Projects like the Imperial Wireless Chain or even a shortwave transmission station in the course of the Second World War had both strategic and commercial considerations: strategic, because Great Britain had to maintain, in times of peace and in times of war, efficient communications with its colonies and other possessions and with other powers; commercial because the economic strength of Great Britain and Canada depended notably on the means of communication. There was no doubt that the problems of communications between the two countries between 1850 and 1950 were a determining factor in Canada's external political relations, and that they led to political unity between the two countries which increased due to the goodwill of the parties involved. The two principles of Canadian autonomy and imperial unity which underlay the relationship between Great Britain and Canada could clearly be seen to have served on many occasions as the catalyst for discussions which resulted in the realisation of these innovative projects and even, perhaps more importantly, for the establishment of new forms of political relationship.

Notes

1. M. de Margerie, *Le réseau anglais de câbles sous-marins* (Paris: A. Pedone, 1909), p. 27.
2. D. R. Headrick, *The Tools of Empire: Technology and European Imperialism in the 19th Century* (Oxford: Oxford University Press, 1981), p. 163.
3. At the end of the nineteenth century, imperialism as it appears cannot be considered from a synchronic perspective. The different regions did not have the same degree of expansion or did not have the same response *vis-à-vis* the control which was exercised over it. In P. Braillard and P. Senarclens, *L'impérialisme* (Paris: Presses universitaires de France, 1980), and more precisely pp. 48–9.
4. H. M. Field, *History of the Atlantic Telegraph* (New York: Charles Scribner & Co., 1867), p. 3. B. Dibner, *The Atlantic Cable* (Toronto, London: Blaisdell Publisher Co., 1964), pp. 6–28, 'Organization begins'.
5. According to the Imperial Year-book for Canada, 'six companies have a terminus in Canada, five on the Atlantic coast, and one on the Pacific. They

are all controlled by foreign interest and several of them merely land at Canso, in Nova Scotia, because of geographical considerations'. In A. E. Southall, *Imperial Yearbook 1915–1916* (Montreal: John Lovell & Sons Ltd., 1915), p. 148.

6. V. J. Coates and B. Finn, *A Retrospective Assessment: Submarine Telegraphy* (San Francisco: San Francisco Press, 1979), pp. 4, 5, 6.

7. A. Moyal, *Clear across Australia* (Melbourne: Thomas Nelson, 1985), p. 92.

8. P. M. Kennedy, 'Imperial Cable Communication and Strategy, 1870–1914', *English Historical Review*, 86 (1974) 728–53. Citation at p. 741.

9. During the war, Bruce Claxton was nominated Parliamentary Secretary to the Prime Minister King.

10. On the American model, see Canada, House of Commons, *Debates* (hereafter *Debates*) Vol. III (Ottawa: J. A. Patenaude, 1937), pp. 2910–11, 2433–4; Canada, *Debates*, (1932), Vol. III, p. 3346; Canada, *Special Committee on radio broadcasting* (Ottawa: J. A. Patenaude, 1932), pp. 64 and others (Augustin Frigon's speech, pp. 414–15). On the British model, see Canada, *Debates* (1936), Vol. IV, pp. 3708–18; *Special Committee . . . (1932)*, p. 517.

11. D. Ellis, *La radiodiffusion canadienne: objectifs et réalités, 1928–1968* (Gouvernement du Canada, Département de Communication, Approvisionnement et Service Canada, 1979), p. 13.

12. On the issue related to propaganda from ennemies, see Canada, Comité spécial de la radiodiffusion (hereafter *CSR*), *Procès-verbaux et témoignages*, Fascicule no. 17 (Ottawa: Edmond Cloutier, 7 juillet 1942), pp. 415, 421. On the collaboration of the British Empire, see Canada, Chambre des communes, *Débats* (hereafter *Débats*) (Ottawa: J.A. Patenaude, 1942), 21 mars 1942, citation of Herbert Bruce).

13. Letter from Gladstone Murray to the Minister of Transportation, C. D. Howe, in Canada, *Special Committee on Radio Broadcasting* (Ottawa: J. A. Patenaude, 28 August 1942), p. 413.

14. Canada, *CSR*, 1942, p. 421; Canada, *Débats*, 19 novembre 1940, p. 229; Canada, *Débats*, 25 novembre 1940, p. 399.

15. CSR 1942, p. 423 (see citation of the *Financial Post*, 9 December 1939).

16. A. Siegel, *Radio Canada International, History and Development* (Oakville and Buffalo: Mosaic Press, 1996), p. 42.

17. Ibid.

18. Ibid., p. 43.

19. Ibid., p. 42.

20. F. Williams, *Press, Parliament and People* (London: William Heinemann Ltd., 1946), p. 64.

21. According to Renée Legris, war propaganda at the international level is based on models and objectives that are different from those generally used in Canada. In R. Legris, *Propagande de guerre et nationalisme dans le radio-feuilleton (1939–59)* (Cap Saint-Ignace: Fides, 1981), p. 19.

22. For the Prime Minister, national unity is a goal, not a means. See J-L. Granatstein, *Conscription in the Second World War, 1939–1945. A Study of Political Management* (Toronto: Ryerson Press, 1969), pp. 13, 74; J. Y.Gravel, 'Le Québec et la guerre', *Études d'histoire du Québec* 7 (Montréal: Fides, 1974): 77 and others.

23. Legris, *Propagande de guerre*, p. 21.

24. Canada, Archives nationales du Canada (thereafter ANC). RG 25, G2, vol. 2931, file 2861–40, *Lettre de Claude Melançon au Très Honorable Ernest Lapointe*, Ottawa, 10 novembre 1941.
25. Ibid.
26. ANC, RG 25, G2, vol 2931, file 2861–40, letter from Peter Aylen (Programme Liaison Officer, Canadian Broadcasting Corporation) to Saul Rae (Department of External Affairs), Ottawa, 4 February 1942.
27. ANC, RG 25, G2, vol. 2931, file 2861-40, Memorandum from L. B. Pearson to M. Robertson. Re *Vichy Propaganda in Canada*, 4 March 1942.
28. *Débats* (11 mai 1942), p. 2354; *La Ligue pour la défense du Canada: ce qu'elle a fait, son attitude présente, ce qu'elle fera* (Montréal, Imprimerie populaire, s.d.), p. 3.
29. ANC, RG 25, vol. 3211, dossier 5353-R-40C pt 1, Political Intelligence Committee, Sub-Committee on French Broadcasts, September 23, 1943; see document entitled *Le Canada parle à la France*.
30. ANC, RG 25, vol. 3211, file 5353-R-40C pt 1, Note for Mr. Cadieux, 29 September 1943. The reports are: *Cabled Summary of Central Directive, Central Directive, Central Directive – Annexes, News Digest, Analysis of French Radio Propaganda, Analysis of B.B.C. French Broadcasts and American Rebroadcasts, Weekly Intelligence Summary for France, Individual Censorship Intercepts, Censorship Reports, Weekly Summary*.
31. ANC, RG 25, vol. 3211, file 5353-R-40C pt 1, Canadian Psychological Warfare Directed to France, 22 December 1943.
32. Ibid.

15
Echoes of Cosmopolitanism: Colonial Penang's 'Indigenous' English Press

Su Lin Lewis

As gateways to China and the Dutch East Indies, the Straits Settlements of Penang, Malacca and Singapore were the citadels of British imperial expansion in East Asia. These flourishing, cosmopolitan port cities – connected to the great Indian Ocean trading routes – had long been centres of economic and cultural exchange. The open-door policies of the British prompted a massive influx of immigration during the colonial period, resulting in a multi-ethnic Straits society that looked not just to London as its metropole, but to China, India, the Arab world and beyond.

By the nineteenth century, new forms of print communications were harnessed most rapidly by the merchants, traders, colonialists and migrants who lived and flowed in these port towns. Newspapers – providing news from abroad, shipping timetables, new colonial regulations and advertisements for merchant wares – were central to the imperial machine of global capitalism. The first newspaper in the Settlements, the *Prince of Wales Government Gazette*, was conceived in Penang in 1806 and targeted a handful of English merchants, planters and government personnel residing in the colony; it published shipping and passenger lists as well as crime and current price reports. It was soon followed by the newspaper considered the first modern Chinese periodical anywhere in the world – the *Chinese Monthly Magazine* in Malacca. In Singapore, the English-language *Straits Times* was launched in 1845, as were other Malay, Chinese and Tamil publications at the close of the century.

Malay, Chinese and Tamil publications gave indigenous and immigrant communities a voice to express shared concerns. As opposed to colonial and missionary presses – as well as the classic colonial institutions of the census, map, and museum[1] – newspapers provided a modern platform for communities to articulate their own group identities. Newspapers solidified communal bonds by standardising shared vernacular languages in print. In 1920, for instance, the introduction of standardised, written Chinese (*guoyu*) allowed Chinese communities – previously separated by dialect – to communicate with each other and link them to the new republican government in China. In segmenting communities through the barriers of language, newspapers led directly to the emergence of communalism and ethno-nationalism in Malaya's diverse communities.

These ethno-centred newspapers perpetuated numerous 'imagined communities' within the territorial confines of one future nation. It is telling that Malaya – fraught with complex local, communal and diasporic solidarities – is largely left out of Benedict Anderson's classic study of the origins of nationalism. It is Indonesia, not Malaya, on which Anderson turns his gaze. Here, by 'curious accident',[2] young Javanese intelligentsia championed Malay as the vehicle of linguistic unity for a deeply heterogeneous community. Rather than Javanese or Dutch, Malay proved to be a 'democratic' language, accessible to all the peoples of the archipelago as the language of the marketplace, diplomacy, religious education and – crucially – the vernacular press, which had used Malay almost exclusively since 1900. As such, Malay – or Bahasa Indonesia – became the unifying symbol of emerging nationalism for a deeply heterogeneous population.

In Malaya, however, the significance of the language took a different trajectory. The flowering of Malay vernacular culture in the 1930s, as elucidated in William Roff's landmark study of the origins of Malay nationalism, parallels Anderson's claim that 'print-language invents nationalism'. During the 1930s, Malay-language periodical publication boomed, with an increasingly literate population and young Malays with literary aspirations taking up journalism as a career. Both reader and writer began to articulate a shared sense of Malay solidarity. As Roff explains, this new solidarity existed less as a vision of nationalism, but as a defensive community of interest against further subordination to economically and politically dominant immigrant communities.[3]

But the 'imagined community' that emerged from Malay print journalism in the 1930s existed only for the racial community of the Malays. It did not reflect the realities of what was rapidly becoming a multi-racial, heteroglossic society. Chinese and Indians spoke their own languages and had their own periodicals. Chinese dialects ranged from Mandarin and Cantonese to Hokkien and Hakka (the latter two particularly in Penang); Indian languages encompassed Singhalese, Tamil and

Hindi, among others. Through Chinese and Tamil publications, the diasporic inhabitants of Penang and Singapore strengthened their links to their homelands. Chinese newspapers translated news from Hong Kong and Shanghai, while Tamil papers used South Asian dailies as their models. The 'imagined communities' of these diasporic inhabitants stretched beyond the territory in which they lived, solidifying links to a faraway home and segregating their exiled communities. As such, the vernacular press in Malaya – unlike Indonesia – proved not unifying but *divisive*.

Parallel to the emergence of ethno-nationalisms through the vernacular press was a new development in the English press, operating outside its original colonial and missionary interests. By the end of the nineteenth century, a non-white community began using the English press to advance their interests and engage with the democratic ideals of empire. The Straits-born Chinese grasped the value of the English press as a tool with which to articulate their vision for society. Among the oldest inhabitants of the Straits Settlements (born British citizens), they viewed themselves as the 'King's Chinese' and pledged their loyalty to the Empire. Because their main cultural influences were simultaneously Chinese, British and Malay, that vision could never be something so narrow as nationalism. For the Straits-Chinese, the English press was to become the mouthpiece of an emerging 'cosmopolitanism' that strove not to divide but to unite Malaya's educated, heterogeneous communities.

The first edition of the Singapore-based monthly *Straits Chinese Magazine*, published in 1897, announced that its audience was 'a large number of Straits-born people of all nationalities who are in every respect better educated than those of a former generation'.[4] The article credited the colonial administration for new advancements in education and the institution of Queen's scholarships, which swept talented Straits citizens to the spires of Oxford and Cambridge. The journal stated that its purpose was to 'champion the cause of any nationality permanently residing in our midst'.[5] Implicit was the suggestion that should any Chinese, Indian or Malay inhabitant of the Straits Settlements suffer injustice on the part of the colonial regime, the magazine was prepared to fight for their cause. The discourse which emerged out of such English periodicals was thus no mouthpiece for colonialism, nor was it narrowly communalist or nationalistic – it was universally democratic and cosmopolitan.

English periodicals such as the *Straits Chinese Magazine* targeted the educated, multi-ethnic inhabitants of the colony. Whereas the

Singapore-based magazine (*c.* 1897–1907) signified an early part of this trend, the Penang-based English daily, *The Straits Echo*, continued to provide a platform for debate between Malaya's multi-ethnic communities throughout the colonial period. As such it provides a valuable case study of a cosmopolitan discourse created by an indigenous population, one that appropriated the language and ideals of empire for its own ends. It articulated a sense of cosmopolitanism rooted in both local multiculturalism as well as the imperial rhetoric of a 'global community'.[6] Unlike past studies of Malaya's plural societies which track the origins of nationalist or communal mentalities, this essay examines the way in which diverse and diasporic communities spoke to one another, exploring their differences as well as their shared common aspirations. Whereas the vernacular presses strengthened communal bonds but isolated communities from each other, the English press provided a new, modern form of celebrating various cultural heritages while striving to find the common bonds between them.

Penang and 'The People's Paper'

A member of one the most established Straits Chinese families in Penang, Lim Seng Hooi left school at the age of 14 to help his father in a small printing business, the Criterion Press. Merchants by trade, the Lim family saw the commercial value of the press in publishing shipping timetables, advertisements and producing local, Penang-based news rather than relying on the Singapore press. In 1894, they launched a Chinese daily paper called the *Penang Sin Poe*, and four years later (in 1898) founded a Malay weekly, the *Chahyah Pulau Pinang*. At the time, these two journals were the only Chinese and Malay newspapers in Penang. In 1903, Lim launched *The Straits Echo*, an English-language paper that served reformist as well as commercial purposes. He employed Chesney Duncan – a swashbuckling Englishman who had previously served in the Korean Merchant Steamship army – as his first editor.

Unlike its long-established predecessor, the government periodical *The Pinang Gazette*, the *Echo* had 'no particular policy – either imperial or colonial'.[7] Its stated purpose was to 'defend the weak against the strong, and the right against the wrong, regardless of nationality, race, or creed'.[8] Like *The Straits Chinese Magazine*, published only six years earlier, the *Straits Echo* relied on 'the innate love of Justice and Fairplay which characterises free peoples the world over'[9] and asked that these ideals apply to all the inhabitants of the Straits. In a playful tone, the paper's *raison d'être* pledged that it would be prepared to criticise the colonial administration and indeed, that such criticism would be healthy and necessary:

> The Administration may appear a flower of perfection, and inten-
> tions of legislators, official and unofficial, simply admirable; but they
> will not wither if in a healthy state when gently agitated by the
> breeze of well-intentioned criticism. They will rather flourish under
> its salubrious influence; and doubtless those in authority may even
> be glad of an opportunity to occasionally see themselves as others
> see them. The *Echo* desires to indicate the points of reasonable differ-
> ence of opinion and to encourage a tone of independent judgement
> upon local as well as Imperial affairs.[10]

Elsewhere in the *Echo*'s first edition, the Government was duly criticised for being 'exceedingly parsimonious' with educational resources. Using the example of the independent British press, the editorial continued that a free press was a bastion for democracy and public opinion:

> it is the first, chief, and most important duty of a free Press to open
> the eyes of the community beyond the actual sphere in which
> individuals move, and by so doing form that body of opinion –
> disinterested and just – which is so fatal to 'relapses' in governing
> bodies. It has ever been the proud boast of the unsubsidised section
> of the British Press that it is fearless, outspoken and strictly impartial
> in the discharge of this duty.[11]

The independent British press was thus the model that Lim appropri-
ated for his newspaper (the *Echo* would often transcribe articles from the left-leaning *Manchester Guardian* and *Review of Reviews*).

The Singapore-based *Straits Chinese Magazine* applauded the noble intentions of the *Echo*, with its 1903 issue stating, 'I am sure all lovers of justice and fair-play and all haters of anti-native feelings and racial prejudices will rejoice and give *The Straits Echo* a warm and hearty welcome.'[12] With a series of left-leaning editors, the *Echo* kept to its intention throughout its existence, gaining a reputation as 'the People's Paper'. After selling the paper in 1926, Lim continued to promote its cause as a prominent Chinese community leader. In the 1939 Chinese New Year edition of the *Echo*, he said of the paper, 'It advocates all worthy causes irrespective of class or creed and may it continue to flourish so that all communities will have a chance of not only expressing their just causes but also have their grievances redressed directly or indirectly through *The Straits Echo*.'[13] The British journalist and travel writer George Bilainkin had a great affection for Lim, and was happy to be one of a series of European editors serving under him for 15 years; like Duncan, he was not averse to criticising the administration. Upon arriving to take up the post of editor in the early 1920s, Bilainkin inherited a staff of between 70 and 80 Chinese, Malays, Tamils, Singhalese and Eurasians, which provided him, he said, with 'a fascinating background from which to learn of the eternal clash of race and colour in the Orient'.[14]

In 1931, Bilainkin was replaced by a Ceylonese sports editor, the 'legendary' Manicasothy Saravanamuttu. Sara, as he was commonly known, became the first non-white editor of a Malayan newspaper – in 1934, a meeting of the editors was unable to convene in the Singapore Club on account of his colour. Sara's outstanding editorship of the paper coincided with the *Echo's* most glorious years. In the 1930s, *The Straits Echo* tripled its circulation and even succeeded in buying out the Singapore-owned *Times of Malaya* and *Pinang Gazette* to take control of the North Malayan newspapers. Educated at Oxford, where training as a Fabian nurtured his socialist ideals, he declared, 'It was natural that my editorial policy should have been mainly that of one "for the people".'[15] Consistent with the early aims of the *Echo* to give the cosmopolitan population of Malaya a voice, in 1939 Sara wrote an editorial citing the Secretary of State to the Colonies:

> As Mr. Malcolm Macdonald pointed out the other day, the main purpose of the British Empire is for the gradual spreading of liberty and the chief aim of British rule in the Colonies is to educate the people to rule themselves . . . hollow is the excuse that the cosmopolitan character of the Malayan population does not easily lend itself to political progress . . . [we] want the various people that have in Malaya their permanent home to be given a greater and greater share in the management of their own affairs, instead of perpetuating the present system of spoon-fed administration. . . . The time has come when the people of this country should emerge from their state of tutelage and be given a chance, step by step, to manage their own affairs. That is the only policy that would be consistent with the aim of the British Empire.[16]

The Straits Echo was thus a child of empire. Quintessentially British notions of 'fair play', Fabian/socialist ideals harboured by British-schooled editors, the example of the unsubsidised British press and the aims of *Pax Britannica* were held up as a mirror to colonialists and compatriots. By using the language and ideals of the coloniser, the paper justified its existence as a means by which the various communities of the Straits Settlements could raise their concerns in a fair and democratic manner. The *Echo* aimed to give people of all races, nationalities and creeds a voice in the administration of the colony.

The *Echo* was also symbolic of wider forces of globalisation. Penang was a port city continually open to the transnational flow of modern ideas and forms of communication, leading it to look beyond nation and empire to an increasingly integrated world. The paper's content and readers' contributions both reflected a cosmopolitan society and perpetuated it. Radio schedules listed programmes from Berlin, Calcutta, Holland, Melbourne, Moscow, Paris, Rome and Tokyo. Local cinemas advertised films ranging from Charlie Chaplin and Greta Garbo silent classics to Cantonese and Tamil talkies. Advertisements – from Kloster beer to Cadbury chocolate and Japanese pearls – suggest a readership plugged into global consumer networks. The high level of foreign news of *The Straits Echo* and other Malayan papers even succeeded in impressing Nehru on his tour of the country.[17] Almost half of Sara's editorials were on foreign topics, taking a pacifist, progressive stance on issues such as the war in Abyssinia, the Palestine question and Congress in India. Frequent commentators such as the retired Muslim scholar H. G. Sarwar contributed military analyses of the war in China and journals from his pilgrimage to Mecca.

As an English-language paper, *The Straits Echo*'s readership was principally composed of multi-racial urbanites educated and versed in English. It was the paper of the English-educated commercial elite, read too by Europeans expatriated and passing through Penang. Yet there is also evidence that the paper reached less affluent members of society – in 1931, a letter from 'Tamil coolies' thanked Mr Cheah Phee Siew for supplying them with drinking water from his ice-cart free of charge, praying 'God may bless him for his charitable spirit'.[18] The level of lively social debate in the paper reflected popular rather than elite culture – according to Sara, Bilainkin's previous attempt to produce a weekly book page interested only a small handful of the European population, whereas the vast majority of his readers, 'particularly the Asians',[19] were far more interested in the daily 'Readers' Page' filled with letters on local topics. The paper thus crossed the boundaries of high and low culture, appealing to Europeans at the top of the social ladder as well as English-speaking Asians at the bottom. It had a global and regional circulation wider than North Malaya – Bilainkin said that in his time, 'the sheets would travel to Siam, Java, India, Sumatra, China, almost everywhere, not omitting Leningrad, where we had one subscriber'.[20] Letters from Taiping, Kuala Lumpur, South Thailand and Singapore suggest a continuation of a wide and active readership at the end of the 1930s.

Language(s) of the cosmopolitan

Debates over language and education underscored the tensions inherent in a cosmopolitan society – one that attempted to reconcile the rich diversity of cultural and linguistic heritages with the opportunities English provided for advancement and cross-cultural dialogue. As an English paper that pledged to defend the causes of diverse communities, *The Straits Echo* found itself at the heart of such debates. In the Readers' Pages, communities wrestled with the demands of modernity and the desire to hang on to their cultural roots. English education provided new opportunities within both colonial society and abroad, but at the risk of forgetting one's heritage. Despite the growing availability of English, diasporic ties to language were still strong. Whereas colonialists, Anglophiles and pragmatists promoted English education, Tamil and Chinese writers wrote in favour of improving the Tamil and Mandarin schools established by immigrants seeking to educate their children in the culture of their homelands. One Tamil reader said,

> The Malays and Chinese have schools where they can learn Malay and Chinese. They have suitable and up-to-date buildings. The teachers in these schools are well trained, and the standard of teaching is quite high. The Indians in Penang have no schools and so most of us who are local born do not know Tamil. It is a great shame, not to know our language.[21]

Language was also a contested issue *within* communities, as evidenced by an inflammatory letter by a Tamil writer who complained that funds were being wasted in popularising Hindi in India: 'With an utter lack of modern Science, Art, Industry, and of political history which are noble in its conception, abounding in instruction, and exalted in its aim, Hindi, as a language, can never become the lingua franca of India and its masses.'[22]

Chinese readers wrote in favour of 'the Beauty of the Chinese Language', disgusted that English-educated youth could not even write their own names in Mandarin.[23] As one reader argued,

Until very recently our Malayan parents have considered a Chinese education inferior to an English education for the children; and that has chiefly been so because English education offers better prospects of a job. We are 'Nanyang Wah Kheow' [Chinese abroad in Malaysia]. The land of our ancestors is China.[24]

Diasporic links to the 'mother-tongue' thus held strong, with language emphasised as a sign of cultural solidarity to one's imaginary homeland. As this reader continued:

Let us encourage our children to study our own language. Since 'it's never too late to mend,' those of us to whom Chinese characters are still hieroglyphics should devote part of our leisure to studying our own mother tongue, not only for the sake of visiting China some day, but chiefly for the purpose of knowing ourselves.[25]

While encouraging such debate in its Readers' Pages, *The Straits Echo* was an ardent supporter of the view that English should be adopted as the mother tongue of Penang's youth, seeing it as the path towards success. Saravanamuttu repeatedly tried to combat the growing tendency of Penang's English-educated youth to creolise the language (mixing it with Penang Chinese and Malay slang) or fail to use it in everyday conversation. He argued that the Ceylonese example should be heeded, whereby youth were discouraged from speaking their mother tongue at school so they could learn to 'think in English'. The editorial pages advised, 'You will not make a success of your life unless you learn one language through and through and that one language must for you be English because it is the language in which the very large majority of you have to earn your living.'[26]

Despite nationalist and extra-national ties to Malay, Chinese, and Indian languages, many *Echo* readers also emphasised the importance of English and lauded its cultural value. As the original Crown Colony, Penang had a pioneering history of English education and a long love affair with the language. Within the Commonwealth, the command of English by Penangites – particularly the Straits-born Chinese – was of stellar quality, better indeed than that of the English themselves. The comments of one Cambridge examiner, reprinted in *The Straits Echo*, attested to this:

Good papers came from West Africa ... and delightful papers from Mauritius in broken English that was half French. But the gem of the collection was a batch of twenty supremely beautiful papers from Penang...every one of them was a work of art, a joy to the eye and a rest to the brain...therefore let us teach our children to write clean sense in simple English words, or let us charter a large ship and invite the entire population of Penang to get aboard of her, come to this island of superstition, slaughter and lies, and undertake the gigantic task of our education.[27]

Some readers argued so persuasively in favour of the English language that they were guilty of sounding 'more British than the British' – an accusation that often befell the Straits-born Chinese. One Straits-born Chinese woman, Miss Lee Kooi Eam, was lauded for writing a beautifully crafted letter on the verbs 'shall' and 'will':

By simply transposing the verbs 'shall' and 'will' an Englishman can indicate that he has discarded politeness and that he is now speaking in a spirit of solemnity by way prophecy, promise, or menace...Truly a language which by such simple means can so clearly define the mental attitude of its user is a glorious heritage, and those of us who read and write the English language besides Englishmen should preserve it, with all its shades of meaning, as a sacred trust.[28]

Malay readers also recognised the importance of English and demanded that English education be more accessible. Some complained that the four years of mandatory vernacular schooling Malays had to undergo before applying to study English set them far behind their Indian and Chinese classmates. Said one Malay reader, 'Laziness should not be thrown at the door of the Malays. They are energetic and as clever as the other nationalities who have outdistanced them by reason of their utter lack of sufficient educational facilities and financial support. This is the only handicap in their race with the other races.'[29] Another reader supported mandatory Queen's scholarships especially given to Malay students.

A Malay writer, Mas M. Akbar, wrote a passionate plea for Malays to learn the English language. Taking the example of other races of Malaya, who had adopted English in quest for further advancement, he argued that English was the key to progress. The Chinese, for example, used English in everyday conversation, 'not because they love their vernacular tongue less but because progress and advancement as a nation lies in the English language'.[30] Like the Chinese and Indian parents who sent their children to English school but spoke to them in their own language at home, Mas Akbar advocated a necessary bilingualism, encompassing love of one's mother tongue alongside English. To be 'modern' did not have to involve 'loving one's vernacular tongue less'; one could nurture one's vernacular tongue at the same time as English. Both were valuable for different purposes – one to advance and communicate with others in the cosmopolitan public sphere, the other for nurturing one's cultural heritage and forging solidarities within a particular community.

If Malays, he went on, continued to conduct their affairs in Malay, their progress compared with other communities would be negligible. In a tone one would expect to hear from an English schoolteacher, he movingly argued:

> To get rid of this language would be as bad and as foolish as 'cutting off the nose to spite the face.' If, like Alice in Wonderland, Miss English was asked – what have you done for us? She will reply: – 'I taught you everything I could, without distinction of cast or creed. I was perfectly honest, straight and fair in all my dealings with you. I did not care whether you were brown or yellow – black or fair. Byron was Byron and Shakespeare was Shakespeare to everyone who had the brains to understand them. I taught you to read the speeches of Milton, Burke, Shelley and a host of other lovers of liberty.... Through me, you studied the problems of your country, you learned economics, statistics, science, arts, geography, history, political science, political institutions and political philosophy. I have trained your scientists and doctors, both to kill or heal mankind. I have taught you to become scientists like Bose – industrialists like Sir Ratan Tate and Sir Henry Ford. Barristers like Jinnah and Braddel, politicians like Chamberlain, Gandhi, Nehru and a host of others. I have helped you in shops, in exports and imports – in trade and in commerce. I have brought culture and civilisation with a modern outlook to your very feet.' I venture to suggest that my Malay brethren here who are aspiring for advancement in many ways than one, should think of the benefits of a change and act on it.[31]

Mas Akbar's eloquent letter, with its allusions to world-historical figures (from America, Britain and India), seemed to view English not only as a pragmatic tool for advancement, but as a way of contributing to world civilisation. In the standard story of the origins of Malay nationalism, voices such as Mas Akbar's are not often heard. They complicate the story, precisely because they fall much more on the side of cosmopolitanism and globalism. They advocate dialogue and connection not simply within an ethno-linguistic community, but between communities – both within and outside the territorial boundaries of nation – connected by the parts they play in *world* history.

As evidenced by the myriad of debates about the nature of language and education in late colonial Penang, language continued to be a contested issue. Among educated urban-dwellers, English was rapidly becoming the *lingua franca* of the archipelago – but not without a fight. Whereas the promotion of Malay created a defensive community of interest against foreigners or immigrant interests, and foretold post-colonial nationalism, the guarding of Mandarin, Tamil and Hindi continued to symbolise a vital link to a faraway home. If print-language invents nationalism, then nationalism – in terms of a singular identity of a people – could never have emerged in Malaya. The proliferation of different languages, and multilingual publications, signified multiple allegiances and solidarities within late colonial, cosmopolitan society. Print-language in English also invented cosmopolitanism. This was not simply due to the self-styled visions of ardent Britons and Americans who desired to make it a universal language.[32] Rather, it was because the demand for English had grown so that English *became* the language of people like urban Penangites, who valued its uses in certain contexts while nurturing their mother tongues in others.

English was a language increasingly accessible to the urban middle class and elite. Within the cosmopolitan port city of Penang and urban centres elsewhere, it acted as a bond between races, offering new possibilities at home and abroad. It was not simply imposed by the coloniser; it was adopted, hybridised, even loved. English, the language of the coloniser, was rapidly becoming the language of the colonised – a tool that enabled different communities to speak to each other and participate in a public sphere which would allow them to voice their grievances. *The Straits Echo*, a newspaper written in English, provided an equal platform by which not only colonial administrators and schoolteachers, but everyday, English-educated Chinese, Indians and Malays could participate in debates on a wide range of issues affecting their society, from the changing position of women to support for cultural associations and overseas wars.[33]

'Global community'

Throughout the 1930s, the *Echo* became associated with cross-cultural understanding and cooperation. Readers of the *Echo* even sought to bridge the boundaries between communities through an association of the papers' readers. One proposed the formation of a 'Straits Echo League', the objects of which would include:

> to foster harmonious relations among the various races of Malaya, to bring them to a common platform of thoughts and strife for the progression of this country, to develop the faculties of the masses by providing facilities for interchange of ideas and the self-expression of views and thoughts, to be the organ instrumental in letting the people to have a voice in the administration of this country.[34]

The suggestion had much support from other readers as well as Saravan-amuttu himself, who organised the first of a series of meetings in response to popular demand. As editor of the paper during its most successful years, Saravanamuttu was an ardent advocate of clubs and associations that promoted progressive, multiracial representation, along with his British colleague and friend F. H. Grummitt, owner of the paper (after Lim Seng Hooi) and president of both the Straits Settlements (Penang) Association and the Rotary Club.[35] Grummitt's association with such clubs promoted the paper's support of a modern, cosmopolitan view associated with imperial ideals of 'global community' and self-improvement.

The paper's support of cross-cultural cooperation at the local level was also a microcosm of a global aspiration. Amidst the pre-war tranquillity of the 1930s, *The Straits Echo* supported the cause of internationalists and idealists who sought to find ways of linking together the various countries and cultures of the world in a spirit of global cooperation. Saravanamuttu's address to the Penang Rotary Club focused on its role as a real force for mutual understanding and world peace, through its fellowship of businessmen and professionals:

> The express purpose of the Fourth Object of Rotary is a creation of the international mind among Rotarians of all races and nations. By an international mind, I mean a mind which, looking out beyond its own racial and territorial boundaries, discerns the essential oneness of all humanity. The things that differentiate men into races, and nations and classes and creeds are of little consequence compared with the compelling unities that binds them all together as members of one great human family. It is not my intention to preach a sermon, although the foregoing sounds very much like a pulpit

utterance, but what I want to do today is to indicate what Rotary has
done and can do to help to break down the barriers that have been
set up between nation and nation and bridge the boundaries
between the various countries.[36]

Saravanamuttu's appeal to the 'international mind' advocated a new
kind of 'globalism' – of thinking and acting on a global basis, in the
common interest of nations and races.[37] The sense of attachment to
the affairs of the world was clearly felt by readers of his paper as well.
In readers' letters one senses tremendous disappointment at the
failure of the League of Nations in securing world peace amidst the
stirrings of Hitler's Germany and militarist Japan. (For instance, a
popular reader's only objection to Straits Echo League was the use of
the word 'League', because it alluded to the 'disastrous League with its
headquarters in Geneva which promised so much but achieved so
little'.)

The globalist outlook of Saravanamuttu and his readers, advocating a
spirit of equal co-operation between the races and nations of the world,
was no doubt idealistic – but it was also rooted in particular histories:
not simply the collective global memory of the First World War, but
also in the injustices of the colour bar in colonial society and the
competitive spirit of immigrants determined to improve their lot in a
diasporic world. Globalism, like cosmopolitanism, had roots in a society
where equal co-operation between communities was essential to individual and social advancement. If globalism was the sense of attachment to a wider, international world, then cosmopolitanism brought
the global into the local and the local into the global – acknowledging
the affairs of the rest of the world as they were connected to the
polyglot port city of Penang.

Conclusion

Between the sunset of empire and the dawn of nationalism lay the
hopeful twilight of cosmopolitanism. Dynamic new forms of media and
communication brought the world closer than ever before. Through the
English press, educated, multi-ethnic inhabitants of the Straits Settlements imbued with a 'sense of complex and multiple belonging'[38]
envisaged a world in which 'justice' and 'fair play' were applicable
beyond race or nationality. Here was an indigenous and diasporic
society extracting – out of the hypocrisy and injustices of empire – the
most humanist of ideals, while savouring its cultural roots. Reader and

writer sought to reform the colonial environment in which non-whites were denied a voice in the administration of the colony, and provide a way in which multi-ethnic communities could speak to and learn from each other in order to grow. The articulation of a necessary multilingualism – which embraced English while nurturing vernacular and diasporic tongues – was symbolic of a society reconciling cultural tradition with modernity and progress. Ideas such as the 'international mind' introduced a vision for the world as well as the future of Malaya, one which rang more true as a modern articulation of their diasporic and multicultural society than the idea of a nation defined by a sole ethnic group.

As noted by contemporary historians of eighteenth- and nineteenth-century cosmopolitanism, the concept has too often been associated with imperial expansion –Van de Veer's cosmopolitan, for instance, is an anthropologist, a missionary, or a colonial officer who displays a willingness to engage with the other. Neglected, he admits, is the way the societies in which Europeans interacted wrote their own history.[39] The press was a hybrid tool (born out of China and the West) of colonial expansion and global communication, which could be appropriated by non-European societies to articulate their own sense of identity. Through the press, cosmopolitanism provided a mode of connecting to imperial centres, modern ideas and world affairs and thus belong to a global identity that was wider and more heterogeneous than nationalism but less exploitative than that of empire. In focusing too often on those 'imagined solidarities' created through the press which led to nationalism and communalism, historians have written such discourses out of history. Local forms of cosmopolitanism, as evidenced in Malaya's 'indigenous' English press, attest to T. N. Harper's assertion that during the late colonial period, 'there were perhaps more people participating in globalisation, more people consciously thinking and acting on a global basis, and from more centres, than at any time since'.[40] In the case of Malaya, what has been lost is a particular and invaluable mode of being that advocated cultural diversity and shared aspirations – cacophony as well as harmony, difference as well as commonality – in celebration of a tangled web of cosmopolitan solidarities.

Notes

1. B. Anderson, *Imagined Communities* (London: Verso, 1991), pp. 163–85.
2. Ibid., p. 132.

248   *Su Lin Lewis*

3. W. Roff, *The Origins of Malay Nationalism* (New York: Oxford University Press, 1994), p. 256.
4. *Straits Chinese Magazine* I, no. 1 (Singapore: March 1897), p. 1.
5. Ibid.
6. T. N. Harper, 'Globalism and the Pursuit of Authenticity: The Making of a Diasporic Public Sphere in Singapore', in *SOJOURN: Journal of Social Issues in Southeast Asia* Vol. 12, No. 2 (Singapore: Institute of Southeast Asian Studies, October 1997), p. 275.
7. *Straits Echo* (Georgetown: Criterion Press), 12 June 1903.
8. Ibid.
9. Ibid.
10. *Straits Echo*, June 1903.
11. Ibid.
12. *Straits Chinese Magazine* Vol. 7, 1903: 61–5.
13. *Straits Echo*, 13 February 1939.
14. G. Bilainkin, *Hail Penang! Being the Narrative of Comedies and Tragedies in a Tropical Outpost, among Europeans, Chinese, Malays, and Indians* (London: Sampson Low, Marston & Co., 1932), p. 25.
15. M. Saravanamuttu, *The Sara Saga, with a Foreword by the Right Honourable Malcolm Macdonald* (Penang: Cathay Printers, 1970), p. 56.
16. *Straits Echo*, 4 January 1939.
17. *Straits Echo*, 10 December 1937.
18. *Straits Echo*, 7 January 1931.
19. Saravanamuttu, *The Sara Saga*, p. 54.
20. Bilainkin, *Hail Penang!*, p. 50.
21. *Straits Echo*, 8 January 1938.
22. *Straits Echo*, 3 February 1938.
23. *Straits Echo*, 30 November 1937.
24. *Straits Echo*, 18 November 1937.
25. Ibid.
26. *Straits Echo*, 27 November 1937.
27. *Straits Echo*, 23 March 1939.
28. *Straits Echo*, 3 February 1938
29. *Straits Echo*, 10 December 1937.
30. *Straits Echo*, 2 April 1939.
31. Ibid.
32. T. N. Harper, 'Empire, Diaspora, and the Languages of Globalism 1850–1914', in A. J. Hopkins (ed.), *Globalization in World History* (London: Pimlico, 2002), p. 155.
33. These debates are elaborated in the author's unpublished MA dissertation on 'Cosmopolitanism and the English Press in Late Colonial Penang', University of London.
34. *Straits Echo*, 7 February 1939.
35. As outlined in Sara's biography, the relationship between these two men was one of friendship and great respect. Grummitt's death in 1947 'someone clipped [his] feathers, and Sara resigned from *The Straits Echo*, later to become Ceylonese High Commissioner to Malaya and Indonesia (Saravanamuttu, *The Sara Saga*, p. 188).
36. *Straits Echo*, 18 November 1937.

37. Harper, 'Empire, Diaspora, and the Languages of Globalism, 1850–1914', p. 142.
38. B. Robbins, 'Introduction', in P. Cheah and B. Robbins (eds.), *Cosmopolitics: Thinking and Feeling Beyond the Nation* (Minneapolis: University of Minnesota Press, 1998).
39. P. Van de Veer, 'Colonial Cosmopolitanism'. in Stephen Vertovec and Robin Cohen (eds.), *Conceiving Cosmopolitanism: Theory, Context, and Practice* (Oxford: Oxford University Press, 2002), p. 178.
40. Harper, 'Empire, Diaspora and the Languages of Globalism', p. 160.

Select Bibliography and Further Reading

Press and empire in Malaya

Andaya, Barbara Watson and Leonard Y. Andaya. *A History of Malaysia*. Second edition (Basingstoke: Macmillan, 1988)

Anderson, Benedict. *Imagined Communities* (London: Verso, 1991)

Anderson, Benedict. *The Spectre of Comparisons: Nationalism, Southeast Asia, and the World* (London: Verso, 1998)

Bilainkin, George. *Hail Penang! Being the Narrative of Comedies and Tragedies in a Tropical Outpost, among Europeans, Chinese, Malays, and Indians* (London: Sampson Low, Marston & Co., 1932)

Breckenridge, Carol A. et al. (eds.). *Cosmopolitanism* (Durham, NC: Duke University Press, 2002)

Cheah, Pheng and Robbins, Bruce (eds.). *Cosmopolitics: Thinking and Feeling Beyond the Nation* (Minneapolis: University of Minnesota Press, 1998)

Harper, T. N. 'Globalism and the Pursuit of Authenticity: The Making of a Diasporic Public Sphere in Singapore', in *SOJOURN: Journal of Social Issues in Southeast Asia* Vol. 12, No. 2 (1997)

Harper, T. N. 'Empire, Diaspora, and the Languages of Globalism, 1850–1914', in A. J. Hopkins (ed.). *Globalization in World History* (London: Pimlico, 2002)

Lent, John A. *Newspapers in Asia: Contemporary Trends and Problems* (Hong Kong: Heinemann Asia, 1982)

McPherson, Kenneth. 'Port Cities as Nodal Points of Change: The Indian Ocean, 1890s–1920s"', in Leila Tarazi Fawaz and C. A. Bayly (eds.). *Modernity and Culture: From the Mediterranean to the Indian Ocean* (New York: Columbia University Press, 2002)

Milner, Anthony. *The Invention of Politics in Colonial Malaya* (Cambridge: Cambridge University Press, 1994)

Roff, William. *The Origins of Malay Nationalism* (New York: Oxford University Press, 1994)

Vertovec, Stephen and Robin Cohen (eds.). *Conceiving Cosmopolitanism: Theory, Context, and Practice* (Oxford: Oxford University Press, 2002)

Imperialism, moral regulation and obscenity

Ballhatchet, Kenneth. *Race, Sex and Class under the Raj: Imperial Attitudes and Policies and their Critics, 1793–1905* (London: Weidenfeld & Nicolson, 1980)

Bland, Lucy. *Banishing the Beast: Sexuality and the Early Feminists* (New York: The New Press, 1995)

Bristow, Edward. *Vice and Vigilance: Purity Movements in Britain since 1700* (Dublin: Gill and Macmillan Ltd, 1977)

Harris, Jose. *Private Lives, Public Spirit: A Social History of Britain 1870–1914* (Oxford: Oxford University Press, 1993)

Harrison, Brian. 'State Intervention and Moral Reform in Nineteenth-Century England', in Patricia Hollis (ed.). *Pressure from Without in Early Victorian England* (London: Edward Arnold, 1974)

Hunt, Alan. *Governing Morals: A Social History of Moral Regulation* (Cambridge: Cambridge University Press, 1999)

Hunter, Ian, David Saunders and Dugald Williamson. *On Pornography: Literature, Sexuality and Obscenity Law* (New York: St. Martin's Press, 1993)

Hyam, Ronald, *Empire and Sexuality: The British Experience* (Manchester: Manchester University Press, 1990)

Marcus, Stephen. *The Other Victorians: A Study of Sexuality and Pornography in Mid-Nineteenth-Century England* (London: Corgi Books, 1966)

Marsh, Joss. *Word Crimes: Blasphemy, Culture, and Literature in Nineteenth-Century England* (Chicago and London: The University of Chicago Press, 1998)

Michaelson, Peter. *Speaking the Unspeakable: A Poetics of Obscenity* (Albany, NY: SUNY Press, 1993)

Mort, Frank. *Dangerous Sexualities: Medico-Moral Politics in England Since 1830.* Second edition (London: Routledge, 2000)

Pease, Alison. *Modernism, Mass Culture, and the Aesthetics of Obscenity* (Cambridge: Cambridge University Press, 2000)

Robb, Peter. 'South Asia and the Concept of Race', in Peter Robb (ed.). *The Concept of Race in South Asia*, SOAS Studies on South Asia Understandings and Perspectives Series (Delhi: Oxford University Press, 1995)

Roberts, M. J. D. 'Morals, Art and the Law: The Passing of the Obscene Publications Act, 1857', *Victorian Studies*, 28, 4 (1985) 625–6

Said, Edward. *Culture and Imperialism* (New York: Vintage Books, 1993)

Sigel, Lisa. 'Filth in the Wrong People's Hands: Postcards and the Expansion of Pornography in Britain and the Atlantic World, 1880–1914', *Journal of Social History*, 33, 4 (2000) 859–85

Stoler, Anne Laura. *Race and the Education of Desire: Foucault's History of Sexuality and the Colonial Order of Things* (Durham, NC: Duke University Press, 1995)

Travis, Alan. *Bound and Gagged: A Secret History of Obscenity in Britain* (London: Profile Books, 2000)

The British press and India

Barns, M. *The Indian Press: A History of the Growth of Public Opinion in India* (London, G. Allen & Unwin 1940)

Barrier, N. G. *Banned – Controversial Literature and Political Control in British India 1907–1947* (Columbia: University of Missouri, Press 1974)

Bayly, C. *Information and Empire: Intelligence Gathering and Social Communication in India 1780–1870* (Cambridge: Cambridge University Press, 1996)

Boyce, G., Curran, J. and Wingate, P. (eds.). *Newspaper History: From the Seventeenth Century to the Present Day* (London: Constable, 1978)

Brake, L., *Print in Transition 1850–1910* (Basingstoke: Palgrave, 2001)

Brake, L., Jones, A. and Madden, L. (eds.). *Investigating Victorian Journalism* (London: Macmillan, 1990)

Briggs, A. and Burke, P., *A Social History of the Media* (Oxford: Blackwell, 2002)

Brown, L. *Victorian News and Newspapers* (Oxford, Clarendon Press, 1985)

Chalaby, J. *The Invention of Journalism* (London: Macmillan, 1998)

Codell, Julie F. (ed.). *Imperial Co-Histories-National Identities and the British and Colonial Press* (London: Fairleigh Dickinson University Press, 2003)

Conboy, Martin. *The Press and Popular Culture* (London: Sage, 2002)

Curran, James, *Media and Power* (London and New York: Routledge, 2002)

Griffiths, D. *The Encyclopedia of the British Press 1422–1992* (New York: St. Martin's Press, 1992)

Hampton, Mark, *Visions of the Press in Britain 1850–1950* (Urbana, IL: University of Illinois Press, 2004)

Harris, M. and Lee, A. (eds.). *The Press in English Society from the Seventeenth Century to the Nineteenth Century* (London: Associated University Presses 1986)

Harris, M. and O'Malley, T. (eds.). *Studies in Newspaper and Periodical History 1994 Annual* (Connecticut: Greenwood Press, 1996)

Israel, M. *Communications and Power: Propaganda and the Press in the Indian Nationalist Struggle, 1920–47* (Cambridge: Cambridge University Press, 1994)

Jones, A. *Powers of the Press: Newspapers, Power and the Public in Nineteenth-Century England* (Aldershot: Ashgate Press, 1996)

Kaul, Chandrika, 'England and India: The Ilbert Bill, 1883. A Case Study of the Metropolitan Press', *The Indian Economic and Social History Review* (New Delhi and London: Sage, Vol. 30, No. 4, October–December 1993), pp. 413–36

—— 'A New Angle of Vision: The London Press, Governmental Information Management and the Indian Empire, 1900–1922', in *Empire, Competition and War: Essays on the Press in the Twentieth Century, Contemporary Record*, special edition (London, Vol. 8, No. 2, Autumn 1994), pp. 213–41

—— 'The Press', in *Contemporary History Handbook*, ed. B. Brivati, A. Seldon and J. Buxton (Manchester: Manchester University Press, 1996), pp. 298–310

—— 'Information Society and the Communications Revolution in India', in D. Derman and J. Lotherington (eds.). *The Communications Revolution* (Ankara: Middle Eastern Technical University, 1996), pp. 118–29

—— 'Some Perspectives on Gender and the Indian Media', in K. Ross and D. Derman (eds.). *Gender and Media* (Ankara: Middle Eastern Technical University, 1996), pp. 249–65

—— 'Imperial Communications, Fleet Street and the Indian Empire, c. 1850s–1920s', in *A Journalism Reader*, (eds.) M. Bromley and T. O'Malley (London, Routledge, 1997), pp. 58–86

—— '*Round Table*, the British Press and India, 1910–22', in A. Bosco and A. May (eds.). *The Round Table Movement, the Empire/Commonwealth and British Foreign Policy* (London: Lothian Foundation Press, 1997), pp. 343–68

—— 'Popular Press and Empire: Northcliffe, India and the *Daily Mail*, 1896–1922', in C. Seymour-Ure, P. Catterall and A. Smith (eds.). *Northcliffe's Legacy: Aspects of the Popular Press 1896–1996* (London: Macmillan, 2000), pp. 45–69

—— *Reporting the Raj, the British Press and India, circa 1880–1922* (Manchester and New York, Manchester University Press/Palgrave, 2003)

Koss, S. *The Rise and Fall of the Political Press in Britain*, 2 vols (Chapel Hill, NC: University of North Carolina Press, 1980)

Lee, A. J. *The Origins of the Popular Press* (London: Croom Helm, 1976)

Linton, D. and Boston, R. (eds.). *The Newspaper Press in Britain* (London: Mansell 1987)

—— *The Twentieth-Century Newspaper Press* (London: Mansell, 1994)

Natarajan, S., *A History of the Press in India* (London: Asia Publishing House, 1962)

Negrine, R. *Politics and the Mass Media in Britain* (London, Routledge, 1994)

P.E.P., *Report on The British Press* (London, 1938)

Peers, D. and Finkelstein, D. (eds.). *Negotiating India in the Nineteenth Century Media*, (Basingstoke: Macmillan 2000)

Read, D. *The Power of News* (Oxford, Oxford University Press 1999)

Seymour-Ure, C. *The British Press and Broadcasting since 1945* (Oxford: Blackwell, 1996)

Startt, J. D. *Journalists for Empire* (Westport, CT: Greenwood Press, 1991)

Thompson, J. L. *Northcliffe Press Baron in Politics 1865–1922* (London: John Murray, 2000)

Wiener, J. H. (ed.). *Innovators and Preachers: The Role of the Editor in Victorian England* (Westport, CT: Greenwood Press, 1985)

—— (ed.). *Papers for the Millions* (New York: Greenwood Press, 1988)

Wilkinson, G. *Depictions and Images of War in Edwardian Newspapers* (London: Palgrave Macmillan 2003)

Churchill's India campaign and the British press

Barty-King, Hugh. *Girdle Round the Earth: The Story of Cable and Wireless and its Predecessors to Mark the Group's Jubilee 1929–1979* (London: Heinemann, 1979)

Bridge, C. *Holding India to the Empire: The British Conservative Party and the 1935 Constitution* (London: Oriental University Press, 1986)

Charmley, J. *Churchill: The End of Glory* (London: BCA, 1993)

Chisholm, A. and Davie, M., *Lord Beaverbrook: A Life* (New York: Alfred Knopf, 1993)

Communications with Australia and New Zealand

Cryle Denis, 'The Empire Press Union and Antipodean Communication: Australian – New Zealand Involvement 1909–1950', *Media History*, 8:1 (June 2002): 49–62

Day, Patrick. *The Making of the New Zealand Press: A Study of the Organisational and Political Concerns of New Zealand Newspaper Controllers* (Wellington: Victoria University Press, 1990)

Fenwick, George. *The United Press Association Formation and Early History* (Dunedin: Otago Times, 1929)

Gilbert, M. *Churchill: Prophet of Truth 1922–1939* (London: William Heinemann, 1976)

Halifax, Earl, *Fullness of Days* (London: Collins, 1957)

Harvey, Ross, 'Bringing the News to New Zealand: The Supply and Control of Overseas News in the Nineteenth Century', *Media History*, 8:1 (June 2002): 12–34

Kaul, Chandrika, 'Imperial Communication Fleet Street and the Indian Empire 1850–1920's', in Michael Bromley and O'Malley Tom (eds.). *A Journalism Reader* (London and New York: Routledge, 1997), pp. 58–86

——— *Reporting the Raj: The British Press and India 1880–1922* (Manchester University Press, Manchester, 2003)

Koss, S. *The Rise and Fall of the Political Press in Britain* (London: Fontana Press, 1990 edition)

Le Sueur, W. D., 'The Jubilee Conference of 1887', in George Johnson (ed.). *The All Red Line: The Annals and Aims of the Pacific Cable Project* (Ottawa: James Hope and Sons, 1903)

Livingston, Kevin, *The Wired Nation Continent. The Communication Revolution and Federating Australia* (Melbourne: Oxford University Press, 1996)

Middlemas, K. and Barnes, J. *Baldwin: A Biography* (London: Weidenfeld & Nicolson, 1969)

Osborne Graeme and Lewis Glen, *Communication Traditions in 20th-century Australia* (Melbourne: Oxford University Press, 2002)

Peele, G. and Cook, C. (eds.). *The Politics of Reappraisal 1918–1939* (London: Macmillan, 1975)

Potter, Simon J., *News and the British World: The Emergence of an Imperial Press System 1876–1922* (Oxford: Clarendon Press, 2003)

Putnis, Peter, 'The Business of Empire: Henry M. Collins and the Early Role of Reuters in Australia', *Australia Journal of Communication*, 24:3 (1997): 11–26

Rantanen, Terhi, 'The Struggle for Control of Domestic News Markets', in Oliver Boyd-Barrett and Rantanen Terhi. *The Globalization of News* (London: Sage, 1998)

Read, Donald, *The Power of News* (Oxford: Oxford University Press, 1992)

Sanders, James, *Dateline-NZPA: The New Zealand Press Association 1880–1980* (Auckland: Wilson and Horton, 1979)

Savory, Gerald Newton. 'Colonial Business Initiatives and the Pacific Cable. A Study in the Role of Private Enterprise in the Development of Imperial Communications', MA diss. (University of Washington, 1972)

Scott, R. Bruce, *Gentlemen on Imperial Service: A Study of the trans-Pacific Telecommunications Cable* (Victoria: Sono Nis Press, 1934)

Select Committee on Press Cable Service in Australian Senate, *Journals* (Melbourne, Australia: Government Printer, 1909), Vol. 1

Storey, Graham, *Reuter's Century 1851–1951* (London: Max Parrish, 1951)

Taylor, A. J. P., *Beaverbrook* (London: Hamish Hamilton, 1972)

Van Cuilenburg Jan and McQuail Denis, 'Media Policy Paradigm Shifts towards a New Communications Policy Paradigm', *European Journal of Communication* 18:2 (2003): 181–208

Winseck Dwayne, 'Back to the Future; Telecommunications Online Service and Convergence from 1840 to 1910', *Media History*, 5:2 (1999): 137–57

Young, K. *Churchill and Beaverbrook: A Study in Friendship and Politics* (London: Eyre and Spottiswoode, 1966)

Empire and New Zealand country newspapers in the nineteenth century

Belich, J. *Paradise Reforged: A History of the New Zealanders from the 1880s to the Year 2000* (Auckland: Penguin, 2001)

Byrne, J. 'The Comparative Development of Newspapers in New Zealand and the United States in the Nineteenth Century', *American Studies International*, 37 (1999)

Cave, R. 'Advertising, Circulation and Profitability: Aspects of the Early Colonial Press', *Bibliographical Society of Australia and New Zealand Bulletin*, 14 (1989) 1–13

Day, P. 'Julius Vogel and the Press', *Turnbull Library Record*, 19 (1986): 103–22

—— *The Making of the New Zealand Press: A Study of the Organizational and Political Concerns of New Zealand Newspaper Controllers, 1840–1880* (Wellington: Victoria University Press, 1990)

Fenwick, G. *The United Press Association: Formation and Early History* (Dunedin: Otago Daily Times & Witness Co., 1929)

Griffth, P., R. Harvey and K. Maslen (eds.). *Book & Print in New Zealand: A Guide to Print Culture in Aotearoa* (Wellington: Victoria University Press, 1997)

Harvey, R. *Union List of Newspapers Preserved in Libraries, Newspaper Offices, Local Authority Offices and Museums in New Zealand* (Wellington: National Library of New Zealand, 1987)

—— 'The Bibliography of Nineteenth-Century New Zealand Newspapers', *Australian and New Zealand Journal of Serials Librarianship*, 2 (1991): 19–33

—— 'Formula for Success: Economic Aspects of the Nineteenth-Century New Zealand Press', in R. Harvey, W. Kirsop and B. J. McMullin (eds.). *An Index of Civilisation: Studies of Printing and Publishing History in Honour of Keith Maslen* (Melbourne: Centre for Bibliographical and Textual Studies, Monash University, 1993), pp. 207–22

—— 'Establishing a Goldfields Newspaper: The Inangahua Herald, Reefton, New Zealand, 1872', in Michael Harris (ed.). *Studies in Newspaper and Periodical History: 1993 Annual* (Westport, CT: Greenwood Press, 1994), pp. 135–46

—— 'The Power of the Press in Colonial New Zealand: More Imagined than Real?', *Bibliographical Society of Australia and New Zealand Bulletin*, 20 (1996): 130–45

—— 'Newspaper Archives in Australia and New Zealand', *Media History*, 5 (1999): 71–80

—— 'Bringing the News to New Zealand: The Supply and Control of Overseas News in the Nineteenth Century', *Media History*, 8 (2002): 21–34

Potter, S. J. *News and the British World: The Emergence of an Imperial Press System* (Oxford: Clarendon, 2003)

Sanders, J. *Dateline – NZPA: The New Zealand Press Association 1880–1980* (Auckland: Wilson & Horton, 1979)

Scholefield, G. H. *Newspapers in New Zealand* (Wellington: Reed, 1958)

Wilson, A. C. *Wire & Wireless: A History of Telecommunications in New Zealand 1890–1987* (Palmerston North: Dunmore Press, 1994)

Press and Empire in South Africa

Beaumont, J. 'The British Press and Censorship during the South African War, 1899–1902', *South African Historical Journal*, 41, November 1999, pp. 267–89

Cuthbertson, G. et al., *Writing a Wider War: Rethinking Gender, Race and Identity in the South African War, 1899–1902* (Athens, OH: Ohio University Press; Cape Town, David Philip, 2002)

Mackenzie, J. M. *Propaganda and Empire: The Manipulation of British Public Opinion, 1880–1960* (Manchester, Manchester University Press, 1986)

Potter, S. J. 'Communication and Integration: The British and Dominions Press and the British World, c. 1876–1914', *The Journal of Commonwealth and Imperial History*, XXXI (2) (May 2003), pp. 190–206

Thompson, A. S. *Imperial Britain: the Empire in British Politics* (Harlow: Longman, 2000)

The press at the Cape, South Africa, in the early nineteenth century

Bayly, C. *The British Empire and the World* (London: Blackwell, 1989)

Botha, H. C. *John Fairbairn in South Africa* (Cape Town: Historical Publication Society, 1984)

Holmes, Rachel. *Scanty Particulars: The Strange Life and Astonishing Secret of Victorian Adventurer and Pioneer Surgeon James Barry* (London: Viking 2002)

Keegan, T. *Colonial South Africa and the Origins of the Racial Order* (London: Leicester University Press, 1996)

Laidlaw, Zoe. *Colonial Connections* (Manchester: Manchester University Press, 2005)

MacKenzie, John M. *The Scots in South Africa: Ethnicity, Identity and Race* (Manchester: Manchester University Press, forthcoming)

Millar, A. K. *Plantagenet in South Africa: Lord Charles Somerset* (Cape Town: Oxford University Press, 1965)

Naidoo, Balasundram, 'David Dale Buchanan as Editor of the Natal Witness, 1846–56', *Archives Year Book of South African History*, 40 (Pretoria, 1982)

Ross, Andrew. *John Philip: Missions, Race and Politics in South Africa* (Aberdeen, 1986)

Vann, J. Don and Van Arsdel. *Rosemary, Periodicals of Queen Victoria's Empire: An Exploration* (London, Mansell, 1996)

Canada, media and empire

Aitken, H. G. J. *The Continuous Wave: Technology and American Radio, 1900–1932* (Princeton, NJ: Princeton University Press, 1985)

Archer, G. L. *History of Radio to 1926* (New York: American Historical Society, 1938)

Baker, W. J. *A History of the Marconi Company* (London: Methuen & Co., 1970)

Beauregard, C. *Guerre et censure au Canada 1939–1945* (Sillery: Septentrion, 1998)

Beauregard, G., Canuel, A. and Coutard, J., *Les médias et la guerre: de 1914 au World Trade Center* (Montréal: Éditions du Méridien, 2002)

Bérard, V. *L'Angleterre et l'impérialisme* (Paris: Armand Colin, 1911)

Brown, F. J. *The Cable and Wireless Communications of the World: A Survey of Present Day Means of International Communication by Cable and Wireless* (London and New York: Sir Isaac Pitman & Son Co., 1927)

Canuel, A. 'La présence de l'impérialisme dans les débuts de la radiophonie au Canada, 1900–1928', *Journal d'études canadiennes*, Vol. 20, No. 4 (1985–86): 45–60

—— 'Le câble sous-marin et la TSF en Allemagne avant la Première Guerre mondiale', *Annales canadiennes d'histoire*, Vol. XXVI (Décembre 1991): 415–29

Chester, G. and Garrison, G. P. 'The Growth of American Radio', *Television and Radio: An Introduction* (New York: Appleton Century Crofts, 1950–56), pp. 20–42

Coates, V. T. and Finn, B. *A Retrospective Technology Assessment: Submarine Telegraphy* (San Francisco: San Francisco Press, 1979)

Elliott, W. Y. *The New British Empire* (New York and London: Whittlesey House, 1932)

Ellis, D. *La radiodiffusion canadienne: objectifs et réalités, 1928–1968* (Hull: Centre d'édition du gouvernement du Canada, 1979)

Finn, B. S. *Submarine Telegraphy: the Great Victorian Technology* (Washington: Smithsonian Institute; Margate: Thanet Press, 1973)

Headrick, D. R. *The Tools of Empire: Technology and the Expansion of European Colonial Empires in the Nineteenth Century* (New York and Oxford: Oxford University Press, 1981)

—— *The Invisible Weapon: Telecommunications and International Politics, 1851–1945* (New York/Oxford: Oxford University Press, 1991)

—— 'Câbles télégraphiques et rivalité franco-britannique avant 1914', *Guerres mondiales et conflits contemporains*, No. 166 (1992): 113–48

Hughes, T. P. *Networks of Power: Electrification in Western Societies, 1880–1930* (Baltimore, MD and London: Johns Hopkins University Press, 1983)

Jacot, B. L. and Collier, D. M. B. *Marconi: Master of Space* (London: Hutchinson, 1935)

Jolly, W. P., *Marconi* (London: Constable, 1972)

Kendle, J. E. *The Colonial and Imperial Conferences (1887–1911): A Study in Imperial Organization* (London: Longmans, 1967)

Kennedy, P. M. 'Imperial Communication and Strategy, 1870–1914', *English Historical Review*, Vol. 86 (1971): 728–53

Kerr, G. D. 'Skirting the Minefield: Press Censorship, Politics and French Canada, 1940', *Canadian Journal of Communication*, Vol. 8, No. 2 (January 1982): 46–69

Landes, D. S. *L'Europe technicienne* (Paris: Gallimard, 1975)

Peers, F. W. *The Politics of Canadian Broadcasting, 1920–1951* (Toronto: University of Toronto Press, 1969)

Sanders, W. *Jack et Jacques: l'opinion politique au Canada pendant la Deuxième Guerre mondiale* (Montréal: Comeau & Nadeau, 1996)

Sturmey, G. S. *The Economic Development of Radio* (London: Gerald Duckworth, 1958)

Toogood, A. *Broadcasting in Canada: Aspects of Regulation and Control, 1923–1969* (Ottawa: Canadian Association of Broadcasters, 1969)

Weir, A. E. *The Struggle for National Broadcasting in Canada* (Montréal and Toronto: Canadian Publishers, 1965)

India, Empire, the press and mid-nineteenth-century British political culture

Bayly, C. A. *Indian Society and the Making of the British Empire* (Cambridge: Cambridge University Press, 1988)

—— *Empire and Information. Intelligence Gathering and Social Communication in India, 1780–1870* (Cambridge: Cambridge University Press, 1996)

Belchem, J. and Epstein, J. 'The Nineteenth-Century Gentleman Leader Revisited', *Social History*, Vol. 22 (London: Routledge, 1997), pp. 174–93

Brake, L., Jones, A. and Madden, L. (eds.). *Investigating Victorian Journalism* (London: Macmillan, 1990)

Brantlinger, P. *Rule of Darkness: British Literature and Imperialism, 1830–1914* (Ithaca, NY: Cornell University Press, 1988)

Dawson, G. *Soldier Heroes. British Adventure, Empire and the Imagining of Masculinities* (London: Routledge, 1994)

Finn, M. *After Chartism: Nation and Class in English Radical Politics, 1848–1874* (Cambridge: Cambridge University Press, 1993)

Hall, C., McClelland, K. and Rendall, J. *Defining the Victorian Nation: Class, Race, Gender and the Reform Act of 1867* (Cambridge: Cambridge University Press, 2000)

Hoppen, K. T. *The Mid-Victorian Generation 1846–1886* (Oxford: Oxford University Press, 1998)

Jones, A. *Powers of the Press: Newspapers, Power and the Public in Nineteenth-Century England* (Aldershot: Ashgate Press, 1996)

Knightley, P. *The First Casualty: The War Correspondent from the Crimea to Vietnam*, (London: Deutsch, 1975)

Metcalf, T. R. *The Aftermath of Revolt: India, 1857–1870* (Princeton, NJ: Princeton University Press, 1965)

—— *Ideologies of the Raj* (Cambridge: Cambridge University Press, 1995)

Palmegiano, E. 'The Indian Mutiny and the Mid-Victorian Press', *Journal of Newspaper and Periodical History*, Vol. 7 (London, 1991): 3–11

Peers, D. and Finkelstein, D. (eds.). *Negotiating India in the Nineteenth Century Media* (Basingstoke: Macmillan, 2000)

Taylor, M. 'Imperium et Libertas? Rethinking the Radical Critique of Imperialism during the Nineteenth Century', *The Journal of Imperial and Commonwealth History*, Vol. 19 (London: Routledge, 1991): 1–23

—— *Ernest Jones, Chartism, and the Romance of Politics 1819–69* (Oxford: Oxford University Press, 2003)

Vernon, J. *Politics and the People: A Study in English Political Culture, c. 1815–1867* (Cambridge: Cambridge University Press, 1993)

—— (ed.). *Re-reading the Constitution. New Narratives in the Political History of England's Long Nineteenth Century* (Cambridge: Cambridge University Press, 1996)

Vincent, D. *Literacy and Popular Culture: England 1750–1914* (Cambridge: Cambridge University Press, 1989)

Film and empire

Campbell-Johnson, A. *Mission with Mountbatten* (London: Robert Hale, 1951)

Chowdhry, P. *Colonial India and the Making of Empire Cinema: Image, Ideology and Identity* (Manchester: Manchester University Press, 2000)

Fielding, R. *The March of Time, 1935–1951* (New York: Oxford University Press, 1978)

Hopkinson, P. *Split Focus: An Involvement in Two Decades* (London: Rupert Hart-Davis, 1969)

Lamb, A. *Incomplete Partition: The Genesis of the Kashmir Dispute 1947–1948* (Hertingfordbury: Roxford Books: 1997)

McKernan, L. (ed.). *Yesterday's News: The British Cinema Newsreel Reader* (London: BUFVC, 2002)

Pandey, G. *Remembering Partition: Violence, Nationalism and History in India* (Cambridge: Cambridge University Press, 2001)

Pronay, N. 'British Newsreels in the 1930s. 1. Audience and Producers', *History*, Vol. 56, No. 188 (October 1971): 411–18

—— 'British Newsreels in the 1930s. 2. Their Policies and Impact', *History*, Vol. 57, No. 189 (February 1972): 63–72

Richards, J. *Visions of Yesterday* (London: Routledge & Kegan Paul, 1973)

Smith, P. *The Historian and Film* (Cambridge: Cambridge University Press, 1976)

Smyth, R. 'The British Colonial Film Unit and Sub-Saharan Africa, 1939–1945', *Historical Journal of Film, Radio and Television*, Vol. 8, No. 3 (1988): 285–98

Turner, J. *Filming History: the Memoirs of John Turner, Newsreel Cameraman* (London: BUFVC, 2001)

Woods, P. ' "Chappatis by Parachute": The Use of Newsreels in British Propaganda in India in the Second World War', *South Asia*, Vol. 23, No. 2 (December 2000): 89–109

—— 'From Shaw to Shantaram: the Film Advisory Board and the Making of British Propaganda Films in India 1940 to 1943', *Historical Journal of Film, Radio and Television*, Vol. 21, No. 3 (August 2001): 293–308

Ziegler, P. *Mountbatten: the Official Biography* (London: Collins, 1985)

Papua New Guinea and the media

Australian Parliament, Joint Standing Committee on Foreign Affairs, Defence and Trade, 'Visit to Bougainville 15–18 March 1999'. Interim report to Parliament, 31 March 1999

Australian Parliament, Joint Standing Committee on Foreign Affairs, Defence and Trade, 'Bougainville: The Peace Process and Beyond'. Completed inquiry presented to Parliament, 27 September 1999

Cass, P. 'A Comparison of the Coverage of the Bougainville Crisis in the *Australian* and the *Times* of PNG', *Australian Journalism Review*, XIV:2 (1992)

Connell, J. and Howitt, R. (eds.). *Mining and Indigenous Peoples in Australasia* (Sydney: Sydney University Press, 1991)

Dorney, S. *Papua New Guinea: People and Politics since 1975* (Sydney: Random House, 1990)

—— *The Sandline Affair* (Sydney: ABC Books, 1998)

Downs, I. *The Australian Trusteeship Papua New Guinea 1945–1975* (Canberra: Australian Government Publishing Service, 1980)

Hudson, W. J. *New Guinea Empire* (Sydney: Cassell, 1974)

Hughes. H. 'Can Papua New Guinea Come Back from the Brink?', *Issue Analysis*, No. 49 (July 2004)

May, R. J. *State and Society in Papua New Guinea: The First 25 Years* (Canberra: Australian National University Press, 2000) at http://epress.anu.edu.au/sspng/mobile_devices/index.html

Mikesell, R. F. *Foreign Investment in Copper Mining: Case Studies of Mines in Peru and Papua New Guinea* (Baltimore, MD: Johns Hopkins University Press, 1975)

O'Callaghan, M. *Enemies Within* (Sydney: Doubleday, 1999)

—— 'The Origins of the Conflict', in A. Carl and L. Garasu (eds.). *Weaving Consensus: The Papua New Guinea–Bougainville Peace Process* (London: Conciliation Resources, 2002)

Ogan, E. 'Business and Cargo: Socio-economic Change among the Nasioi of Bougainville', *New Guinea Research Bulletin*, No. 44 (1972)

Ogan, E. 'The Bougainville Conflict: Perspectives from the Nasioi', *State, Society and Governance in Melanesia*, Discussion Paper 99/3.

Radio Australia, *Time to Talk*, programme two, 'Women and Land in Bougainville', at http://abc.net.au/timetotalk/english/issues_two.htm

Somare, M. *Sana: An Autobiography* (Port Moresby: Nuigini Press, 1975)

Stephen, D. *A History of Political Parties in Papua New Guinea* (Melbourne: Lansdowne Press, 1972)

Strathern, A. J. and Stewart P. J. ' "Mi les long yupela usim flag bilong mi": Symbols and Identity in Papua New Guinea', *Pacific Studies*, XXIII:1/2 (2000)

Turner, M. *Papua New Guinea: the Challenge of Independence* (Melbourne: Penguin, 1990)

Whitlam, G. 'Into the Seventies with Labor', 1969 Election Policy Speech, Sydney Town Hall, 1 October 1969

—— 'Decolonisation of Papua New Guinea', Keynote address, University House, Canberra, 3 November 2002

Windybank, S. and Manning, M. 'Papua New Guinea on the Brink', *Issue Analysis*, No. 30 (March 2003)

Media and the exile of Seretse Khama, 1948–56

Benson, Mary. *Tshekedi Khama* (London, Faber and Faber, 1960)

Crowder, Michael. 'Professor Macmillan Goes on Safari: The British Government Observer Team and the Crisis over the Seretse Khama Marriage, 1951', in Hugh Macmillan and Shula Marks (eds.). *Africa and Empire. W. M. Macmillan, Historian and Social Critic* (London: Temple Smith/Institute of Commonwealth Studies, 1989)

Douglas-Home, Charles, *Evelyn Baring: The Last Proconsul* (London: Collins, 1978)

Dutfield, M. *A Marriage of Inconvenience: The Persecution of Seretse and Ruth Khama* (London: Unwin Hyman 1990)

Hyam, Ronald and Henshaw, Peter. *The Lion and the Springbok: Britain and South Africa since the Boer War* (Cambridge: Cambridge University Press, 2003)

Morton, Fred and Ramsay, Jeff (eds.). *The Birth of Botswana: A History of the Bechuanaland Protectorate from 1910 to 1966* (Gaborone: Longman Botswana, 1987)

Parsons, Neil, Henderson, Willie and Tlou, Thomas. *Seretse Khama 1921–1980* (1995; rpt. Braamfontein, South Africa: Macmillan Boleswa, 1997)

Redfern, John. *Ruth and Seretse. 'A Very Disreputable Transaction'* (London: Victor Gollancz, 1955)

Seretse, Gasebalwe, *Tshekedi Khama: The Master Whose Dogs Barked At (A Critical Look at Ngwato Politics)* (Gaborone, Botswana: Gasebalwe Seretse, 2004)

Tlou, Thomas, and Campbell, Alec. *History of Botswana.* (1984; rpt. Gaborone: Macmillan Botswana, 2001)

British press and decolonization in Africa

Anderson, D. *Histories of the Hanged: Britain's Dirty War in Kenya and the End of Empire* (London: Weidenfeld & Nicolson, 2005)

Baker, C. *States of Emergency: Crisis in Central Africa, Nyasaland 1959–1960* (London: Tauris, 1997)

Clough, Marshall S. *Mau Mau Memoirs: History, Memory and Politics* (Boulder, CO: Lynne Rienner, 1998)

Elkins, Caroline. *Britain's Gulag: The Brutal End of Empire in Kenya* (London: Jonathan Cape, 2005)

Evans, Harold. *Downing Street Diary: The Macmillan Years, 1957–1963* (London: n.p., 1981)

Howe, Stephen. *Anticolonialism in British Politics: The Left and the End of Empire, 1918–1964* (Oxford: Oxford University Press, 1993)

Lamb, Richard. *The Macmillan Years 1957–63: The Emerging Truth* (London: John Murray, 1995)

Lewis, J. 'Daddy Wouldn't Buy Me a Mau Mau: The British Popular Press and the Demoralisation of Empire', in E. S. Atieno Odhiambo and John Lonsdale (eds.). *Mau Mau and Nationhood* (Oxford, James Currey, 2003)

Kyle, K. *The Politics of the Independence of Kenya* (Basingstoke: Macmillan, 1999)

Macmillan, Harold. *Pointing the Way, 1959–1961* (London, Macmillan, 1972)

Murphy, Philip. *Alan Lennox-Boyd: A Biography* (London, Tauris, 1999)

—— (ed.). *British Documents on the End of Empire: Central Africa* (London: Stationery Office, 2005).

Index